Growing Old at Willie Nelson's Picnic

and Other Sketches of Life in the Southwest

Edited by **Ronald B. Querry**

 Texas A&M University Press: College Station

Library of Congress Cataloging in Publication Data
Main entry under title:

Growing old at Willie Nelson's picnic and other
    sketches of life in the Southwest.

    1. Southwest, New—Social life and customs—
Addresses, essays, lectures.   2. Indians of North
America—Southwest, New—Social life and customs—
Addresses, essays, lectures.   3. Southwest, New—
Fiction.   I. Querry, Ronald B. (Ronald Burns),
1943–
F787.G76   1983   306'.0979   83-45106
ISBN 0-89096-164-6
ISBN 0-89096-172-7 (pbk.)

Manufactured in the United States of America
FIRST EDITION

For my mother, Beverly Corbett;
and for my daughter, Isabel;
and to the memory of Max—the best of his kind.

Contents

Tales

Acknowledgments

FOR their generous encouragement and suggestions in the making of this collection I am grateful to my colleagues David Mair, Ronald Schleifer, and Alan Velie, whose teaching and friendship will remain among the great fortunes of my days at the University of Oklahoma. Too, I am grateful to A. T. Austin of Santa Rosa, New Mexico, who first showed me the lay of the Southwest land. And to Leslie Upsher—of my heart's country—who gently intervened on several occasions to prevent my making some unusual mistakes, I am most grateful.

Appreciation is due the following for permission to use copyrighted material:

Excerpt from *The Way to Rainy Mountain*, by N. Scott Momaday. Copyright © 1969 by N. Scott Momaday. Reprinted by permission of the University of New Mexico Press.

"The Old Man," by Larry L. King. Copyright © 1971 by Larry L. King. Reprinted by permission of the author.

"The Great Candy Exchange," excerpted from *On The Border*, chapter 14, by Tom Miller. Copyright © 1981 by Tom Miller. Reprinted by permission of Harper & Row, Publishers, Inc.

Excerpt from *The Long Road North*, by John Davidson, first printed in a slightly different form in an article entitled "The Long Road North" in *Texas Monthly*. Copyright © 1977 by Mediatex Communications Corporation. Copyright © 1978, 1979 by John Davidson. Reprinted by permission of Doubleday & Company, Inc.

"On the Trail," by Joseph G. McCoy. Reprinted by permission of the publishers, The Arthur H. Clark Company, from *Cattle Trade of the West and Southwest*, by Joseph G. McCoy.

"Nineteen Cows," by John Graves. Reprinted by permission of the author from *From a Limestone Ledge*. Copyright © 1980 by John Graves.

"The End of the Trail," by Al Reinert. Reprinted with permission from the November, 1978, issue of *Texas Monthly*. Copyright © 1978 by *Texas Monthly*.

"The Hopi Snake Dance," by D. H. Lawrence, from *Mornings in Mexico*. (Reprinted in slightly different form in *The Later D. H. Lawrence*, edited by W. Y. Tindall, 1952.) Copyright © 1927 by Alfred A. Knopf, Inc. Reprinted by permission of the publishers, Alfred A. Knopf, Inc.

"The Penitentes of New Mexico," by Earle R. Forrest. Reprinted by permission of the publishers, The Arthur H. Clark Company, from *Missions and Pueblos of the Old Southwest*, by Earle R. Forrest.

"The Old Soldier's Joy," by Larry McMurtry. Copyright © 1968 by Larry McMurtry; first printed in *Texas Quarterly* and reprinted with the author's permission.

"A Rodeo Memoir," by Kirk Purcell, first printed in a slightly different version in an article entitled "Comic Relief" in *D Magazine*. Reprinted by permission.

"The Rites of Autumn," by Gary Cartwright. Reprinted with permission from the October, 1977, issue of *Texas Monthly*. Copyright © 1977 by *Texas Monthly*.

"Growing Old at Willie Nelson's Picnic," by William C. Martin. Reprinted with permission from the October, 1974, issue of *Texas Monthly*. Copyright © 1974 by *Texas Monthly*.

"Native American Muses," by Arrell Morgan Gibson, first printed in *The New Mexico Historical Review*. Reprinted with permission of the Regents of the University of New Mexico and the editor.

"The High Road to Taos," by Trent Elwood Sanford. Reprinted from *The Architecture of the Southwest*, by Trent Elwood Sanford, by permission of W. W. Norton & Company, Inc. Copyright © 1950 by W. W. Norton & Company, Inc. Copyright renewed 1978 by Dorothy D. Sanford.

"A Geronimo Story," by Leslie Marmon Silko, from *The Man to Send Rain Clouds*, edited by Kenneth Rosen. Copyright © 1974 by Leslie Marmon Silko. Reprinted by permission of Viking Penguin, Inc.

Excerpt from *The Man Who Killed the Deer*, by Frank Waters. Copyright © 1942, 1970 by Frank Waters. Reprinted by permission of the publishers, Ohio University Press/Swallow Press.

Excerpt from *Portrait of an Artist with Twenty-Six Horses*, by William Eastlake. Copyright © 1963 by William Eastlake. Reprinted by permission of the author.

Excerpt from *Honkytonk Man*, by Clancy Carlile. Copyright © 1980 by Clancy Carlile. Reprinted by permission of Simon & Schuster, a Division of Gulf & Western Corporation.

"There Could Be No More to It," by Lawrence Wharton. Copyright © 1982 by Lawrence Wharton. By permission of the author.

*Growing Old at Willie Nelson's Picnic and
Other Sketches of Life in the Southwest*

Introduction

THIS book is about the Southwest. It is a collection of works by a score of writers. One of the selections first appeared in print more than a hundred years ago; another appears here for the first time. Among the writers represented are a Texas-born journalist—a high school dropout—who moved East and wrote a smash Broadway musical about the Lone Star State; a Laguna Pueblo woman; a British novelist whose work was for many years banned in this country; an architectural historian; a trial lawyer; and a Kiowa Indian who has won the Pulitzer Prize for fiction. My intention has been to bring together diverse voices that speak to and from the Southwest in the belief that only through such a montage of attitudes and subjects can we begin truly to appreciate the uniqueness of that region of the United States.

In his introduction to *In a Narrow Grave: Essays on Texas*, Larry McMurtry speaks of the difficulty that writers from and about the Southwest have sometimes experienced in finding an audience for their work: "As a regionalist, and a regionalist from an unpopular region, I find the problem of how to get heard rather a fascinating one. I haven't found it especially depressing, but then I wouldn't have gone in for writing if I hadn't liked talking to myself. I quite recognize that there have always been literary capitals and literary provinces, and that those who choose for whatever reason to abide in the provinces need not expect a modish recognition."

My experience as a student and teacher of the literature of the Southwest has, from time to time, led me to conclude—at least in my darker moments—that we in the Southwest sometimes see ourselves as outside the mainstream of American Culture, as though art, culture, and literature take place elsewhere, in the "literary capitals," if you will. Recently, to be sure, the picture has been changing. Economic blight and fuel shortages, along with the oil boom, have resulted in the "discovery" of the Sunbelt as a good region in which to live and work. New York and Paris have witnessed svelte models dressed in the fashion of Hopi women—the "Santa Fe Look." Broadway has seen a highly successful musical called *The Best Little Whorehouse in Texas*. The Southwest is no longer the unpopular region of which Mr. McMurtry speaks. It has, it would seem, gained its "modish recognition."

The Southern writer Willie Morris tells about a friend who is quite certain that the Deep South ends and the Southwest begins about three miles past a certain filling station on Texas Highway 79, somewhere between Hearne and Austin. In his essay in this book, Larry McMurtry locates the boundary north and west of a line running between Fort Worth and Dallas. Cartographers often include southern California in the Southwest, and a recent collection of Southwest fiction adds Arkansas. My own notion confines the region to Arizona and New Mexico, the western two-thirds of Oklahoma, and West Texas. For our purposes here, however, I have chosen to rely upon what I perceive to be the generally accepted geographical region of Texas, Oklahoma, New Mexico, and Arizona as the Southwest.

The selections that follow range from autobiographical portraits to historical sketches, from architectural descriptions to imaginative literature. Their subjects go from Hopi Indian dancers in Arizona who hold live rattlesnakes in their teeth to sunburned, beer-drinking revelers at a red-neck rock concert in Texas. The common thread that runs throughout these works—indeed, that holds them together—is the sense of *place* that informs them.

The land is of primary importance to even the most elementary understanding of the Southwest. It is a land of great distances and of rare, if sometimes harsh, beauty. It is a commonplace of conversation that the Southwest is a place of clean, pure air. As a region, it has mostly been spared the gray/brown pollution of the more industrialized areas of the country. The high, dry air over mountains and the arid deserts of New Mexico and Arizona make for a brilliant blue sky above beautifully colored earth. Painters have long since discovered that the bright, clear atmosphere results in a purity of color peculiar to the region—red and salmon-colored buttes and white limestone cliffs against a turquoise sky.

There are great cities in the Southwest, to be sure. But for the most part it remains an area of uncrowded space. Scott Momaday, reminiscing about his Kiowa ancestors, who "reckoned their stature by the distance they could see," looks out across the plains of Oklahoma: "Loneliness is an aspect of the land. All things in the plain are isolate; there is no confusion of objects in the eye, but *one* hill or *one* tree or *one* man. To look upon that landscape in the early morning, with the sun at your back, is to lose the sense of proportion. Your imagination comes to life, and this, you think, is where Creation was begun."

Momaday's words echo those of D. H. Lawrence, who upon first seeing the sun rise over the deserts of Santa Fe remarked that "in the magnificent fierce morning of New Mexico one sprang awake, a new part of the soul woke up suddenly." But Lawrence also saw the harshness of the land when later he described the Hopi village of Hotevilla in Arizona, where he was to witness the Snake Dance: "Hotevilla is a tiny little village of grey little houses, raggedly built with undressed stone and mud around a little oblong plaza, and partly in ruins. . . . It is a parched, grey country of snakes and eagles, pitched up against the sky."

While a sense of place is essential to an appreciation of the Southwest, of equal importance is the relationship between the people and their land. Clearly the people/land relationship is an integral part of any culture and therefore any region. Perhaps it is better not to insist that the land here exerts some special hold over its inhabitants, but rather that the *manifestation* of that relationship is somehow special.

When the nameless Indian in Frank Waters's *The Man Who Killed the Deer* sets out to find his injured friend, he is prompted to do so because his own heartbeat is somehow out of sync with that of the sacred mountain at the base of which he lives—he goes because he cannot do otherwise: "It was as if an invisible hand was pulling at his spirit. . . . And the beat, from deep within, from the heart of the world, pulsed steadily, inaudibly, like the beat of the man's blood. Each was the echo of the other, indivisible. But they were not quite in tune." I do not suggest that this mystical bond between Indian and Earth is easily understood. Indeed, I am not certain that such a thing is understandable, in our time and in a non-Indian culture. What I do suggest is that it is quite wonderful.

Other parts of the country lay claim to a kind of regional culture. New England and the Deep South come to mind. The Southwest, however, is a unique blend of three cultures—Indian, Spanish, and Anglo. This latter term, *Anglo*, is unsatisfactory, but it is the term of the region.

The Navajo Nation makes up the largest tribal group in the United States; by the early 1980's its reservation alone covered more than twenty-five thousand square miles of Arizona, New Mexico, and Utah. The ruins at Old Oraibi, on the Hopi Third Mesa in what is now Arizona, date to about 1100 A.D., and we must suppose that the Hopis were an ancient people long before the first stone at Oraibi was laid. Historians tell us that the richly cultured pueblo city-state of Taos in northern New Mexico has been more or less continuously occupied for more than seven hundred years. It is worth remarking that within about sixty miles of that ancient pueblo this country developed and built its first atomic bomb at Los Alamos.

There remain today towns and villages in the Southwest where Spanish is the everyday language of the people and where Penitentes continue to practice the bizarre religious rites described by a contributor to this volume. Strictly Anglo influence—in money and in commerce—is most observable in Texas and Oklahoma and in the larger cities of New Mexico and Arizona. Though often at odds with one another, the Indian, Spanish, and Anglo influences have come together to produce in today's Southwest a unique tri-cultural personality.

Still, how each of the separate cultures views itself and the others is addressed time and again in the works included here. A Yuma, Arizona, sixth grader in Tom Miller's look at attitudes along the U.S.–Mexican border says that the Mexicans who walk past his house wear "big long things called *sarapes* and big hats and eat beans and tortillas every day," while his counterpart at the Escuela Rodríguez in Sonora, Mexico, prefers the food in Yuma "'cause they've got Kentucky Fried Chicken!" Leslie Silko's Indian scouts in "A Geronimo Story" lead the white soldiers in their search for the outlaw Apache chief and shake their heads in wonder at the folly of the cavalry officers. Larry King's father in "The Old Man" is surprised to find that "Meskins," as he calls them, visit the Alamo.

The selections that follow represent the many approaches that the serious student may expect to encounter in a regional study. They are gathered into sections according to the various aspects of the life and the land that they demonstrate. The first section, "Legacies," explores, in two distinctly different voices, examples of the ancestral heritage that so marks the Southwest. "Borderlines" looks at some of the attitudes and impulses that bear upon the special relationships among people along the borders of Mexico. The cattle industry—both as it was and as it is—is the subject of "Livestock." One of the world's greatest modern novelists looks at an ancient Indian ritual and a historian describes an even stranger religious cult in "Ceremonies." Set against these ceremonies of another time are examples of modern-day "Diversions" in the Southwest, including an old-time fiddlers' reunion and a college football weekend. The development of Indian arts and an architectural tour of northern New Mexico occupy the section entitled "Art." And the final portion of the book, "Tales," is a collection of imaginative responses to the distinctive qualities of the land, the people, and the historical experiences addressed in the preceding sections.

The book's arrangement is intended to facilitate the reader's movement among its different facets. Each of the pieces included stands alone, to be sure, and the order in which one approaches the selections may vary. Taken as a whole, however, they come together in a montage of features that form the basis for the unique richness that is the Southwest.

LEGACIES

N. Scott Momaday

N. Scott Momaday was born at the Kiowa and Comanche Indian Hospital at Lawton, Oklahoma, in 1934. He is listed on the Kiowa tribal rolls as "7/8 degree Indian blood." Momaday was raised on the Navajo Reservation in New Mexico and Arizona and at Jemez Pueblo in central New Mexico. A master storyteller, a poet and an artist, Momaday's finest work is *House Made of Dawn*, the Pulitzer Prize–winning novel for 1969. Besides fiction and poetry, Momaday has written two memoirs, *The Way to Rainy Mountain* and *The Names*, which tell about his childhood and his family heritage. *The Way to Rainy Mountain* follows in legend and historical fact the migration of the Kiowas from their ancestral home in what is now Montana to the plains of Oklahoma. The book's introduction recounts Momaday's pilgrimage along the route taken by the Kiowas from the headwaters of the Yellowstone River to Rainy Mountain near Mountain View, Oklahoma. The book itself is arranged in three sections, with each section divided into short chapters—really almost *verses*. These chapters are, in turn, divided into three parts: a legend or story, a historical observation or anecdote, and a personal reminiscence by the author. For each of the three parts the voice of the narrator is distinct—that is, the voice for the first part, the story, is one appropriate to the oral "telling" of a tale; the history is formal, at times anthropological; and the personal section is lyrical, almost poetic. In the original work, the typescript for each part is different as well. Included here are the Introduction and three of the triparted chapters.

From *The Way to Rainy Mountain*

A single knoll rises out of the plain in Oklahoma, north and west of the Wichita Range. For my people, the Kiowas, it is an old landmark, and they gave it the name Rainy Mountain. The hardest weather in the world is there. Winter brings blizzards; hot tornadic winds arise in the spring, and in summer the prairie is an anvil's edge. The grass turns brittle and brown, and it cracks beneath your feet. There are green belts along the rivers and creeks, linear groves of hickory and pecan, willow and witch hazel. At a distance in July or August the steaming foliage seems almost to writhe in fire. Great green and yellow grasshoppers are everywhere in the tall grass, popping up like corn to sting the flesh, and tortoises crawl about on the red earth, going nowhere in the plenty of time. Loneliness is an aspect of the land. All things in the plain are isolate; there is no confusion of objects in the eye, but *one* hill or *one* tree or *one* man. To look upon that landscape in the early morning, with the sun at your back, is to lose the sense of proportion. Your imagination comes to life, and this, you think, is where Creation was begun.

I returned to Rainy Mountain in July. My grandmother had died in the spring, and I wanted to be at her grave. She had lived to be very old and at last infirm. Her only living daughter was with her when she died, and I was told that in death her face was that of a child.

I like to think of her as a child. When she was born, the Kiowas were living the last great moment of their history. For more than a hundred years they had controlled the open range from the Smoky Hill River to the Red, from the headwaters of the Canadian to the fork of the Arkansas and Cimarron. In alliance with the Comanches, they had ruled the whole of the southern Plains. War was their sacred business, and they were among the finest horsemen the world has ever known. But warfare for the Kiowas was preeminently a matter of disposition rather than of survival, and they never understood the grim, unrelenting advance of the U.S. Cavalry. When at last, divided and ill-provisioned, they were driven onto the Staked Plains in the cold rains of autumn, they fell into panic. In Palo Duro Canyon they abandoned their crucial stores to pillage and had nothing then but their lives. In order to save themselves, they surrendered to the soldiers at Fort Sill and were imprisoned in the old stone corral that now stands as a military museum. My grandmother was spared the humiliation of those high gray walls by eight or ten years, but she must have known from birth the affliction of defeat, the dark brooding of old warriors.

Her name was Aho, and she belonged to the last culture to evolve in North America. Her forebears came down from the high country in western Montana nearly three centuries ago. They were a mountain people, a mysterious tribe of hunters whose language has never been positively classified in any major group. In the late seventeenth century they began a long migration to the south and east. It was a journey toward the dawn, and it led to a golden age. Along the way the Kiowas were befriended by the Crows, who gave them the culture and religion of the Plains. They acquired horses, and their ancient nomadic spirit was suddenly free of the ground. They acquired Tai-me, the sacred Sun Dance doll, from that moment the object and symbol of their worship, and so shared in the divinity of the sun. Not least, they acquired the sense of destiny, therefore courage and pride. When they entered upon the southern Plains they had been transformed. No longer were they slaves to the simple necessity of survival; they were a lordly and dangerous society of fighters and thieves, hunters and priests of the sun. According to their origin myth, they entered the world through a hollow log. From one point of view, their migration was the fruit of an old prophecy, for indeed they emerged from a sunless world.

Although my grandmother lived out her long life in the shadow of Rainy Mountain, the immense landscape of the continental interior lay like memory in her blood. She could tell of the Crows, whom she had never seen, and of the Black Hills, where she had never been. I wanted to see in reality what she had seen more perfectly in the mind's eye, and traveled fifteen hundred miles to begin my pilgrimage.

Yellowstone, it seemed to me, was the top of the world, a region of deep lakes and dark timber, canyons and waterfalls. But, beautiful as it is, one might have the sense of confinement there. The skyline in all directions is close at hand, the high wall of the woods and deep cleavages of shade. There is a perfect freedom in the mountains, but it belongs to the eagle and the elk, the badger and the bear. The Kiowas reckoned their stature by the distance they could see, and they were bent and blind in the wilderness.

Descending eastward, the highland meadows are a stairway to the plain. In July the inland slope of the Rockies is luxuriant with flax and buckwheat, stonecrop and larkspur. The earth unfolds and the limit of the land recedes. Clusters of trees, and animals grazing far in the distance, cause the vision to reach away and wonder to build upon the mind. The sun follows a longer course in the day, and the sky is immense beyond all comparison. The great billowing clouds that sail upon it are shadows that move upon the grain like water, dividing light. Farther down, in the land of the Crows and Blackfeet, the plain is yellow. Sweet clover takes hold of the hills and bends upon itself to cover and seal the soil. There the Kiowas paused on their way; they had come to the place where they must change their lives. The sun is at home on the plains. Precisely there does it have the certain character of a god. When the Kiowas came to the land of the Crows, they could see the dark lees of the hills at dawn across the Bighorn River, the profusion of light on the grain shelves, the oldest deity ranging after the solstices. Not yet would they veer southward to the caldron of the land that lay below; they must wean their blood from the northern winter and hold the mountains a while longer in their view. They bore Tai-me in procession to the east.

A dark mist lay over the Black Hills, and the land was like iron. At the top of a ridge I caught sight of Devil's Tower upthrust against the gray sky as if in the birth of time the core of the earth had broken through its crust and the motion of the world was begun. There are things in nature that engender an awful quiet in the heart of man; Devil's Tower is one of them. Two centuries ago, because they could not do otherwise, the Kiowas made a legend at the base of the rock. My grandmother said:

Eight children were there at play, seven sisters and their brother. Suddenly the boy was struck dumb; he trembled and began to run upon his hands and feet. His fingers became claws, and his body was covered with fur. Directly there was a bear where the boy had been. The sisters were terrified; they ran, and the bear after them. They came to the stump of a great tree, and the tree spoke to them. It bade them climb upon it, and as they did so it began to rise into the air. The bear came to kill them, but they were just beyond its reach. It reared against the tree and scored the bark all around with its claws. The seven sisters were borne into the sky, and they became the stars of the Big Dipper.

From that moment, and so long as the legend lives, the Kiowas have kinsmen in the night sky. Whatever they were in the mountains, they could be no more. However tenuous their well-being, however much they had suffered and would suffer again, they had found a way out of the wilderness.

My grandmother had a reverence for the sun, a holy regard that now is all but gone out of mankind. There was a wariness in her, and an ancient awe. She was a Christian in her later years, but she had come a long way about, and she never forgot her birthright. As a child she had been to the Sun Dances; she had taken part in those annual rites, and by them she had learned the restoration of her people in the presence of Tai-me. She was about seven when the last Kiowa Sun Dance was held in 1887 on the Washita River above Rainy Mountain Creek. The buffalo were gone. In order to consummate the ancient sacrifice—to impale the head of a buffalo bull upon the medicine tree—a delegation of old men journeyed into Texas, there to beg and barter for an animal from the Goodnight herd. She was ten when the Kiowas came together for the last time as a living Sun Dance culture. They could find no buffalo; they had to hang an old hide from the sacred tree. Before the dance could begin, a company of soldiers rode out from Fort Sill under orders to disperse the tribe. Forbidden without cause the essential act of their faith, having seen the wild herds slaughtered and left to rot upon the ground, the Kiowas backed away forever from the medicine tree. That was July 20, 1890, at the great bend of the Washita. My grandmother was there. Without bitterness, and for as long as she lived, she bore a vision of deicide.

Now that I can have her only in memory, I see my grandmother in the several postures that were peculiar to her: standing at the wood stove on a winter morning and turning meat in a great iron skillet; sitting at the south window, bent above her beadwork, and afterwards, when her vision failed, looking down for a long time into the fold of her hands; going out upon a cane, very slowly as she did when the weight of age came upon her; praying. I remember her most often at prayer. She made long, rambling prayers out of suffering and hope, having seen many things. I was never sure that I had the right to hear, so exclusive were they of all mere custom and company. The last time I saw her she prayed standing by the side of her bed at night, naked to the waist, the light of a kerosene lamp moving upon her dark skin. Her long, black hair, always drawn and braided in the day, lay upon her shoulders and against her breasts like a shawl. I do not speak Kiowa, and I never understood her prayers, but there was something inherently sad in the sound, some merest hesitation upon the syllables of sorrow. She began in a high and descending pitch, exhausting her breath to silence; then again and again—and always the same intensity of effort, of something that is, and is not, like urgency in the human voice. Transported so in the dancing light among the shadows of her room, she seemed beyond the reach of time. But that was illusion; I think I knew then that I should not see her again.

Houses are like sentinels in the plain, old keepers of the weather watch. There, in a very little while, wood takes on the appearance of great age. All colors wear soon away in the wind and rain, and then the wood is burned gray and the grain appears and the nails turn red with rust. The windowpanes are black and opaque; you imagine there is nothing within, and indeed there are many ghosts, bones given up to the land. They stand here and there against the sky, and you approach them for a longer time than you expect. They belong in the distance; it is their domain.

Once there was a lot of sound in my grandmother's house, a lot of coming and going, feasting and talk. The summers there were full of excitement and reunion. The Kiowas are a summer people; they abide the cold and keep to themselves, but when the season turns and the land becomes warm and vital they cannot hold still; an old love of going returns upon them. The aged visitors who came to my grandmother's house when I was a child were made of lean and leather, and they bore themselves upright. They wore great black hats and bright ample shirts that shook in the wind. They rubbed fat upon their hair and wound their braids with strips of colored cloth. Some of them painted their faces and carried the scars of old and cherished enmities. They were an old council of warlords, come to remind and be reminded of who they were. Their wives and daughters served them well. The women might indulge themselves; gossip was at once the mark and compensation of their servitude. They made loud and elaborate talk among themselves, full of jest and gesture, fright and false alarm. They went abroad in fringed and flowered shawls, bright beadwork and German silver. They were at home in the kitchen, and they prepared meals that were banquets.

There were frequent prayer meetings, and great nocturnal feasts. When I was a child I played with my cousins outside, where the lamplight fell upon the ground and the singing of the old people rose up around us and carried away into the darkness. There were a lot of good things to eat, a lot of laughter and surprise. And afterwards, when the quiet returned, I lay down with my grandmother and could hear the frogs away by the river and feel the motion of the air.

Now there is a funeral silence in the rooms, the endless wake of some final word. The walls have closed in upon my grandmother's house. When I returned to it in mourning, I saw for the first time in my life how small it was. It was late at night, and there was a white moon, nearly full. I sat for a long time on the stone steps by the kitchen door. From there I could see out across the land; I could see the long row of trees by the creek, the low light upon the rolling plains, and the stars of the Big Dipper. Once I looked at the moon and caught sight of a strange thing. A cricket had perched upon the handrail, only a few inches away from me. My line of vision was such that the creature filled the moon like a fossil. It had gone there, I thought, to live and die, for there, of all places, was its small definition made whole and eternal. A warm wind rose up and purled like the longing within me.

The next morning I awoke at dawn and went out on the dirt road to Rainy Mountain. It was already hot, and the grasshoppers began to fill the air. Still, it was early in the morning, and the birds sang out of the shadows. The long yellow grass on the mountain shone in the bright light, and a scissortail hied above the land. There, where it ought to be, at the end of a long and legendary way, was my grandmother's grave. Here and there on the dark stones were ancestral names. Looking back once, I saw the mountain and came away.

Before there were horses the Kiowas had need of dogs. That was a long time ago, when dogs could talk. There was a man who lived alone; he had been thrown away, and he made his camp here and there on the high ground. Now it was dangerous to be alone, for there were enemies all around. The man spent his arrows hunting food. He had one arrow left, and he shot a bear; but the bear was only wounded and it ran away. The man wondered what to do. Then a dog came up to him and said that many enemies were coming; they were close by and all around. The man could think of no way to save himself. But the dog said: "You know, I have puppies. They are young and weak and they have nothing to eat. If you will take care of my puppies, I will show you how to get away." The dog led the man here and there, around and around, and they came to safety.

A hundred years ago the Comanche Ten Bears remarked upon the great number of horses which the Kiowas owned. "When we first knew you," he said, "you had nothing but dogs and sleds." It was so; the dog is primordial. Perhaps it was dreamed into being.

The principal warrior society of the Kiowas was the Ka-itsenko, *"Real Dogs," and it was made up of ten men only, the ten most brave. Each of these men wore a long ceremonial sash and carried a sacred arrow. In time of battle he must by means of this arrow impale the end of his sash to the earth and stand his ground to the death. Tradition has it that the founder of the* Ka-itsenko *had a dream in which he saw a band of warriors, outfitted after the fashion of the society, being led by a dog. The dog sang the song of the* Ka-itsenko, *then said to the dreamer: "You are a dog; make a noise like a dog and sing a dog song."*

There were always dogs about my grandmother's house. Some of them were nameless and lived a life of their own. They belonged there in a sense that the word "ownership" does not include. The old people paid them scarcely any attention, but they should have been sad, I think, to see them go.

If an arrow is well made, it will have tooth marks upon it. That is how you know. The Kiowas made fine arrows and straightened them in their teeth. Then they drew them to the bow to see if they were straight. Once there was a man and his wife. They were alone at night in their tipi. By the light of the fire the man was making arrows. After a while he caught sight of something. There was a small opening in the tipi where two hides were sewn together. Someone was there on the outside, looking in. The man went on with his work, but he said to his wife: "Someone is standing outside. Do not be afraid. Let us talk easily, as of ordinary things." He took up an arrow and straightened it in his teeth; then, as it was right for him to do, he drew it to the bow and took aim, first in this direction and then in that. And all the while he was talking, as if to his wife. But this is how he spoke: "I know that you are there on the outside, for I can feel your eyes upon me. If you are a Kiowa, you will understand what I am saying, and you will speak your name." But there was no answer, and the man went on in the same way, pointing the arrow all around. At last his aim fell upon the place where his enemy stood, and he let go of the string. The arrow went straight to the enemy's heart.

The old men were the best arrowmakers, for they could bring time and patience to their craft. The young men—the fighters and hunters—were willing to pay a high price for arrows that were well made.

When my father was a boy, an old man used to come to Mam-
medaty's house and pay his respects. He was a lean old man in
braids and was impressive in his age and bearing. His name was
Cheney, and he was an arrowmaker. Every morning, my father
tells me, Cheney would paint his wrinkled face, go out, and pray
aloud to the rising sun. In my mind I can see that man as if he
were there now. I like to watch him as he makes his prayer. I
know where he stands and where his voice goes on the rolling
grasses and where the sun comes up on the land. There, at
dawn, you can feel the silence. It is cold and clear and deep like
water. It takes hold of you and will not let you go.

Mammedaty was the grandson of Guipahgo, and he got on well most
of the time. But, you know, one time he lost his temper. This is how
it was: There were several horses in a pasture, and Mammedaty
wanted to get them out. A fence ran all the way around and there
was just one gate. There was a lot of ground inside. He could not get
those horses out. One of them led the others; every time they were
driven up to the gate, that one wheeled and ran as fast as it could to
the other side. Well, that went on for a long time, and Mammedaty
burned up. He ran to the house and got his bow and arrows. The
horses were running in single file, and he shot at the one that was
causing all that trouble. He missed, though, and the arrow went deep
into the neck of the second horse.

In the winter of 1852–53, a Pawnee boy who had been held as a
captive among the Kiowas succeeded in running away. He took with
him an especially fine hunting horse, known far and wide as Guadal-
tseyu, "Little Red." That was the most important event of the winter.
The loss of that horse was a hard thing to bear.

Years ago there was a box of bones in the barn, and I used to go
there to look at them. Later someone stole them, I believe. They
were the bones of a horse which Mammedaty called by the
name "Little Red." It was a small bay, nothing much to look at, I

have heard, but it was the fastest runner in that whole corner of the world. White men and Indians alike came from far and near to match their best animals against it, but it never lost a race. I have often thought about that red horse. There have been times when I thought I understood how it was that a man might be moved to preserve the bones of a horse—and another to steal them away.

Larry L. King

Larry L. King was born on New Year's Day in 1929 in Putnum, Texas. His early days were spent as a farmboy, an oil-field worker, a high school dropout, and a soldier. He attended Texas Tech in Lubbock for, as he says, "about thirty minutes." He has been a newspaperman in Texas and New Mexico, an aide to congressmen and presidents in Washington, a Nieman Fellow in Journalism at Harvard, a visiting professor at Duke and Princeton universities, and a contributing editor for several major magazines—*Harper's* and *Texas Monthly* among them. Besides his work as a journalist, King has published a novel, *The One-Eyed Man*, and a memoir, *Confessions of a White Racist*, and he has collected his magazine articles into several volumes, . . . *and Other Dirty Stories* and *Of Outlaws, Con Men, Whores, Politicians, and Other Artists* to name but two. King's biggest success has been his smash Broadway musical, *The Best Little Whorehouse in Texas*, and his subsequent account of that success, *The Whorehouse Papers*. King's finest writing, however, may well be found in the following selection. It is King's reminiscence of his father and of a trip the two of them, along with the author's two children, took from Midland, Texas, to the state capitol in Austin and the Alamo in San Antonio just weeks before The Old Man's death.

The Old Man

While we digested our suppers on The Old Man's front porch, his grandchildren chased fireflies in the summer dusk and, in turn, were playfully chased by neighborhood dogs. As always, The Old Man had carefully locked the collar of his workday khakis. He recalled favored horses and mules from his farming days, remembering their names and personalities though they had been thirty or forty years dead. I gave him a brief thumbnail sketch of William Faulkner—Mississippian, great writer, appreciator of the soil and good bourbon—before quoting what Faulkner had written of the mule: "He will draw a wagon or a plow but he will not run a race. He will not try to jump anything he does not indubitably know beforehand he can jump; he will not enter any place unless he knows of his own knowledge what is on the other side; he will work for you patiently for ten years for the chance to kick you once." The Old Man cackled in delight. "That feller sure knowed his mules," he said.

Sons rarely get to know their fathers very well, less well, certainly, than fathers get to know their sons. More of an intimidating nature remains for the father to conceal, he being cast in the role of example-setter. Sons know their own guilty intimidations. Eventually, however, they graduate their fears of the lash or the frown, learn that their transgressions have been handed down for generations. Fathers are more likely to consider their own sins to have been original.

The son may ultimately boast to the father of his own darker conquests or more wicked dirkings: perhaps out of some need to declare his personal independence, or out of some perverted wish to settle a childish score, or simply because the young—not yet forged in the furnace of blood—understand less about that delicate balance of natural love each generation reserves for the other. Remembering yesterday's thrashings, or angry because the fathers did not provide the desired social or economic advantages, sons sometimes reveal themselves in cruel ways.

Wild tigers claw the poor father for failures real or imagined: opportunities fumbled, aborted marriages, punishments misplaced. There is this, too: a man who has discovered a likeness in his own image willing to believe (far beyond what the evidence requires) that he combines the natural qualities of Santa Claus, Superman, and the senior saints, will not easily surrender to more mature judgments. Long after the junior partner has ceased to believe that he may have been adopted or that beating off will grow hair on the hand while the brain slowly congeals into gangrenous matter, the father may pose and pretend, hiding bits and pieces of yesterday behind his back. Almost any father with the precious stuff to care can adequately conceal the pea. It is natural in sons to lust—yes, to *hunger* for—an Old Man special enough to have endowed his progeny's genes with genius and steel. Or, failing the ideal, to have a father who will at least remain sturdy, loyal, and *there* when life's vigilantes come riding with the hangman.

You see the fix the poor bastard is in, don't you? He must at once apologize and inspire, conceal and judge, strut and intervene, correct and pretend. No matter how far he ranges outside his normal capabilities, he will remain unappreciated through much of the paternal voyage—often neglected, frequently misread, sometimes profaned by his own creation. For all this, the father may evolve into a better man: may find himself closer to being what he claims, a strong role having ways of overpowering the actor. And if he is doubly blessed, he may know a day when his sons (by then, most likely, fathers themselves) will come to love him more than they can bring themselves to say. Then, sometimes, sons get to know their fathers a bit; perhaps a little more than nature intended, and surely more than yesterday would have believed.

There was that blindly adoring period of childhood when my father was the strongest and wisest of men. He would scare off the bears my young imagination feared as they prowled the night outside our Texas farmhouse, provide sunshine and peanut butter, make the world go away. I brought him my broken toys and my skinned knees. He did imitations of all the barnyard animals; when we boxed he saw to it that I won by knockouts. After his predawn winter milkings, shivering and stomping his numb feet while rushing to throw more wood on the fire, he warned that tomorrow morning, by gosh, he planned to laze abed and eat peach cobbler while his youngest son performed the icy chores.

He took me along when he hunted rabbits and squirrels, and on alternate Saturdays when he bounced in a horse-drawn wagon over dirt roads to accomplish his limited commercial possibilities in Putnam or Cisco. He thrilled me with tales of his own small-boy peregrinations: an odyssey to Missouri, consuming two years, in covered wagons pulled by oxen; fordings of swift rivers; and pauses in Indian camps where my grandfather, Morris Miles King, smoked strong pipes with his hosts and ate with his fingers from iron kettles containing what he later called dog stew. The Old Man taught me to whistle, pray, ride a horse, enjoy country music, and, by his example, to smoke. He taught that credit buying was unmanly, unwise, and probably unforgivable in heaven; that one honored one's women, one's flag, and one's pride; that, on evidence supplied by the biblical source of "winds blowing from the four corners of the earth," the world was most assuredly flat. He taught me the Old Time Religion, to bait a fishhook and gut a butchered hog, to sing "The Nigger Preacher and the Bear."

I had no way of knowing what courage was in the man (he with no education, no hope of quick riches, no visible improvements or excitements beckoning to new horizons) that permitted him to remain so cheerful, shielding, and kind. No matter how difficult those depression times, there was always something under the Christmas tree. When I was four, he walked five miles to town in a blizzard, then returned as it worsened, carrying a red rocking chair and smaller gifts in a gunny-sack. Though he had violated his creed by buying on credit, he made it possible for Santa Claus to appear on time.

I would learn that he refused to accept the largess of one of FDR's recovery agencies because he feared I might be shamed or marked by wearing to school its telltale olive-drab "relief shirts." He did accept employment with the Works Progress Administration, shoveling and hauling wagonloads of dirt and gravel for a road-building project. When I brought home the latest joke from the rural school—WPA stands for We Piddle Around—he delivered a stern, voice-quavering lecture: "Son, the WPA is an honest way some poor men has of makin' their families a livin'. You'd go to bed hungry tonight without the WPA. Next time some smart aleck makes a joke about it, you ought to knock a goddamned whistlin' fart out of him."

Children learn that others have fathers with more money, more opportunity, more sophistication. Their own ambitions or resentments rise, inspiring them to reject the simpler wants of an earlier time. The son is shamed by the father's speech, dress, car, occupation, and table manners. The desire to flee the family nest (or to soar higher in it; to undertake some few experimental solos) arrives long before the young have their proper wings or before their parents can conceive of it.

The Old Man was an old-fashioned father, one who relied on cor-poral punishments, biblical exhortations, and a ready temper. He was not a man who dreamed much or who understood that others might require dreams as their opium. Though he held idleness to be as use-less and as sinful as adventure, he had the misfortune to sire a hedonist son who dreamed of improbable conquests accomplished by some magic superior to grinding work. By the time I entered the trouble-some teen-age years, we were on the way to a long, dark journey. A mutual thirst to prevail existed—some crazy stubborn infectious con-tagious will to avoid the slightest surrender.

The Old Man strapped, rope whipped, and caned me for smoking, drinking, lying, avoiding church, skipping school, and laying out at night. Having once been very close, we now lashed out at each other in the manner of rejected lovers on the occasion of each new disappoint-ment. I thought The Old Man blind to the wonders and potentials of the real world; could not fathom how current events or cultural habits so vital to my contemporaries could be considered so frivolous—or worse. In turn, The Old Man expected me to obediently accept his own values: show more concern over the ultimate disposition of my eternal soul, eschew easy paths when walking tougher ones might somehow purify, be not so inquisitive or damnfool dreamy. That I could not (or would not) comply puzzled, frustrated, and angered him. In desperation he moved from a "wet" town to a "dry" one, in the foolish illusion that this tactic might keep his baby boy out of saloons.

On a Saturday in my fifteenth year, when I refused an order to dig a cesspool in our backyard because of larger plans downtown, I fought back: it was savage and ugly—though, as those things go, one hell of a good fight. But only losers emerged. After that we spoke in terse mumbles or angry shouts, not to communicate with civility for three years. The Old Man paraded to a series of punishing and uninspiring jobs— night watchman, dock loader for a creamery, construction worker, chicken butcher in a steamy, stinking poultry house, while I trekked to my own part-times jobs or to school. When school was out I usually repaired to one distant oil field or another, remaining until classes began anew. Before my eighteenth birthday I escaped by joining the army.

On the morning of my induction, The Old Man paused at the kitchen table, where I sat trying to choke down breakfast. He wore the faded old cross-gallus denim overalls I held in superior contempt and carried a lunch bucket in preparation of whatever dismal job then rode him. "Lawrence," he said, "is there anything I can do for you?" I shook my head. "You need any money?" "No." The Old Man shuffled uncertainly, causing the floor to creak. "Well," he said, "I wish you good luck." I nodded in the direction of my bacon and eggs. A moment later the front door slammed, followed by the grinding of gears The Old Man always accomplished in confronting even the simplest machinery.

Alone in a Fort Dix crowd of olive drab, I lay popeyed on my bunk at night, chain smoking, as Midland High School's initial 1946 football game approached. The impossible dream was that some magic carpet might transport me back to those anticipatory tingles I had known when bands blared, cheerleaders cartwheeled sweet tantalizing glimpses of their panties, and we purple-clads whooped and clattered toward the red-shirted Odessa Bronchos or the Angry Orange of San Angelo. Waste and desolation lived in the heart's private country on the night that opening game was accomplished on the happiest playing field of my forfeited youth. The next morning, a Saturday, I was called to the orderly room to accept a telegram—a form of communication that had always meant death or other disasters. I tore it open with the darkest fantasies to read MIDLAND 26 EL PASO YSLETA 0 LOVE DAD. Those valuable communiqués arrived on ten consecutive Saturday mornings.

With a ten-day furlough to spend, I appeared unannounced and before a cold dawn on the porch of that familiar frame house in Midland. The Old Man rose quickly, dispensing greetings in his woolly long-handles. "You just a first-class private?" he teased. "Lord God, I would a-thought a King would be a general by now. Reckon I'll have to write ole Harry Truman a postcard to git that straightened out." Most of the time, however (when I was not out impressing the girls with my PFC stripe) a cautious reserve prevailed. We talked haltingly, carefully, probing as uncertainly as two neophyte premed students might explore their first skin boil.

On the third or fourth day The Old Man woke me on the sleeping porch, lunch bucket in hand. "Lawrence," he said, "your mother found a bottle of whisky in your suitcase. Now, you know this is a teetotal home. We never had a bottle of whisky in a home of ours, and we been married since 19-and-11. You're perfectly welcome to stay here, but your whisky's not." I stiffly mumbled something about going to a motel. "You know better than that," The Old Man scolded. "We don't want you goin' off to no blamed motel." Then, in a weary exasperation not fully appreciated until dealing with transgressions among my own offspring: "Good God, son, what makes you want to raise ole billy hell all the time?" We regarded each other in a helpless silence. "Do what you think is right," he said, sighing. "I've done told you how me and your mother feel." He went off to work; I got up and removed the offending liquids.

The final morning brought a wet freeze blowing down from Amarillo by way of the North Pole. The Old Man's car wouldn't start; our family had never officially recognized taxis. "I'll walk you to the bus station," he said, bundling in a heavy sheepskin jumper and turning his back, I suspect, so as not to witness my mother's struggle against tears. We shivered down dark streets, past homes of my former schoolmates, by vacant lots where I played softball or slept off secret sprees, past stores I remembered for their bargains in Moon Pies and then Lucky Strikes and finally Trojans. Nostalgia and old guilts blew in with the wind. I wanted to say something healing to The Old Man, to utter some gracious good-bye (the nearest thing to retroactive apologies a savage young pride would permit), but I simply knew no beginnings.

We sat an eternity in the unreal lights of the bus station among crying babies, hung-over cowboys, and drowsing old Mexican men, in mute inspection of those dead shows provided by bare walls and ceilings. The Old Man made a silent offering of a cigarette. He was a vigorous fifty-nine then, still clear-eyed, dark-haired, and muscular, but as his hand extended that cigarette pack and I saw it clearly— weather cured, scarred, one finger crooked and stiff-jointed from an industrial accident—I suddenly and inexplicably knew that one day The Old Man would wither, fail, die. In that moment, I think, I first sensed—if I did not understand—something of mortality; of tribes, blood, and inherited rituals.

At the door to the bus The Old Man suddenly hugged me, roughly, briefly: not certain, perhaps, such an intimacy would be tolerated by this semistranger who bore his name. His voice broke as he said, "Write us, son. We love you." I clasped his hand and brushed past, too full for words. For I knew, then, that I loved him, too, and had, even in the worst of times, and would never stop.

We took a trip last summer, one The Old Man had secretly coveted for a lifetime, though, in the end, he almost had to be prodded into the car. "I hate like the devil to leave Cora," he said of his wife of almost six decades. "She's got to where her head swims when she walks up and down the steps. She taken a bad spill just a few weeks ago. I try to stay close enough to catch her if she falls."

The Old Man did not look as if he could catch much of a falling load as he approached eighty-three. Two hundred pounds of muscle and sinew created by hard work and clean living had melted to a hundred-sixty-odd; his senior clothing flapped about him. He had not worn his bargain dentures for years, except when my mother insisted on enforcing the code of some rare social function, because, he complained, they played the devil with his gums, or gagged him, or both. The eagle's gleam was gone from eyes turned watery and rheumy; he couldn't hear so well any more; he spoke in a wispy voice full of false starts and tuneless whistles requiring full attention.

He was thirteen years retired from his last salaried job, and he had established himself as a yard-tender and general handyman. He mowed lawns, trimmed hedges, tilled flower beds, grubbed stumps, painted houses, performed light carpentry or emergency plumbing. In his eightieth year my mother decreed that he might no longer climb trees for pruning purposes. Though he lived with that verdict, his eyes disapproved it just as they had when his sons dictated that he might no longer work during the hottest part of the desert summer days. The Old Man surrendered his vigor hard, each new concession (not driving a car or giving up cigarettes) throwing him into a restless depression. He continued to rise each morning at five, prowling the house impatiently on rainy days, muttering and growling of all the grass that needed mowing or of how far behind Midland was falling in unpainted fences. At such times he might complain because the Social Security Administration refused him permission to earn more than twelve hundred dollars annually while continuing to merit its assistance; he sneaked in more work by the simple expediency of lowering his prices. Except on the Sabbath (when, by his ethic, the normal joy of work translated to sin), he preferred the indoors only when eating or sleeping. He had long repaired to a sleeping porch of his own creation, where it was always twenty degrees cooler in winter and correspondingly hotter in the summertime; one of the curses of modernity, he held, was "refrigerated air."

On my mother's reassurances that she would spend a few days with her twin sister, we coaxed The Old Man into my car. Years earlier I had asked him whether he wanted to see some particular place or thing and whether I might take him there. To my surprise (for The Old Man had never hinted of secret passions) he said yes, he had wanted since childhood to visit the state capitol in Austin and the Alamo in San Antonio: he had read of them in books his mother had obtained when his father's death had cut off his schooling. I had long procrastinated. Living in the distant Sodoms and Gomorrahs of the East, I wandered in worlds alien to my father in search of ambitions that surely mystified him. There were flying trips home: an hour's domino playing here, an evening of conversation there. Then the desert would become too still, dark, and forbidding: I would shake his worn old hand, mutter promises and excuses, grab a suitcase; run. Last summer my wife effectively nagged me to deliver on my old pledge. And so, one boiling morning in July, we departed my father's house. He sat beside me on the front seat, shrunken and somehow remote, yet transmitting some youthful eagerness. The older he had grown, the less The Old Man had ever troubled to talk, contenting himself with sly grins or solemn stares so well timed you sometimes suspected he heard better than advertised. Deliver him a grandchild to tease and he would open up: "Bradley Clayton King, I hear turrible things on you. Somebody said you got garments on your back, and you have ancestors. And word come to me lately that you was seen hesitatin' on the doorstep." With others, however, he was slow to state his case.

Now, however, we had hardly gone a mile before The Old Man began a monologue lasting almost a week. As we roared across the desert waste, his fuzzy old voice battled with the cool cat's purr of the air conditioner; he gestured, pointed, laughed, praised the land, took on new strength.

He had a love for growing things, a Russian peasant's legendary infatuation for the motherland; for digging in the good earth, smelling it, conquering it. "Only job I ever had that could hold a candle to farmin'," he once said, "was blacksmithin'. Then the car come along, and I was blowed up." Probably his greatest disappointment was his failure as a farmer—an end dictated by depressed prices in his most productive years and hurried by land worn down through a lack of any effective application of the basic agrarian sciences. He was a walking-plow farmer, a mule-and-dray-horse farmer, a chewing-gum-and-baling-wire farmer. If God brought rain at the wrong moment, crops rotted in the mud; should He not bring it when required, they baked and died. You sowed, tilled, weeded, sweated: if heaven felt more like reward than punishment, you would not be forced to enter the Farmer's State Bank with your soiled felt hat in your hand.

World War II forced The Old Man off the family acres: he simply could not reject the seventy-odd cents per hour an oil company promised for faithful drudgery in its pipeline crew. And he felt, too, deep and simple patriotic stirrings: perhaps, if he carried enough heavy pipe quickly enough, the fall of Hitler and Tojo might be hastened. He alternately flared with temper fits and was quietly reflective on the fall day in 1942 when we quit the homestead he had come to in a covered wagon in 1894; later, receiving word of the accidental burning of that unpainted farmhouse, he walked around with tears in his eyes. He was past seventy before giving up his dream of one day returning to that embittered soil, of finally mastering it, of extracting its unkept promises.

As we left behind the oil derricks and desert sand hills last summer, approaching barns and belts of greenery, The Old Man praised wild flowers, dairy herds, shoots of cotton, fields of grain. "That's mighty good timberland," he said. "Good grass. Cattle could bunch up in them little groves in the winter and turn their backsides to the wind." He damned his enemies: "Now, Johnson grass will ruin a place. But mesquite trees is the most sapping thing that God lets grow. Mesquites spreads faster than gossip. A cow can drop her plop on a flat rock, and if she's been eatin' mesquite beans they'll take a-holt and grow like mornin' glories."

One realized, as The Old Man grew more and more enthusiastic over roadside growths and dribbling little creeks, just how fenced in he had been for thirty years; knew, freshly, the depth of his resentments as gas pumps, hamburger outlets, and supermarkets came to prosper within two blocks of his door. The Old Man had personally hammered and nailed his house together in 1944, positioning it on the town's northmost extremity as if hoping it might sneak off one night to seek more bucolic roots. Midland had been a town of maybe twelve thousand then; now it flirted with seventy thousand and the chamber of commerce mindlessly tub-thumped for more. The Old Man hated it: it had hemmed him in.

We detoured to Eastland County so he might take another glimpse of the past. He slowly moved among the tombstones in a rural cemetery where his parents rested among parched grasses and the bones of their dear friends: people who had been around for the Civil War; God-fearing, land-grubbing folk who had never dreamed that one day men would fly like birds in the sky or swim like fishes beneath the sea. Though he had on his best suit, he bent down to weed the family plot. I kneeled to help; my young son joined us. We worked in silence and a cloaking heat, sharing unspoken tribal satisfactions.

We drove past stations he recognized as important milestones: "Right over yonder—the old house is gone now, been gone forty years—but right there where you see that clump of them blamed mesquites, well, that was where your brother Weldon was borned. Nineteen-and-fifteen, I reckon it was. We had two of the purtiest weepin' willers you ever seen. I had me a dandy cotton crop that year."

We climbed an unpaved hill, the car mastering it easily, where the horses or mules of my youth had strained in harness, rolling their eyes under The Old Man's lash. "This durn hill," he said. "I come down it on a big-wheel bicycle I'd borrowed when I was about fifteen. First one I'd seen, and I was taken with it. Didn't know no more about ridin' it than I did about 'rithmetic. Come whizzin' down so fast my feet couldn't match them pedals: didn't have sense enough to coast. Well-sir, I run plumb over in the bar ditch and flipped over. It taken hair, hide and all." He laughed, and the laugh turned into a rasping cough, and the cough grew so violent that veins hammered at the edge of his sparse hair and the old face turned crimson. Through it all he joyously slapped his leg.

We stopped for lunch in a flawed little village where my father had once owned a blacksmith shop. The café was crammed by wage hands and farmers taking their chicken-fried steaks or bowls of vegetable soup seriously, men who minutely inspected strangers and muted their conversations accordingly. Weary of the car and the road, The Old Man chose to stand among the crowded tables while awaiting his order. He was grandly indifferent to the sneaked upward glances of the diners, whose busy elbows threatened to spear him from all sides, and to the waitress who, frowning, danced around him in dispensing hamburgers or plates of hot corn bread. "Tell granddad to sit down," my teenage daughter, Kerri, whispered. "He's all right," I said. "Well, my *gosh*! At least tell him to take off his *hat*!"

The Old Man startled a graybeard in khakis by gripping his arm just in time to check the elevation of a spoonful of mashed potatoes. "What's your name?" he inquired. The old nester's eyes nervously consulted his companions before he surrendered it. "Don't reckon I know you," my father said. "You must not of been around here long." "Twenty-some years," the affronted newcomer mumbled. "I had me a blacksmith shop right over yonder," The Old Man said. He pointed through a soft-drink sign and its supporting wall. "It was in the 1920s. My name's Clyde King. You recollect me?" When the old nester failed the quiz, my father abandoned him to his mashed potatoes. "What's *your* name?" he inquired of a victim mired in his blackberry pie. My twelve-year-old son giggled; his sister covered her humiliated face.

He walked along a diminutive counter of ketchup bottles, fruit pies, and digestive aids, reading only those faces grizzled enough to

remember. An aging rancher, deep in his iced tea, nodded: "Yeah, I remember you." The Old Man pumped his hand, beaming. "I was just a kid of a boy," the rancher said. "I was better acquainted with your brother Rex. And the one that run the barbershop. Claude, wasn't it? Where they at now?" The Old Man sobered himself. "Well, I buried 'em within three weeks of one another last month. Claude was seventy-eight and Rex was seventy-four. I'm the only one of the King boys still kickin'. Oldest of the bunch, too. If I live to the eighteenth of next February, the Lord willin', I'll be eighty-three years old." "Well, you look in right good shape," the rancher said.

When The Old Man sat down at our booth my daughter asked, too sweetly, "Granddad, you want me to take your hat?" He gave her an amused glance, a look suggesting he had passed this way before. "Naw," he said. "This a-way, I know where it's at if this café catches a-fire and I need it in a hurry." Then he removed the trespass to his outer knee and slowly crumbled crackers into the chili bowl before bending to feed his toothless face.

His bed was empty when I awoke in an Austin motel shortly after sunrise. He could be seen in contemplation of the swimming pool, turning his direct gaze on all who struggled toward their early jobs. Conversing with a black bellhop when I claimed him, he was full of new information: "That nigger tells me he averages a dollar a head for carryin' suitcases. I may buy me some fancy britches and give him some competition. . . . Folks sure must be sleepyheaded around here. I bet I walked a mile and didn't see two dozen people. . . . Went over yonder to that governor's mansion and rattled the gate and yelled, but didn't nobody come to let me in." "Did you *really*?" I asked, moderately appalled. "Thunder, yes! I'm a voter. Democrat, at that." Then the sly country grin flashed in a way that keeps me wondering in the night, now, whether he really had.

We entered a coffee shop. "Lord God," The Old Man said, recoiling from the menu. "This place is high as a cat's back. You mean they git a dollar eighty-five for two eggs and a little dab a bacon?" I smiled— how much did he think our motel room had cost? "Well, the way things is now, I expect it run ten or twelve dollars." No, the price had been thirty dollars. His old eyes bulged: "For *one night*? Lord God, son, let's git us a blanket and go to the wagonyard!"

"This here's a heap bigger place than I thought it would be," he said in a hushed voice as he inspected the polished chambers of the Texas House of Representatives. He read the faces of past governors hanging in the rotunda, pointing out his favorites (selecting three good men and two rank demagogues). He stood shyly, not having to be reminded to remove his hat, when introduced to a few stray legislators and when led into Governor Preston Smith's office. Probably he was relieved to find the governor was absent, for The Old Man had never prospered in the company of "big shots": a big shot may be defined as one who wears neckties in the middle of the week or claims a title; I was never certain what fine distinctions The Old Man made in his mind between a United States senator and a notary public.

He marveled at the expanse of grass on the capitol grounds, inspected its flower beds, inquired of an attendant how many gallons of water the grounds required each day, and became stonily disapproving when the hired hand did not know. In the archives of the General Land Office he painstakingly sought out the legal history of that farm his father had settled in the long ago. He was enchanted by the earliest maps of Texas counties he had known as a boy.

That night he sat on his motel bed recalling the specifics of forgotten cattle trades, remembering the only time he got drunk (at age sixteen) and how the quart of whisky so poisoned him that he had promised God and his weeping mother that, if permitted to live, he would die before touching another drop. He recited his disappointment in being denied a preacher's credentials by the Methodist hierarchy on the grounds of insufficient education. "They wanted note preachers," he said contemptuously. "Wasn't satisfied with preachers who spoke sermons from the heart and preached the Bible pure. And that's what's gone wrong with churches."

A farmhand and apprentice blacksmith, he had not been smitten blind by his first encounter with my mother at a country social. "I spied another girl I wanted to spark," he grinned. "Next day I seen that girl and several others go into a general store by the blacksmith shop. I moseyed over like I was out of chewin' tobacco. Lord God, in the daylight that girl was ugly as a mud fence! I couldn't imagine wakin' up to that of a-mornin'." He laughed. "Then I taken a second look at Cora—she was seventeen—and she had the purtiest complexion and eyes and . . . well, just *ever*thing." Scheming to see her again, he pep

talked his faint heart to encourage the boldness to request a date.

"Didn't seem like I'd ever do it," he confessed. "I'd go up to her at socials or church and make a bow and say, 'Miss Cora.' And she would bob me a little curtsy and say, 'Mister Clyde.' Then I'd stand there like a durned lummox, fiddlin' with my hat, and my face would heat up, and I couldn't think of a consarned thing to say." He laughed in memory of the callow swain that was. "It was customary in them days for young women to choose young men to lead singin' at church. I know within reason, now, that it was to help tongue-tied young hicks like myself, but I was pea green then and didn't know it. One night Cora picked me. Lord God, it excited me so that I plumb forgot the words to all the hymns I knowed." One could see him there in that lantern-lighted plank church, stiff in his high collar and cheap suit, earnest juices popping out on his forge-tanned forehead, sweet chaos alive in his heart. His voice would have quavered as he asked everyone to please turn to number one-forty-three, while matchmaking old women in calico encouraged him with their wise witch's eyes and young ladies with bright ribbons in their hair giggled behind fluttering fans advertising Sunday-school literature or pious morticians.

"Somehow I stumbled through it. Never heard a word the preacher said that night—I was tryin' to drum up nerve to approach Miss Cora, you see. Quick as the preacher said amen to his last prayer I run over fat women and little kids to get there before I got cold feet: 'Miss Cora, may I have the pleasure of your company home?' When she said, 'Yes, if you wish,' my heart pounded like I was gonna faint!

"Her daddy—ole man Jim Clark, *Lord God*, he was a tough case—he didn't allow his girls to ride in no buggies. If you wanted to spark a Clark girl, you had to be willin' to walk. Wellsir, I left my team at the church. Walkin' Cora home I asked if I could pay a call on her. I never dated no other woman from then on. There was another young feller had his eye on Cora. Once I had paid her three or four courtin' calls, I looked him up to say I didn't want him tryin' to spark her no more. Because, I said, I had it in mind to marry her. 'What'll you *do* about it?'—he got his back up, you see. I said, 'Whatever I got to do. And if you don't believe me, by God, just you try me!' He never give me no trouble."

The Old Man revealed his incredulous joy when, perhaps a year later, his halting proposal had been accepted. "Do you remember what you said?" my intrigued daughter asked. "Durn right! *Ought* to. I practiced on it for some weeks." He laughed a wheezing burst. "We had just walked up on her daddy's porch one evening and I said"—and here The Old Man attempted again the deeper tones of youth, seeking the courtly country formality he had brought into play on that vital night, reciting as one might when called upon in elocution class in some old one-room schoolhouse—"'Miss Cora, I have not got much of this world's goods, and of education I haven't none. But I fancy myself a man of decent habits, and if you will do me the honor of becoming my wife, I will do the best I can by you for always.'" He bowed his head, hiding his tears. "Granddad," my daughter asked, "did you kiss her?" "Lord God, *no!*" The Old Man was sincerely shocked, maybe even a bit outraged: "Kissin' wasn't took lightly in them days."

Between Austin and San Antonio we drove through San Marcos; a prominent sign proclaimed that Lyndon B. Johnson had once earned a degree at the local teachers college. "That's a mighty fine school," The Old Man said. I remained silent. "Yessir," he said, "a *mighty* fine school." Only the purring air conditioner responded. The Old Man shifted elaborately on the seat. "Why, now, I expect that school's as good a school as the New-nited States has." By now he realized that a contest was joined: whatever joke he wished to make must be accomplished in the absence of my feeding straight-line. "I doubt if that Harvard outfit up yonder could hold a candle to this school," he said. "I expect this school would put that Harvard bunch in the shade." My son, less experienced in such games, provided the foil: "Granddad, why is it such a good school?" "*Got* to be," The Old Man said. "It learned ole Lyndon to have sense enough to know he couldn't get elected again." He enjoyed his chortle no less for the delay.

"Didn't you like President Johnson?" my son asked.

"Naw, LBJ told too many lies. I wouldn't a-shoed horses on credit for him."

"Who was your favorite president?"

"Harry Truman. Harry wasn't afraid to take the bull by the horns. Wasn't no mealymouth goody-goody in him like in most politicians. Old Ike, now, they blowed him up like Mister Big and all he ever showed me was that silly grin."

"Did you ever vote for a Republican?" my son asked.

"Yeah, in 19-and-28. Voted for Herbert Hoover. And he no more than put his britches on the chair till we had a depression. I promised God right then if He wouldn't send no more depressions, I wouldn't vote for no more Republicans."

"Do you think God really cares who's president?" I asked.

"I reckon not," The Old Man said. "Look at what we got in there now."

What did The Old Man think of this age of protest and revolt?

"It plagues me some," he admitted. "I got mad at them young boys that didn't want to fight in Vietnam. Then after the politicians botched it so bad nobody couldn't win it, and told lies to boot, I decided *I* wouldn't want to risk dyin' in a war that didn't make sense."

It was suggested that no wars made sense.

"Maybe so," The Old Man said. "Bible says, 'Thou shalt not kill.' Still yet, the Bible's full of wars. Bible says there'll be wars and rumors of wars. I don't think war is what all the ruckus is about, though. I think young people is just generally confused."

"Why?"

"They don't have nothing to cling to," he said. They had been raised in whisky homes; their preachers, teachers, politicians, and daddies had grown so money-mad and big-Ikey nothing else counted. Too much had been handed today's kids on silver platters: they got cars too soon and matching big notions. They went off chasing false gods. Well, didn't guess he much blamed 'em: they didn't have nothing waiting at home except baby-sitters, television, and mothers that cussed in mixed company or wore whisky on the breath.

"I seen all this coming during the Second World's War," The Old Man said. "People got to moving around so much with good cars. Families split up and lost their roots. The main thing, though, was the women. Women had always stayed home and raised the kids: that was their job. It's just nature. And the man of the family had to be out scratchin' a living. But during the Second World's War, women started workin' as a regular thing and smokin' and drinkin' in public. Triflin' started, and triflin' led to divorces. I knowed then there was gonna be trouble because *somebody's* got to raise the kids. You can't expect kids to turn out right if you shuffle 'em off to the side."

There was little a divorced man could say.

"I'm thankful I raised my family when I did," he said. "World's too

full of meanness and trouble these days. Every other person you meet
is a smark aleck, and the other one's a crook. Them last few years I was
workin' for wages, there wasn't one young feller in fifty willin' to work.
All they had in mind was puttin' somethin' over on somebody. Down at
the creamery docks, the young hands would slip off to play cards or talk
smut or sit on their asses any time the boss man wasn't standin' over
'em. They laughed at me for givin' a honest day's work. I told 'em I'd
hired out to work, by God. I wouldn't a-give a nickel for any of 'em.
Didn't put no value on their personal word. I'd lift them heavy milk
crates—lift a dozen to their one—and when the drivers come in and
their trucks had to be swamped out and cleaned, I'd look around and
be the only hand workin'." He shook his head. "They didn't care about
nothin'. Seemed like life was . . . well, some kind of a joke to 'em.

"Now," he said, "I think the niggers is raisin' too much sand.
Maybe I'd be raisin' ole billy myself if I'd been kinda left out of it like
them. I dunno—it's hard to wear the other feller's shoes. But I just
wasn't raised up to believe they're supposed to mix with us. It don't
seem natural."

"Dad!" I said, *"Dad* . . . Dad . . ."

"Oh, I know," he said. Impatience was in his voice. This was an
old battle fought between us many times without producing a victor—
even though we had selectively employed the Bible against each other.

"You still mowing Willie's lawn?" I asked.

"Every Thursday," The Old Man said. "Durn your hide," he
chuckled. Then: "Naw, Willie's moved off to Houston or someplace."
Willie was a male nurse and had been the first black man to move into
my father's neighborhood eight years ago. Not long after that community despoiling I visited home: great were the dire predictions having
to do with Willie's staying in his place. Six months later we were sitting
on the front porch. The black man walked into the yard. "Hey there,
Old-Timer," he said.

I stiffened: surely The Old Man would burn a cross, bomb a
school, break into "The Nigger Preacher and the Bear."

Instead he said mildly, "How you, Doctor?"

"Can you do my lawn a couple days early next week? I'm having
some people over for dinner Tuesday night."

"Reckon so," The Old Man said. "Whatcha gonna have to eat?"

The black man smiled and said he thought he might burn some
steaks on the grill.

"You can *tip* me one of them beefsteaks," The Old Man said, looking mischievous. "I'm a plumb fool about beefsteak."

They laughed; the black man complimented my father on his flower beds before giving him instructions on exactly how he wanted his shrubbery trimmed. The Old Man walked with him across the street to inspect the particulars. When he returned to ease back into his chair, I said—affecting the flattest possible cracker twang—"Boy Hidy, if that chocolate-coated sumbitch don't stay in his *place.* . . ." The Old Man's grin was a bit sheepish. "I wouldn't mind 'em if they was all like ole Willie," he said. "He works hard, he keeps hisself clean, to my knowledge he don't drink, and I don't believe he'd steal if he was hungry." Then came one of those oblique twists of mind of which he was capable: "I don't take his checks though. I make 'im pay cash."

Now, some years later, we were approaching San Antonio. "I always figgered this for just another little ole Meskin town except for havin' the Alamo," he said. Soon he was marveling at the city's wonders, at the modern office buildings, old Spanish-style homes, green parks and easy-riding rivers. The Old Man happily waved to passing paddle boats as we idled under a tree at a riverfront café, laughing through the tears at himself when—mistaking a bowl of powerful peppers for stewed okra—he spooned in a country mouthful requiring a hard run on all available ice water.

He approached the Alamo with a reverence both enthusiastic and touching. "Right here," he proclaimed—pointing to a certain worn stone slab—"is where Travis drew a line with his sword and told all the boys willin' to die for the right to step across. All of 'em stepped across except Jim Bowie, who was sick on a cot, and he had his buddies *carry* him across." Just why he had selected that particular stone not even historians may attest: the much-restored Alamo must make do with the smaller original artifacts and the wilder romanticisms. Indeed, where much of the blood was spilled a prestige department store now stands.

He moved among display cases containing precious bits and pieces of a more vigorous time: wooden pegs serving purposes later to be preempted by metal hinges, square-headed nails, early Colt firearms, crude chisels and hand-operated bellows, arrowheads, saddlebags, oxen yokes, tintype photos, the earliest barbed wire, a country doctor's bag with crude equipment such as an old uncle had carried in the long ago. He assembled his descendants to explain the uses of each relic, carefully associating himself—and his blood's blood—with that older time and place. He came to a new authority; his voice improved. Soon a group of tourists followed him about, the bolder ones asking questions. The Old Man performed as if he had been there during the siege. Choosing a spot on the outer walls, he said with conviction that right over yonder was where the invaders had fatally broken through. ("Daddy," my daughter whispered, "will you *please* get him to stop saying 'Meskin'?")

Taking a last look, he said, "Ma bought me a book on the Alamo. I must of read it a hundred times. I read how them damn Meskins done Travis and his brave boys, how ole General Santa Anna had butchered all them Texas heroes, and I promised myself if I ever seen one of them greaser sons-a-bitches, why, I'd kill him with my bare hands." He laughed at that old irrationality. "But did you notice today, half the people in that Alamo was *Meskins*? And they seemed to think just as much of it as we do."

Now it was late afternoon. His sap suddenly ran low; he seemed more fragile, a tired old head with a journey to make; he dangerously stumbled on a curbstone. Crossing a busy intersection, I took his arm. Though that arm had once pounded anvils into submission, it felt incredibly frail. My children, fueled by youth's inexhaustible gases, skipped and cavorted fully a block ahead. Negotiating the street, The Old Man half laughed and half snorted: "I recollect helpin' you across lots of streets when you was little. Never had no notion that one day you'd be doin' the same for me." Well, I said. Well. Then: "I've helped that boy up there"—motioning toward my distant and mobile son— "across some few streets. Until now, it never once occurred that he may someday return the favor." "Well," The Old Man said, "he will if you're lucky."

Three o'clock in an Austin motel. The Old Man snores in competition with jet aircraft. On an adjoining bed his grandson's measured breathing raises and lowers a pale banner of sheets. Earlier, the boy had exorcised his subconscious demons through sheet-tugging threshings and disjointed, indistinct private cries. The Old Man snores on, at peace. *Night battles never plagued me*, he once said in explaining his ability to sleep anyplace, anytime. *I never was one to worry much. What people worry about is things they can't do nothin' about. Worryin' always seemed like a waste to me.*

The bridging gap between the two slumbering generations, himself an experienced insomniac, sits in the dark judging whether he would most appreciate a cold six-pack or the world's earliest sunrise. Out of deference to The Old Man, he has known only limited contacts with those bracing stimulants and artificial aids for which his soft, polluted body now begs. The only opium available to him is that hallucinogenic agent the layman calls "memory"—a drug of the most awful and powerful properties, one that may ravish the psyche even while nurturing the soul. Stiff penalties should be affixed to its possession, for its dangerous components include disappointing inventories, blocked punts, lumpy batters, and iron buckets of burden. It is habit forming, near-to-maddening in large doses, and may even grow hair on the palms.

I remembered that we had compromised our differences in about my twentieth year. My own early assumption of family responsibilities proved healing: in the natural confusions of matrimony, one soon came to appreciate The Old Man's demanding, luckless role. Nothing is so leavening to the human species as to gaze upon the new and untried flesh of another human being and realize, in a combination of humility, amazement, and fear, that you are responsible for its creation and well-being. This discovery is almost immediately followed by a sharply heightened appreciation of more senior fathers.

We discovered that we could talk again. Could even sit at ease in long and mutually cherished silence. Could civilly exchange conflicting opinions, compete in dominoes rather than in more deadly games, romp on the lawn with our descendants, and share each new family pride or disappointment. For some four years in the early 1950s we lived in close proximity. The Old Man came to accept my preference for whisky as I came to accept his distaste for what it represented; he learned to live with my skeptic's atheism as I came to live with his belief that God was as tangible an entry as the Methodist bishop.

The Old Man was sixty-six and I was twenty-five when I went away for good. There were periodic trips back home, each of them somehow more hurried, fleeting, and blurred. Around 1960 it dawned on me that The Old Man and his sons had, in effect, switched roles. On a day I cannot name, he suddenly and wordlessly passed the family crown. Now the sons were solicited for advice or leadership and would learn to live uneasily in the presence of a quiet and somehow deeply wrenching paternal deference. (*Weldon, you reckon it would be all*

right if I got a better car? Well, now, Dad, I believe I'd go slow on
that. Maybe you don't see and hear well enough to drive in traffic very
much. *Lawrence, what would you say to me and your mother goin'
back to the farm?* Now, dad, why in the world? People have been
starving off those old farms for fifty years. What would you do out there
in the sticks, miles from a doctor, if you or mother got sick?)

The heart of the young blacksmith continued to beat in that
shrinking frame, however. He could not drive a car any more; he nodded off in the middle of the sermon at Asbury Methodist; meddlers had
barred him from climbing trees. He remained very much his own man,
however, in vital areas. Living by his sweat, The Old Man saved
an astonishing amount of his paltry pensions and earnings, fiercely
guarded his independence, took pride in his age, seldom rode when he
could walk, tended the soil, ate well, and slept regularly.

On that motel bed slept a man who, at age twelve, had fallen heir
to the breadwinner's role for a shotgun-widowed mother and eight
younger siblings. He had accepted that burden, had discharged it
without running off to sea: had drawn on some simple rugged country
grace and faith permitting him no visible resentments then or later. He
had sweated two family broods through famines and floods, Great Depressions and World Wars, industrial and sociological revolutions.
Though a child of another century, really, he walked through the chaos
and tediums of his time determinedly—as Faulkner wrote of women
passing through grief and trouble—"able to go through them and
come out on the other side."

The faintest dawn showed through the windows when The Old
Man sat up in bed, yawning: "Lord God, is it dinnertime? Must be,
you bein' awake!" He examined my face: "Didn't you get no sleep?"
Some. "How much?" Three or four hours, I lied. "You ain't gonna live
to see fifty," The Old Man predicted. "What you ought to do is buy you
a cotton farm and work it all day. I bet you'd sleep at night, then."

He almost hopped into his trousers from a standing position,
amazingly agile in that fresh hour he most cherished. Noting my inspection he asked, "Reckon you can do that at eighty-two?" Hell, I
said, I can't do it at forty-one. The Old Man celebrated this superiority
with a pleased grin. The previous night he had insisted on playing
dominoes past midnight in the home of a favorite nephew, Lanvil
Gilbert, talking it up like a linebacker: *Say you made five? Why, that*

makes me so mad I'll play my double-five—and gimme fifteen while you got your marker handy. . . . I forgot to tell you boys I run a domino school on the side. Got a beginner's class you might be able to git in. Back at the motel he had again explored the distant past until his grandchildren yawned him to bed. *Old Man,* I thought, *what is the secret? What keeps you interested, laughing, loving each breath?* I remembered his enthusiastic voice on the telephone when I told him I had given my son his middle name: "I'm puttin' a five-dollar bill in the mail to buy him his first pair of long pants. Put it up and keep it. I want that exact five-dollar bill to pay for my namesake's first long pants." Grand satisfaction had visited his face earlier on our Austin trip when my son brought him a gigantic three-dollar pocket watch. The boy had shoved it at him—"Here, granddad, this is for you, I bought it out of my allowance"—and then had moved quickly away from the dangers of sentimental thanks and unmanly hugs.

As we started down to breakfast, The Old Man said, "Why don't we take Bradley Clayton with us?" Sure, if he wants to go. The Old Man gently shook the boy. "Namesake," he said, "Wake up, namesake, you sleepyhead." The boy rolled over with reluctance, blinking, trying to focus. "Git up from there," the Old Man said in feigned anger. "Time I was your age, I had milked six cows and plowed two fields by this time-a-day."

"What?" the boy said, incredulous.

"I'll make you think what!" The Old Man said, then repeated his improbable claim.

The boy, pulling his wits together, offered The Old Man a sample of the bloodline's baiting humor: "Was *that* what made you rich?"

The Old Man whooped and tousled the boy's hair, then mock-whipped him toward the bathroom.

We talked late on my final night. The Old Man sat in his jerry-built house, on a couch across from a painting of Jesus risking retina damage by looking directly into the celestial lights. Pictures of his grandchildren were on the walls and on the television top, along with a needlework replica of the Dead Kennedys appearing to hover over the U.S. Capitol, and a Woolworth print depicting a highly sanitized village blacksmith. One of his sons, thinking to please The Old Man, had given him the latter: while he appreciated the thought, he had been amused by the artist's concept. "Lord-a-mercy," he had chuckled, "the feller that painted that thing never *seen* a horse shod or a blacksmith shop either one." The painting revealed a neat, sweatless man effortlessly bending a horseshoe as he worked in an imposing brick edifice surrounded by greenery, while little girls in spotless dresses romped happily among gleaming anvils possibly compounded of sterling silver. The Old Man enjoyed comparing it with the realities of a photo made in the 1920s, showing him grease stained and grimy in a collapsing wooden structure filled with indescribable debris.

His hands—always vital to his lip movements—swooped and darted, described arcs, pointed, performed slow or vigorous dances according to the moment's chin music. Just before bed I asked in a private moment whether he had any major regrets. "Two," he said. "I wish I could of done better financially by your mother. I never meant for her to have such a hard life. And I wish I could of went to school."

On the morning of my departure he was spry and fun filled. Generally such leave-takings were accomplished in tensions and gloom; for a decade the unspoken thought had hovered that this might be the final good-bye. Last July, however, that melancholy tune was but faintly heard: The Old Man was so vigorously alive that I began to think of him as a sure centenarian. I left him standing on the front porch, wearing his workman's clothes, shaking a friendly fist against what he would do if I didn't write my mother more often.

Six weeks later he gathered a generous mess of turnip greens from his backyard vegetable garden, presenting them to his wife with the request that she concoct her special corn bread. A few hours after his meal he became dizzy and nauseated. "I just et too many of them turnip greens," he explained to his wife. Persuaded to the hospital for examination and medications, he insisted on returning home on the grounds he had never spent a night in a hospital bed and was too old to begin. The next morning, in great pain, he consented to again be loaded into my brother's car.

The Old Man mischievously listed his age as sixteen with a crisp hospital functionary filling out the inevitable forms. He ordered nurses out when a doctor appeared, extracting a promise from my brother that "no womenfolk" would be permitted to intimately attend him. When the examining physician pressed his lower abdomen, The Old Man jerked and groaned. "Is that extremely sore, Mr. King?" Well, yes, it was a right-smart sore. "How long has it been that way?" About ten days, he reckoned. "Why didn't you tell me?" my exasperated brother inquired. The old eyes danced through the pain: "Wouldn't a done no good, you not bein' no doctor."

He consented to stay in the hospital, though he did complain that his lawn mower and supporting tools had been carelessly abandoned: would my brother see that they were locked in the backyard toolshed? Then he shook my brother's hand: "Weldon, thank you for everything." He shortly lapsed into the final chills and fevers, and before I could reach home he was gone. I saw him in his final sleep and now cannot forget those magnificently weathered old hands. They told the story of a countryman's life in an eloquent language of wrinkles, veins, old scars and new. The Old Man's hands always bore some fresh scratch or cut as adornment, the result of his latest tangle with a scrap of wire, a rusted pipe, a stubborn root; in death they did not disappoint even in that small and valuable particular. No, it is not given to sons to know everything of their fathers—mercifully, perhaps—but I have those hands in my memory to supply evidence of the obligations he met, the sweat he gave, the honest deeds performed. I like to think that you could look at those hands and read the better part of The Old Man's heart.

Clyde Clayton King lived eighty-two years, seven months, and twenty-five days. His widow, four of five children, seven of eight grandchildren, six great-grandchildren, and two great-great-grandchildren survive. His time extended from when "kissin' wasn't took lightly" to exhibitions of group sex; from five years before men on horseback rushed to homestead the Cherokee Strip to a year before man's first walk on the moon; from a time when eleven of twelve American families existed on average annual incomes of $380 to today's profitable tax-dodging conglomerates; from the first presidency of Grover Cleveland to the mid-term confusions of Richard Nixon. Though he had plowed oxen in yoke, he never flew in an airplane. He died owing no man and knowing the satisfaction of having built his own house.

I joined my brother and my son in gathering and locking away The Old Man's tools in that backyard shed he had concocted of scrap lumbers, chipped bricks, assorted tins, and reject roofing materials. Then, each alone with his thoughts, we moved in a concert of leaky garden hose and weathered sprinklers, lingering to water his lawn.

Afterword

When Willie Morris was my editor at *Harper's*, titillated by my whisky stories about The Old Man, he urged me several times to write about him. Each attempt failed. Only six weeks before The Old Man died, I tried again. A month later, on a damp day over drinks in a Lexington Avenue bar when I felt unusually used up, I morosely confessed failure: "Goddammit, I'm intimidated by it. I guess I just don't understand him well enough." Willie generously said he agreed with my first declaration, though he doubted the latter.

Flying home for The Old Man's funeral, I began to sort him out in my mind. Though not aware of doing so, I probably was beginning the writing process even then. I remember openly and carelessly puffing several sticks of pot between Washington and Dallas, and seeing mystical, tantalizing, undefinable clues to what it was all about in the puffy drifting cumulus formations outside the sealed window. When Willie Morris telephoned his condolences about two hours after we had buried The Old Man, I blurted, "Willie, I can write it now."

The task required about thirty days or, more accurately, nights. Emotional ones; I cried a lot. Though the article came in at about twelve thousand words, I wrote nearer to forty thousand in the original draft. Always it was a process of defining, of evaluating, of winnowing and cutting down. To my amazement, I discovered much about The Old Man—and about myself, and larger subjects—that I had not previously suspected. I came to believe that perhaps what life is all about, with its uncertain currents and puzzling tugging tides, is the extensions of the generations trying to work it all out. I once read somewhere that writing is, ideally, an act of discovery; certainly it was for me in that case.

"The Old Man" brought other satisfactions. One was hearing my mother say, almost two years after its publication, "Rereading that piece about your daddy gives me back a little of him for a while." Another occurred one night shortly after I learned the article had several times been reprinted abroad. Swooshing down a dark Texas highway, the headlights showing only vast empty reaches and the car radio thrumming indigenous country music, I thought: *By God, they're reading about old Clyde King tonight in Warsaw and Moscow!* It was a great feeling, like giving to someone you love, only slightly dampened by the thought that I would have given anything to hear the wry, self-deprecating thing The Old Man might have said about such an absurdity. A third windfall came when I heard my son precisely quoting something The Old Man had said in the article: "'A cow can drop her plop on a flat rock, and if she's been eatin' mesquite beans they'll take a-holt and grow like mornin' glories.'" He quoted his grandfather with a pleased smile, and with a chant sensing not only the rhythm but the poetry of the utterance. In that moment I could have wished or imagined no greater reward.

BORDERLINES

Tom Miller

Tom Miller lives in Tucson, Arizona. He is a journalist who has contributed to the *New York Times, Esquire, New West,* and other publications, and he is the author of *The Assassination Please Almanac* and *On the Border: Portraits of America's Southwestern Frontier,* from which the following is excerpted. In writing *On the Border,* Miller spent four months traveling from Kopernik Shores, near Brownsville, Texas, to San Ysidro, California—a distance of some two thousand miles of Mexican–United States border. In the selection here—"The Great Candy Exchange"—Miller visited with a group of elementary school children in Yuma, Arizona, and with children of the same age group at the Escuela Abelardo L. Rodríguez in San Luis Río Colorado, Sonora, Mexico.

The Great Candy Exchange

To get other impressions of this country between America and Mexico we visited with fourth-, fifth-, and sixth-grade students at a Yuma, Arizona elementary school. Without hesitation they spoke their minds about the difference between Yuma and nearby San Luis Río Colorado, Sonora.

"The streets are made of dirt in Mexico!"

"Yeah, they're bumpy and they don't fix them up. They're full of holes."

"And they have a lotta rocks, too. They're too poor to pave them."

"The houses are smaller there."

"Yeah, they don't got no wood to build no houses."

"The schools are real tall. If you go there and you don't know Spanish, they put you in the first grade."

"And their teachers are real strict. My cousin is in school there and she told me."

Among the Yuma students were recently naturalized citizens as well as a number of green-card children, whose parents were Mexicans allowed to live and work on the U.S. side. Many of the students spoke English and Spanish interchangeably, and those who conversed only in Spanish learned English in special classes. One of the recently naturalized students preferred her American school. "They don't have trash cans at the school I went to in Mexico. And we get more education than they do."

"They think different in schools down there," a boy said slowly. "They teach math but it's different. They know how to do it but they do it in a different way."

Most of the Yuma children had relatives or close friends across the line and visited them regularly. When they visit San Luis they bring something for their friends, such as—

"Shoes! Some kids over there don't have any shoes."

"Clothes!"

"I once brought my cousin a bike."

"I gave my old skateboard to Margo. She lives in San Luis."

"I have some cousins over there, and they said they would like to have our president."

"Money. Sometimes we bring money."

They all knew money. I held up a ten-peso note—worth approximately forty-five cents—in one hand and a dollar bill in the other, and asked which they would rather have.

"That one! The dollar!"

"But this bill says 'one' on it and the other says 'ten.' Wouldn't you rather have ten than one?"

"*Noooooooooooo.*"

"Why aren't they the same?"

"Their money's different because it's lower."

"Yeah, that's the way the president wants it."

"One time I was in a store with my Mom, and this Mexican man, he pulled out a Mexican dollar. He thought he could buy some bread."

"You can get stuff cheaper over there than here," chimed in a classmate. "Like if you only have a hundred dollars you can buy anything 'cause they only make seventy-five dollars a month."

"They don't have too much work over there. That's why."

"Yeah, they don't have any money. They have to go get their water outside the house and drink it."

"And the bathrooms are outside, some of them. And they're wooden."

"Their president steals too much from the poor people."

"I feel sad when I see people so poor," a girl added.

A sixth grader waved his hand frantically. "Sometimes people come across the border and they walk right by our house. The people who sneak across wear those big long things called *sarapes* and big hats. They eat beans and tortillas every day."

"I heard they swim across. But I don't know where they swim at."

"This whole school used to be an ocean," a neighboring fourth grader patiently explained. "And they used to swim across here."

A more knowledgeable classmate spoke up. "There's a dam. The All-American Dam, it's called. The people who come across hide in the bushes down there. We went down there once and saw the Border Patrol. If they see footprints, they'll follow them."

"Yeah, they pick up wetbacks. They pick 'em up and take 'em across the border."

"Sometimes when people are picking lemons and the Border Patrol comes around, everyone runs."

"My friend from San Luis told me they hit him with a belt," one Mexican boy said.

"Some of them get killed, I heard," another quickly added.

"They won't let you across if you don't have a *pasaporte*. Otherwise you have to stay in Mexico."

"The kids come across through a hole and they go to that park by the fence," said a boy as everyone giggled. "One of them put a *thing* on an old lady and they took her purse. Now they don't let them come across anymore." The giggling stopped.

"The Border Patrol is real strict. If Mexicans are walking down the street and they look like they're real poor, they get asked questions. If they don't speak English, the Patrol takes them in."

"They're *mean*, the Patrol," said a girl, making a face. "You're supposed to have papers to get by the border—I hate them. One time my brother was going to work and they were checking the little green cards, and my brother didn't have his and they brought him back to the border. And my brother said, 'I wish I could get a gun and shoot them.' They kicked him."

A classmate from Mexico nodded his head vigorously. "I think everybody ought to have the liberty to go anywhere they wanna. Mexico doesn't bother people from here going to Mexico. Not like the United States bothers us."

A shy girl in the second row spoke up. "I still can't get it why people from here go down there and Mexico doesn't do nothing to them. But people from down there come here and if they don't have no papers, they'll get in trouble by the *migra*."

"It's scary!"

"But all they're coming over for is jobs."

I asked if Mexico had a Border Patrol that picked up Americans who sneaked over looking for work. They laughed and laughed. Imagine, Mexico having a Border Patrol!

"A friend of my mom's got fired so a Mexican lady could work," said a tall girl in the back. "I don't think Mexicans should be allowed to come over and work."

A hush fell over the room. No one said a word.

The teacher broke the awkward silence. "You don't see so many of the little boys selling Chiclets and colored rocks any more. Why is that?"

"I guess they finally got fed up with not selling anything," one boy suggested.

I asked what some of the nice things about the other side were.

"Cheese! You can't get Mexican cheese here."

"They have a different kind of chocolate. I think it's called *cajeta*."

"Candy!" "Yeah, the candy!" "Mmm, I love their candy." "Their candy is different from ours." A chorus of *yums* went round the room. The feeling was unanimous. The candy was better on the other side.

"And Mexican suckers. I like Mexican suckers. My dad always buys me some when we go across."

"Yeah, they got sno-cones and stuff like that."

"And they have real nice decorated clothes."

"They dress different. Their shirts have pockets all over."

"I love their tortillas. They make good tortillas."

"And they have big Mexican flowers, paper flowers."

"They have different shoes."

"Yeah, their sandals are called *huaraches* and they all wear them."

"Also there's not any shoeshine boys over here, but there's plenty over there."

"And here you have to call on the phone for a taxi, but over there they have taxis all around."

"San Luis has lots of doctors and dentists. It's cheaper to go to one there."

"My Mom says they do a better job."

"Well, I like Mexico better," one recent immigrant asserted. "I was born there and grew up there."

"I like it 'cause you can get firecrackers there," said his neighbor.

"When you come back they check at the border to see if you're carrying any firecrackers or things like that."

"We get firecrackers over there for the Fourth of July," explained one girl. "When we bring them back we hide them under the pillows so the inspectors won't find them."

"Yeah? My dad hides them under the table in our camper."

"One time at the border they checked in the back of our trunk to see if we were bringing back a Mexican."

"They check in front, too. But we go through there all the time and they don't hardly check anymore."

"Once when we came back they checked the back of our van and we had our dog with us. They took the dog away for a while, so now we hide him. We put him down and pull covers over him."

"They also check to see if you're bringing any marijuana back with you."

"I know. Sometimes they pull your car over and put a search dog in it to look for drugs."

Lunchtime was approaching, and the children started talking about food again. Are the restaurants in Mexico very different? I asked.

"Yes. On all the walls they got big pictures of people on horses and things. They have those big forks and spoons which you can't get over here."

"When I walk into a restaurant there I notice the flies."

"They got little stools."

"A lot of their restaurants don't have menus, either."

"They don't got Burger Kings!"

"It isn't fair that we have so much and they have so little."

No matter what we talked about—food, clothing, schools, any-thing—in one form or another the children always commented on the poverty. Students who had family in Mexico said their relatives wanted to move to the United States.

"They should allow people to come in."

"Yeah, this is a free country. Isn't it?"

The bell rang and the children of Yuma scrambled for the door. A couple of them stopped as we prepared to leave. "Why don't you stay for lunch? You could eat with us."

"That's very nice of you. What are you having?"

"Let's see. Today is Monday. *Enchiladas quemadas, claro.*"
Burned enchiladas, of course.

In San Luis Río Colorado, the state's oldest and biggest elementary school is named for Abelardo Rodríguez, a former governor and later president of Mexico. Professor Horacio Pompa, the school's principal, invited us to speak with his students at Escuela Abelardo L. Rodríguez about life along the border.

The students stood at attention when we walked into the classroom; that was the first difference. They spoke only Spanish; that was the second. But after that, the fourth, fifth, and sixth graders in Mexico had observations remarkably similar to their Yuma counterparts. Most of their mothers and fathers were employed, and over half of the parents worked in the United States.

"They prefer things that way," one student announced.

"There is more work in the U.S., and more money." The parents from San Luis who found work in Arizona and California toiled in lemon groves and lettuce fields, they drove tractors and made furniture. One sold car parts and another worked at Yuma Chevrolet.

Shy at first, the students soon began to voice their thoughts loudly about the other side.

"Their clothes—they have so many more of them!"

"Yes, and their clothes are much better. Our relatives are always bringing us some."

"They have more variety in what they wear."

"And their ice cream is good—we don't have it like that here."

"And you get good service in restaurants!"

"In our cafés all we have is chile and frijoles."

"We prefer the food in Yuma—"

"—'cause they've got Kentucky Fried Chicken!"

"They have candy over there we can't get."

"Oooo yes, our friends bring us American candy when they come over." "Their candy tastes delicious." "I like American candy." A chorus of *yums* went around the room. The feeling was unanimous. The candy was better on the other side.

The school's Drum and Bugle Corps was practicing outside the classroom window for the upcoming Yuma Rodeo Parade. Many of the students planned to attend. They liked listening to American music.

"American music is all John Travolta!"

"And the Bee Gees."

"All American music is rock 'n' roll and disco," a boy in front said. The class laughed when he said "rock 'n' roll."

"All we have is *ranchero* music."

I tried my money game again, asking whether they preferred the bill marked "10" or the one with a "1."

"That one! That one!" they cried out in unison, pointing to the dollar bill.

"Why are pesos and dollars different?"

"I know." A fifth grader on the side shot up his hand. "The peso is twenty-two-point-six to one!" No doubt a future financier. Or street vendor.

On and on our conversation continued through the morning.

"The roads on the other side are cleaner and wider," one student said, "with no holes." "They have green on the sides of the roads there," another added. "And most of them are paved, too," a third emphasized.

"They have fewer students in each classroom on the other side, and they go home from school earlier."

"We go over there to go shopping or to visit. But every time we cross," a girl complained, "we need papers."

"Sometimes we go over to play in Amistad Park on the border. We just go through a hole in the fence."

"It's easier for Americans to cross over here than for us to go there." Everyone nodded in agreement.

"Maybe we should hassle Americans like they hassle us."

"No," a classmate replied, "we need American visitors."

"Yeah, a lot of gringos go to our beaches."

They all had something to say about the Border Patrol: "*la migra!*"

"They watch people so they don't jump the fence."

"They catch the ones that don't have *pasaportes*—"

"—and take them away."

"It's better to work over there and live here," one boy proudly stated. "We're more used to living here. We're strangers on the other side."

When we finished, the students applauded in appreciation. As we were leaving the school grounds, we saw Professor Pompa tending the school garden. He came over to say goodbye and give us a flower.

John Davidson

John Davidson was born and raised in Fredericksburg, a small ranching community in the Texas Hill Country. He attended the University of Texas at Austin (B.A., 1969) and served as a Peace Corps volunteer in Peru. He taught English for two years at La Universidad Católica de Puerto Rico and has traveled extensively throughout Latin America. *The Long Road North* is Davidson's first book. The selection which follows first appeared in *Texas Monthly*.

From *The Long Road North*

When I asked Javier what it was like to be a wetback, he smiled at the implausibility of summing up five years of experience, and then he looked thoughtfully at his hands. We had just met and were sitting on a shady curb next to a hamburger stand in West San Antonio; it was one of those first hot weeks toward the end of May when you know it won't be cool again till fall. Javier's hands, I noticed, looked too old for his twenty-four years. The fingers were squeezed out of shape from heavy labor and the skin so thick it was like permanent work gloves. He absently rubbed a scar on the back of his left hand as if it might come off and said:

"Two years I worked on a roofing crew. I worked hard and the boss treated me like I was part of the family. His brother was my supervisor and we became compadres. I went to live in his house and shared a room with his son. His wife cooked and took care of my clothes like she did for all the rest. Every Saturday—we worked six days a week except when it rained—we got paid, and every Saturday the boss said he was holding my Saturday wages to save for me. After almost two years of work, I spilled hot tar on my hand. I went to the boss and said I need to go to a doctor, but he told me to just put dirt on the burn. I went to the doctor anyway and missed a day of work. Not too long after that, I got a cold. It was a bad cold, and I had to stay in bed for a week. When I went back to work, my boss was angry. He told me, 'Javier, you're no good and you're lazy. Get out of here! Go back to Mexico where you belong!' None of what he said was true and it made me mad. I told him I was leaving but I wanted my Saturday wages. That's when he said, 'What wages?' He robbed me of almost two thousand dollars and there was nothing I could do. If I had complained too much, he would have turned me in to the Border Patrol."

I commiserated with Javier and said that if I could spend some time with him in San Antonio, follow him around to see how he lived, I might be able to write his story. Javier shook his head and said he was getting ready to leave for Jalisco; he had just received word from his family that he was needed at home. Perhaps when he got back.

"How will you come back?" I asked.

"Swim the river and walk."

"Then why don't I go with you," I suggested.

"Do you mean in a car?" Javier asked.

"No, swim and walk." I explained that I didn't want to alter the trip, but would just follow along and do whatever he normally did. "I'll be your shadow," I proposed.

Javier looked at me doubtfully. "It's the wrong time of year. The grass is too high; too many snakes."

"It would make a good story," I countered.

Javier looked away, squinting as if to imagine the trip and then began to smile. "If you made the trip," he nodded his head in approval, "then you would know what it's like to be a wetback. Así podrías sacar el chiste: that way you could get the joke."

And so two hours later we left for Mexico. Nonstop—except for sleeping on bus station floors—we traveled eight hundred miles to Jalisco, spent forty-five minutes with Javier's family, picked up his younger brother, and started back to Texas. Both in Mexico and after we crossed the river and started walking toward San Antonio, I was struck by Javier and his brother's attitude toward time and space. It is based on the active knowledge that distance—fifty to a hundred and fifty miles—breaks down into footsteps, which in time accumulate and overcome terrain. It is reinforced by a dependence on walking as a major means of transportation. Keeping up with them was one of the most strenuous things I've ever attempted.

While in Mexico, I achieved a surprising anonymity in the company of Javier. Unlike other trips I had made, no one treated me like a tourist or showed the least curiosity that I spoke Spanish. In Jalisco, none of Javier's family asked who I was or why I was with him, nor did his brother during the entire trip. It was as if traveling with Javier, speaking nothing but Spanish, I had submerged my identity. By the time we were headed north, I began to feel that I was indeed Javier's shadow.

When Javier woke, the bus was splashing slowly through water. It cut a wake that lapped at the houses along the street, and stranded cars rocked gently as the bus proceeded into deeper water. "*Está hundido Nuevo Laredo*," a voice in the dark softly exclaimed the obvious. Looking at the flooded streets, Javier thought of the river. If it was flooding, they couldn't swim. A smuggler would have to take them across. Too tired to worry, Javier leaned his head against the window and closed his eyes.

The bus pulled into the Nuevo Laredo terminal at 3 A.M. Javier shook his brother Juan to wake him, and they gathered their belongings to get off. Downtown, the water had run off into the river, and the streets were deserted. Momentarily lost, the two brothers stood in the milky neon glow in front of the Estrella Blanca bus station until Javier went inside to ask about a cheap hotel. He waited meekly at the counter for the clerk to notice him and finally reached out and touched his sleeve.

In Nuevo Laredo Javier and Juan were as easily identifiable as businessmen on a flight to New York City. Their congenital humility and fundamental silence mark them as campesinos. As does their appearance—strong white teeth from a childhood without Cokes and candy, and whites of the eyes slightly discolored from a lifelong deficiency of vitamins and minerals. An informed observer could accurately speculate that the two brothers were coming from an economically depressed agricultural area, probably from the Central Plateau north of Mexico City, and that they were going to cross the Rio Grande illegally. There would be no other reason for two campesinos to come to the border.

Directed toward a cheap hotel the clerk described as "*baratito*," they started down the empty street, Juan carrying a small cardboard box tied with a string and Javier an orange canvas flight bag with black straps. From Javier's clothes—brown-and-white-plaid double-knit trousers, a dark brown shirt, dark green velvet jacket trimmed with silver braid, and a black baseball cap—it is clear that he's been to Texas before. On a white patch on the front of the cap, a red stitched caption demands, "What's your handle?" and an imperative red thumb indicates an appropriate blank, which Javier left nameless.

At 24, Javier is tall and rangy. Five eleven, he is easily the tallest in his family. He estimates he has between eight and eleven brothers and sisters, but he's uncertain how many have died and been born in the five years since he first left Mexico. As to his exceptional height, Javier alternately attributes it to childhood "exercise"—his father took him out of school after the second grade to work in the fields—and to "medicine"—a car ran over him when he was four and he received considerable doctoring. Sparse black bristles on his face intend a moustache and goatee and recall Oriental villains. High sharp cheekbones, a long, slightly flattened nose, and acne scars contribute to the villainous impression, but it is quickly dispelled when he smiles. Juan, younger and smaller than Javier, wears sky-blue pants, a paler blue shirt, and has heavy black hair, fine features, and a resolutely impenetrable nature.

At the hotel, they got a small windowless room with a double bed for two dollars. Without bothering to remove his clothes or black boots, Juan pulled the green bedspread back and lay down on the spotted gray sheets. Javier took off his shirt and then his cowboy boots, which, to discourage scorpions, he propped upside down in the corner before switching off the bare bulb in the ceiling and lying down next to Juan.

Tired after the fifteen-hour bus ride from Jalisco they fell asleep and didn't wake until late the next morning. Outside, when they left the hotel, it was already hot, and the humidity rose off the damp ground and pavement. Javier and Juan walked directly to the bridge and followed a chain-link fence west along the riverbank. Garbage thrown from nearby houses was scattered along the trail, and a sweet smell of putrefaction filled the air. At the river's edge, they could see the results of the storm—dense brown water pocked by whirling eddies, and farther out, rafts of river trash and the stately progression of floating tree trunks that marked the current's velocity.

"Can you swim?" Javier asked his younger brother.

"Some," Juan answered.

"But not in this," Javier said, and smiled. "You would get caught in the trash or a log would hit you. Then you would drown." He squatted on his heels to watch the river. "I wonder how many have drowned here?"

Juan looked at him.

"No one knows what happens to the ones trying to cross. In the river, we're neither here nor there, so no one counts."

Juan shrugged indifferently and settled on his heels to watch the river. They turned in unison as a man came around a bend in the trail. His pants legs were rolled above the knee and his bare feet were stuck in an old pair of unlaced shoes. He was carrying his shirt. "Lots of water," Javier greeted him.

"Enough," the man agreed.

"How long will the river be up?"

"Who knows," the man answered as he passed. "A week. Maybe more."

They watched the man till he disappeared around the next bend, then turned back to the river. "What do you think?" Javier asked. "Will we make it our not?"

"*Pues, sí*," Juan shrugged, unconcerned.

"We'll see," Javier said and stood up.

Climbing out of the river bottom, Javier indicated what appeared to be an impenetrable thicket of mesquite. Grass rose a foot and a half to an intricate crisscross of mesquite limbs that formed a green wall. "The first fifty miles," he said, "it's like this. Only worse." He turned and climbed the bank to the railroad tracks.

In town, they waded through the jam of American tourists and Mexican vendors on the narrow sidewalks. Away from the bridge and past the market and curio shops, they found an inexpensive restaurant where each ordered carne guisada, tortillas, frijoles, and Pepsi Cola. They ate slowly, using pieces of tortilla to delicately tear the stewed meat into shreds, which they rolled with beans and *salsa* into small tacos. When he finished, Javier cleaned his teeth with a napkin and got out his cigarettes.

From the restaurant, they walked to a small corner grocery store. Javier selected two plastic net shopping bags: one blue-and-green plaid and the other orange and yellow. He asked the woman behind the counter for six cans of refried beans, six cans of large sardines, a small bottle of *salsa picante*, two loaves of Bimbo white bread, five packages of crackers, four packs of Parade cigarettes, several boxes of matches, and a bottle of rubbing alcohol. Javier distributed the purchases between the two plastic bags, tied the strap of his canvas bag to the plastic handles of one shopping bag, and draped them both over his right shoulder like saddlebags. Juan transferred the shirt and pair of pants from the cardboard box into his own shopping bag.

At a hardware store, Javier bought a compass for himself and a white straw hat for Juan, which, on closer inspection, turned out to be plastic. So equipped, they retraced their steps down Avenida Guerrero toward the bridge, turned west, and in the early afternoon sun, walked out past the railroad station and the cemetery into the slums of Nuevo Laredo.

On the low side of the streets, the soggy contents of houses were draped on fences and shrubs or piled on any dry surface to catch the sun. Block after block, the houses became poorer until the town finally petered out with one last corner grocery. Squatting in the shade against the wall, a man watched them approach. "Hey, where you going?" he called when they got closer.

"*Más allá,*" Javier evaded. Farther on.

"Toward Carrizo?" The man stood to face them. Beneath his straw hat, he had yellow eyes and a three-day growth of beard. "A truck is coming that will take you."

"We'll see," Javier answered and they walked into the store. Inside, he asked the *señora* for a half-gallon plastic milk bottle and then bought himself and Juan a Pepsi. When they walked back out, a man was sitting in an old red pickup parked in the shade of the building next to the man with yellow eyes. The driver looked at Javier and Juan with their boots, hats, and plastic net shopping bags. "I imagine you want to cross the river," he said.

"It is a possibility," Javier admitted.

"I can take you both toward Carrizo where a man has a boat. Twenty dollars."

"Ten each?" Javier asked.

"That's right. Ten each."

Javier gave him a ten and put his bags in the back of the truck. "What about your friend?" the man asked.

Javier looked at Juan and shrugged. "He doesn't have any money."

"You could loan it to him," the man suggested.

"Not when I have barely enough to cross the river," Javier answered and started climbing in.

"Fifteen for both," the man offered.

"Leave him here," Javier said coldly, and sat down in the back of the truck to indicate he was ready to leave. The driver shrugged and started the engine. As the truck drove away from the store, Juan and

Javier looked at each other but made no sign. As the truck pulled onto the road, the driver glanced into the mirror and saw Juan standing forlornly with his shopping bag. He stepped on the clutch and brake, leaned out the window, and shouted angrily, "All right. Get in!"

The truck ran west along the gravel road a mile south of and parallel to the river. Where the land was low and flat, standing water came up to the truck's axle and the flooded mesquite flats looked like swamps shimmering with heat, reflecting the blue sky with its stray white clouds. Speaking above the sound of crunching gravel and the partially submerged muffler, Javier touched Juan's arm and said, "We may have to walk all of tonight in water."

Impassive, Juan blinked once like a shiny black crow inwardly focused on not falling off its wire. "We cross today?"

"At sunset. If we can get away from the river at night, the little airplane won't see us."

"Little airplane?"

"From *emigración*. They patrol with the airplane and in jeeps and trucks." Then, pointing at the submerged pasture, "Do you think you can sleep in water?"

"I'd rather walk in it."

"Walk enough, and you can sleep anywhere," Javier assured him.

The truck faltered twice before reaching dry land and going on toward Carrizo. After fifty minutes of driving they came to a large white warehouse closed and overgrown with weeds and sunflowers. On the far side of the building, the driver stopped the truck in front of the solitary shack. "For ten dollars," he complained when he got out of the truck, "this is as far as I can take you."

As Juan and Javier climbed down with their belongings, an undernourished adolescent in a large cowboy hat and black jeans tucked into cowboy boots loped out from the shack and stopped before them. "You want to cross the river," he said, his pale eyes tracking independent of each other. Not knowing which eye focused and which stared into space, Javier hesitated and the driver said, "Hector, where's Rodrigo?"

"He's coming now. Any minute," the boy promised. He was so thin—a backbone inside a ragged white T-shirt—it appeared unlikely that he could propel the cowboy boots. "Three others are already waiting. We'll take them all today."

"Then I'll leave these two with you," the driver said, and got back in his truck. As he drove away, Juan and Javier followed Hector to the shack, which was circumscribed by a ring of trash as far as the arm could throw. Away from the road, the tin shack, its roof weighted down with worn-out tires, had been expanded by a makeshift awning covered with huisache branches and a lean-to kitchen. An old Formica-and-chrome kitchen table and chairs sat in the shade of the awning.

"Perhaps you have a cigarette you can give me?" Hector asked. Javier took out his pack, gave Hector and Juan each a cigarette, and took one himself. He started to sit down at the table beneath the awning after they had lighted the cigarettes. "Not here," Hector stopped him. "Sometimes the *federales* come; you had better hide in the bushes." He led them beyond the circle of trash and into the mesquite, where three men sat at the edge of a clearing around a washed-out campfire. Two of the men had paper bags at their sides and the third a black plastic shaving kit. "They're going too," Hector said by way of introduction, and the three men nodded. Javier and Juan dropped their bags in the ring of ashes and sat down on the ground in the long shadows of the mesquite trees. "Very soon and Rodrigo will be here," Hector assured them one last time before going back to the shack.

They watched Hector leave and then Javier asked the men where they came from. "*Veracruz—donde no vale la vida*," the round-faced man sitting in the middle answered for the three. "And you?"

"Jalisco," Javier echoed. "Where life has no value." Javier stretched out on the ground, put his canvas bag beneath his head, and pulled a weed to chew on. "How long have you been waiting here?"

"Since midday," the same man answered. "What time is it now?"

Javier looked at his wristwatch. "Four o'clock." To the west he could see cumulus clouds building as if for the sunset.

"Rodrigo is probably getting drunk somewhere," the man speculated. "The skinny one with the eyes said they took nine this morning."

"Nine," Javier repeated. "That's a good business."

"Yes, but it's not a regular harvest."

"It never is," Javier agreed. "You've been before?"

"Yes, but not the others," the man answered.

"Then you're the one that knows the way?"

"I can look at the sky and tell which way is north."

"That's good," Javier said and pulled the long stem of the weed through his teeth to shred it. "The first time I went, one of us had a compass. We walked for three days and came to a big river. At last we thought we were getting out of the brush. We were so happy. We spent most of a morning looking for a place to cross before we realized it was the Rio Grande."

"You walked in a circle," the man said.

"That's right," Javier smiled. "The one with the compass didn't know how to read it. Like idiots, we almost crossed back into Mexico."

"But you made it."

"Barely," Javier sat up, stretched, and then propped up on one elbow. "Just barely."

"How many days did it take?"

"Eleven to San Antonio. We almost starved in the brush before we got to Carrizo and had to stop at a ranch and work for food. They gave us each two dollars for three days of cutting mesquite posts and said if we didn't leave they would call *la emigración*."

"Be glad they didn't need more posts. You would have worked more days for the same amount of money."

"True," Javier said and sat up farther. Gazing toward the man, he had noticed that beneath the cuffs of his green polyester trousers hung a set of plaid double-knit cuffs. The two other men also had double sets of cuffs hanging above their boots. "You're wearing two pair of pants," Javier observed.

The three men looked down at their cuffs and then up. "For the snakes," the man in the middle explained.

"They must be bad now."

"Perhaps the rain makes them crawl up in the trees to stay dry."

Javier studied the mesquite around them for signs of snakes and concluded, "That way they would strike us in the face or on the arms, rather than on our boots." Juan shifted uneasily, attracting Javier's attention. "Are you frightened?" Javier asked.

"Psssh," Juan exhaled genuine disgust and turned away.

"The last time," the man in the middle went on, "we found a corpse. Snakebit, we decided."

"Many say they've seen bodies. Thank god, I never have."

Hector reappeared to say that Rodrigo would be there any minute. Impatient, the man in the middle got up and said they would walk further up the river to see if anyone else had a boat. "Rodrigo comes and you're not here," Hector warned, "he won't wait for you. He'll be

angry that you left." The man shrugged; the three of them picked up
their belongings and started for the road.

Javier watched them go, then lay back down, resting his head on
the canvas bag. "If we cross by sunset," he said, "that's soon enough."
He pulled the brim of his baseball cap over his eyes and drifted off
to sleep.

It was dusk when they heard the pickup. There was honking, then
shouting and drunken laughter. Confident it wasn't *federales*, Javier
and Juan picked up their bags and walked out toward the road. In the
half-light, they could see a blur of activity between the shack and an
old truck. Hector, when he saw them, brought Rodrigo out to talk.
Powerfully built, dressed completely in black, Rodrigo acted as surly as
he looked. "You want to cross," he said, and hitched his pants higher.
When he opened his mouth, splayed, tusklike teeth sprouted from his
upper gum.

Yes, they wanted to cross, Javier answered politely.

"You can pay?" he looked them over as if it might be by the
pound.

Yes, Javier answered, they could pay.

"Tomorrow morning when it gets light, I'll take you across. You
can sleep tonight behind the warehouse."

Javier and Juan sat on the warehouse loading dock and ate a can of
refried beans. Above them they could hear bats swoop, and before
them the tops of six-foot-tall sunflowers swayed at the edge of the dock.
Juan reached for the empty milk container and started to get up.
"Where are you going?" Javier asked.

"To ask for water."

"Don't ask them for anything. If they don't rob us, we'll be lucky.
Let them forget we're here."

At the edge of sleep, Javier heard someone on the steps to the
dock. Hector came toward them carrying a large bundle. "You want
these?" he said and dropped a couple of blankets. They spread one
blanket beneath them and pulled the other over. "Tonight," Javier said
happily as dirt sprinkled onto them from the blanket, "we sleep like
the president."

Javier woke with the first gray light. He sat on the dock and
watched the shack. A rooster crowed, but the shack remained silent.
The sun rose and Javier lay back down to wait. When he woke again,

Rodrigo was climbing the steps to the dock. He squatted down in a friendly way at the end of their blankets. "How much money do you have?" he asked.

"Twenty."

"Each?" he said and sucked his upper lip down over his teeth.

"Together," Javier answered.

As if annoyed, Rodrigo ran a hand through his wavy hair. On his forearm, a lopsided "lov you" was scratched with blue ink. "You think I can take you for that?"

"It's all we have," Javier replied.

"You'll have to give me more—a wristwatch or something of value," Rodrigo said and left the dock without waiting for a response.

Thirty minutes later, Hector appeared to say they should follow him. Carrying their plastic shopping bags, they trotted behind him across the road and through a cornfield toward the river. Overhead, the sun had broken through the morning haze. The damp ground was steaming. They came out of the field onto a road that turned toward the river. From behind, they heard horses and saw Rodrigo approaching in a wagon, which contained a boat. Hitched to two red nags, the wooden relic, adapted with tires, was too large for the horses, but bolting, eyes rolling, they caught up with Javier and Juan and forced them off the road.

Hector led the two brothers down a path into a ravine where they could see Rodrigo waiting on a small knoll next to the now-empty wagon. The boat—which was actually two automobile hoods welded together—floated below in the water. As if barring the way, Rodrigo stood to face them. "How much can you pay me?" he started over.

"Twenty dollars," Javier repeated.

"That's not enough," Rodrigo said angrily. "I take *la raza* across; I help *la raza*. It's a good thing I do, but I must be paid. If caught, I go to prison and my family starves."

"It's all I have."

"What about your wristwatch? What kind is it?"

Javier looked at the dial. "Timex. It's old but I need it. I can't give it to you."

Rodrigo scowled at Juan. "What about you?"

"*Nada*," Juan said and showed empty hands.

Rodrigo turned his back on them. Hector and the two men looked from Javier to Rodrigo and back to see who would give. The tension mounted until Javier repeated, "I promise, it's all I have."

"Then give me the money," Rodrigo relented.

They slid slowly down the bank on their heels to the boat, which had three crossboards for seats. Rodrigo stationed the two brothers and their belongings at either end and climbed into the middle seat. Before telling Hector to push them out, he studied the dense trees and brush on the opposite bank for movement. The mile of river they could see from bend to bend was clear, and the silence revealed no warning hum of Border Patrol surveillance plane or patrol boat. Hector shoved the boat into the swirling brown water, and Rodrigo dug in with oars made of plywood squares nailed to long sticks. With each heavy stroke, the two ends of the boat twisted at the welded seam, but by keeping within shelter of the bank, Rodrigo managed to row against the current without the two hoods splitting apart. The boat moved laboriously upstream until Rodrigo lifted the left oar and dug hard with the right to swing the boat into the current, and then dug with both oars to propel them across the forty yards of river before it could sweep them too far downstream. Javier started to speak, but Rodrigo hushed him—a voice carried too far on water—and there was only the steady thunk of the oars in the notches cut into the side of the boat.

The prow of the boat hit bank at the edge of a canebrake and the two brothers scrambled out into ankle-deep mud. Rodrigo handed up their bags and Juan shoved the boat back into the current. Staggering from the weight of the mud on their boots, they crashed through the cane to dry ground and pushed their way up an overgrown ravine to a dry bank, where Javier sat down to slice thick wedges of mud off the bottom of his boots with a stick. He handed the stick to Juan and, breathing hard, whispered, "We have to get away from the river fast. No more noise." He stood, swung the plastic shopping bag counterbalanced by the weight of the canvas bag over his shoulder, and started north.

The heat of the river bottom was oppressive. The trees and brush gave off more humidity than shade, and the lack of breeze was claustrophobic. Following behind, Juan noticed Javier's dark brown shirt beginning to soak black and the empty water container bouncing loose in the plastic shopping bag. From the top of a steep dirt bluff, beyond a barbed-wire fence and dirt road that ran along the rim, they could see flat pastureland, and below, a curving sweep of river and the lower Mexican bank. Javier stepped on a fence wire and jumped over. Juan followed and they sprinted across the road and through the open part of the pasture to the cover of a clump of mesquite trees. The ground was clear and they wove quickly through the mesquite until they came to another fence that separated the pasture from a field of corn. Again they jumped the fence and ran crouching between two rows of corn to the next fence. The midday sun was fierce in the open field and they were both covered with sweat and panting for breath. The next pasture, where they spooked a small herd of cows, brought them uncomfortably near a farmhouse. They circled away through the mesquite, crossed another fence, and kept going until they heard the clear whine of pickup tires on hot asphalt.

Breathing hard, Javier came to a halt beneath a large mesquite tree where he dropped his bags and sprawled on the ground. "*Carretera*," he rasped, and nodded toward the highway when Juan dropped beside him; he was so dry, the cotton was edging out in gray flecks at the corner of his mouth. Juan sat fanning himself with his white hat and staring as Javier rummaged in his canvas bag and took out the compass to check directions. Sure they were going north, Javier climbed the mesquite as high as its limbs would take him and looked out toward the road. A car whined past and when it disappeared, he dropped back to the ground. "We have to cross a bridge," he said, and swung his bags over his shoulder.

Through the tops of the mesquite they could see a taller line of cottonwood and sycamore indicating a creek. Thick brush protected their approach to the bridge and from its base they saw the water still running muddy from the storm. Javier dropped his bags at the foot of a concrete rampart. "Stay here," he whispered when Juan started to follow him down to the creek. Juan sat down and watched Javier crouch beyond a clump of willow to fill the water container. From above, he could see a large black water moccasin uncoil in the willow and slide into the water.

"Did you see the snake?" Juan asked when Javier handed up the jug.

"I wish it were the last!" he answered. His baseball cap was tilted back, his face was wet, and drops of water hung in the sparse hairs on his moustache and goatee. He watched Juan drink the brown water from the jug. When Juan finished, Javier refilled the jug and put it in his shopping bag. "One at a time, we cross the bridge," he instructed.

"Wait till I'm across and hidden, then you come. Listen for cars." On all fours he crawled up the rampart to the bridge. As he was about to haul himself over the concrete railing, they heard a diesel semi-trailer. He squatted down and waited for the truck to swoop thunderously past and drone into the distance. Grinning at Juan, he pulled his ball cap snug, climbed over the railing, and ran crouching across the bridge. In turn, Juan did the same.

On the far side of the bridge, Javier was waiting out of sight at the bottom of the road's embankment. Juan waded down through knee-deep grass, they crossed the fence, and started through another pasture. The grass gave way to a hard sandy crust shaded by mesquite trees where they picked up the parallel tracks of a road. Javier looked back and stopped when he noticed Juan walking in one of the sandy tracks. "Step on the grass," he said. "You won't leave footprints." He turned and walked on.

The terrain began to change to hard rocky ground cut with shallow gullies and covered with low-lying scrub brush. Without the cover of mesquite trees, they were exposed to the hot sky. Looking for relief, Javier cut away from the road through the thickest stand of brush until he came to an eroded ditch. At a clump of scrub oak that spanned the ditch the two men dropped in, crawled into the shade, and got out the water jug. By now it was midafternoon.

"What do you think?" he asked his younger brother.

"It's not so bad," Juan answered.

"We haven't begun."

Javier took a can of sardines out of the net shopping bag and cut it open with a pocketknife. He put a piece of white bread on his palm, laid a large Mexican sardine on the bread, poured a little tomato sauce from the can, and rolled it up like a tortilla.

After they finished the sardines and half the loaf of bread, they drank more water and smoked a cigarette. Javier took the dark green velvet jacket out of his canvas bag and draped it over his head and ball cap to keep off the black flies, then leaned back against the ditch wall. "Rest!" he said from behind the dark veil and snuggled his body against the ground.

Juan tilted his white hat over his eyes and crossed his arms, but a rock beneath his shoulder, then the flies, and finally Javier's heavy breathing distracted him. He crawled up on the edge of the ditch to stretch out flat, found that more comfortable, and dozed off. He woke to the sound of a four-wheel-drive vehicle winding through the brush. Not thinking they could have been seen in the brush, but remembering his footsteps in the road, he cautiously slipped back into the ditch where Javier slept soundly. A pickup door slammed, a dog barked, and he heard a man's voice. In the ensuing silence, Juan sat in the ditch and stared down at the ground before him. Next to a dry leaf on the sand, movement focused his eyes on a scorpion scuttling his way. Meditatively, listening to the silence, Juan picked up a twig and stuck the end of it in the scorpion's path. Violently, the scorpion swung the stinger at the end of its long tail over its back at the twig, turned and crabbed in the opposite direction. Again Juan blocked it with the twig, and again the scorpion swung its stinger and turned. Each time intercepted, the scorpion ran back and forth in the silence, back and forth as the truck started and wound away into the brush, back and forth across the sand until Juan crushed it with the twig.

Javier breathed more deeply beneath his dark veil until abruptly, he pulled away his jacket and blinked.

"I dreamed I was snoring and the dream woke me up."

"It was no dream," Juan said.

Javier shook his head with sleepy amusement and then noticed his wristwatch. "Four o'clock! Two hours I slept!"

"You're sleeping a lot," Juan commented.

"I wonder why," Javier said as he sat up. And then with irony, "I guess because it's my vacation."

Javier checked the compass, and they drank more water before crawling out of the ditch. Beyond the fence, the land turned stony and the low rolling hills were covered with an unbroken thicket of brush. Parting the way with a cedar stick he had picked up at the fence, Javier waded in, Juan following. Thorns snagged each step, and stones, unseen beneath the foliage, staggered them. The brush rolled from swell to swell; the dark green troughs of blackbrush and ironwood were dappled with ashen ceniza and reefs of pale prickly pear, and the crests were light green with fernlike guajillo. Above, white blocks of cumulus marched east toward the Gulf and a late afternoon breeze rippled the surface of green.

Within the brush, the ground held the afternoon heat. Javier's shirt soaked black with perspiration; their accumulated scratches stung with sweat. They held the shopping bags before them like shields, but the constant nag of thorns was inescapable. The first variation in the landscape, a short caliche ledge, forced them down into a trough of huisache. In the pallid light below the bushes they saw a skeletal lattice of pale branches and a long ditch of stagnant water. The ground was sodden caliche, and white clay clung to their boots miring each step. Slipping and staggering, goaded by moist suffocation, they forced their way through the thicket until the ditch dried and they were able to climb the opposite bank.

Climbing out, Juan stumbled and grabbed a branch of blackbrush, driving three of the long straight thorns into his palm. He gave the branch a careful yank to pluck out the spines and then watched as three drops of dark blood formed at the punctures.

Thirsty, tired, red in the face, they pushed through the brush. At the top of a swell, they saw a small cloud of dust moving along the ground from east to west and, as it came closer, heard the crunch of tires on gravel.

The ground had been cleared for fifty feet on either side of a dirt road, increasing the danger of exposure. At the edge, they listened for traffic before dashing across the open space, crossing the fence, the road, another fence, and back into the brush. They kept going through the thinner secondary growth until Javier dropped his bags in a clearing on a slight rise and sat down in the evening shadow of a mesquite tree. Juan sank to the ground, Javier took out the jug, and they both drank. Due east on the horizon, near the road, they could see a windmill. Javier unbuttoned his soaked shirt and flapped the breeze to dry it. "This is going to smell," he grimaced. And then noticing that Juan was relatively dry, "Why don't you sweat?"

"Too thirsty," he answered.

Javier handed him the jug and watched him tilt it for another swallow. A layer of silt approached the neck of the jug as Juan drank. Javier asked him, "Now, what do you think? Think we'll make it?"

Juan handed him the jug and shrugged.

"At any rate, we've had luck," Javier said. "The little airplane hasn't seen us." He took another swallow of the water and then handed it to Juan. When Juan finished, the jug was essentially empty.

"Where do we get more water?" Juan asked.

"Windmills," Javier answered.

"That one?" Juan pointed to the one in view.

"It's too far out of the way. We'll come to others."

"Yes?"

"There are thirteen before Carrizo. With luck, we will sleep next to one tonight." Javier took the compass out of his bag and checked directions. A light evening breeze had begun to blow and the sun's rays were beginning to lose their intensity. "Let's walk," Javier said, and got to his feet. "These are the good hours."

And on they went, one step after another, Javier always in front carrying a cedar stick he'd picked up, Juan just behind wearing his white plastic hat. They never complained and rarely remarked the armadillos and rabbits that crossed their paths.

Two more roads and they came to a windmill. They opened the tap beneath the storage tank, let the water run clear, and Javier leaned down to drink. Juan drank as much of the salty water as he could and they took turns holding their heads beneath the stream and running the cool water over their hands and arms. Javier took off his soaked brown shirt, rinsed it, and stored it in the net shopping bag. He put on a dark green shirt he'd been carrying in his canvas bag, they filled the jug with water, and, as there was another hour of light, checked the compass and moved on.

The sun neared the dark horizon, its long rays refracting pink on remnants of cloud: the sky turned an intense and late blue. In the last light, they crossed another dirt road. In the secondary growth of mesquite beyond it, Javier picked out a cleared spot that looked relatively snake-free. The sun touched the edge of the horizon and abruptly, as at sea, was gone.

The two brothers sat on the ground beneath the lilac sky eating refried beans spread thick on pieces of white bread. Juan had discovered that either the jug of water had leaked or Javier's wet shirt had soaked the bread, but after considering spreading the slices out to dry overnight with the shirt, they went ahead and ate the bread wet. With their boots they stamped out places on the ground to sleep. Javier put on his velvet jacket and they both lay down on the ground, their heads resting on their bags. In the dark, his back to Javier, Juan asked, "The life in San Antonio; is it a good life?"

Javier thought a moment before answering. "It's work."

"But it's better than Mexico."

"Harder than Mexico. More work. That's all it is—work."

"But you have a car."

"To go to work." Javier raised himself on one elbow to speak more clearly. "Everyone who goes thinks he'll make lots of money; that he'll have a chance. But you never have a chance."

"Then why are you going?"

"Who knows," Javier said. "For the chance."

Javier lay back and didn't speak again. After a moment, his body jerked once and Juan could sense his falling asleep. In the night air, after the day's heat, it was suddenly cool, and Juan pushed his back to Javier's for warmth. The last thing he heard before dropping off was a high-pitched chorus of coyotes singing in the brush.

A quarter moon rose at eleven. At twelve, they started walking again. The dark shiny leaves of the blackbrush and ironwood reflected the pale light, and the ceniza stood spectral. From the contour of the brush and the feel of the cedar stick, Javier was able to guide them through. When the ground was rough, he warned Juan. When the brush was eye-level thorny, he held it back with the stick. They watched the sky to set their course and stopped often to light matches and look at the compass. What relief there was from the heat was negated by the insecurity of each step.

At a thicket of prickly pear, they veered to the east to try to outflank it, but, after pushing through dense brush, were stopped by an arm of the thicket. They backtracked and forced their way to the west, but again found themselves outflanked. The prickly pear appeared to encircle them, as if like fish they had swum into a trap. Within the thicket, the brush and the dark prevented their seeing where they had entered, and they were unable to gauge the depth of the prickly pear they would have to penetrate. Slightly disoriented, Javier checked the compass and then sighted a narrow indentation to the north. He placed the end of his cedar stick against a branch of the obtruding cactus and pushed until it broke with a vegetable crunch and fell out of the way. With the end of the cedar stick, he slowly and patiently pushed a narrow hole through a four-foot-high wall of prickly pear and on they went.

Coyotes sang in the night, the sky turned gray, they lay down to sleep again. By eight o'clock the next morning it was hot in the brush and again they were walking. By noon, they had all but depleted the salty water just to keep their mouths wet. Their faces were a perpetual shade of red beneath their hats; their clothing soaked with sweat; their eyes stinging with perspiration. They stopped to rest beneath a mes-quite, and, too hot and too dry to want them, ate beans spread on soda crackers, which, since they had no saliva, stuck to their teeth and gums.

They rested till two before starting again. The brush quivered with heat under the afternoon sun, and the sky was devoid of clouds. Though they had crossed two dirt roads, they hadn't come to any more windmills and began to think they'd passed them in the night. From the sun and sweat, Javier's left eye started to itch and turn red. Occasionally, when they stopped to wet their mouths—an act that only defined the thirst—Javier would look up at the blank sky and shake his head, *"No quiere nublarse."* It doesn't want to cloud up, he would say, and smile sadly as if it were a small favor that he was being sense-lessly denied.

One sip after another of the water which, at the end, was merely provocation, and finally the jug was empty. Their lips burned from the sun and they became acutely aware of their thirst. Tongue, palate, lining of the mouth: it felt as if they would slowly swell and stick to-gether. What wasn't the heat, a branch in the face, or the next footstep was beyond their attention. Twice they saw rattlesnakes—one coiled and one moving through the grass—and twice ignored them.

At five they came to a windmill. The water was salty, but they no longer cared. It freed their mouths and they took off their shirts to soak with water and sponge themselves. After they had slaked their thirst, they sat beneath the water tank to rest. "How far?" Juan asked.

Javier thought of how long they had walked before saying, "To-morrow we come to a highway not far from Carrizo, from there, it's ninety miles to San Antonio."

"Ninety miles," Juan repeated.

"But who knows," Javier consoled him. "Perhaps someone will give us a ride."

They walked till sundown, ate, and slept. When the moon rose, they walked. At dawn, they found a windmill where they rested until the morning heat drove them on. Again the sky was cloudless; the heat, visible, audible. The brush trembled with the transmission of the sun's rays passing through, rebounding up from the ground, and shimmering humidly above; the heat's reverberation climbed slowly, reaching higher and higher cycles, yet hitting no limit.

During the night, Javier's eye had continued to itch, and with the renewed heat and sweat and rubbing, started to swell closed. By midmorning, his eyelids had swollen into a puffed slit through which Juan could see bloodshot veins radiating out from the black iris. When they stopped at noon, the eye was sealed shut, they were low on water, and they discovered a new torment. Black lusterless flies, small and flat, clung to their pants legs and rode along peacefully until they came to a halt. Then, in a swarm, they attacked hands, faces, and necks, sending the two brothers into a slapping frenzy. Spurred by the flies, they moved on through the heat of the day.

After more than an hour without water, Javier and Juan saw a windmill on the horizon. Their relief, however, slowly turned into despair when, goal in view, they saw how tedious their progress was. With the afternoon heat growing to a crescendo, in their thirst and exhaustion, the windmill appeared to advance before them on the horizon.

The windmill, they found, was surrounded by a deer-proof fence; large mesquite trees drooped around a dark pond of motionless water. The gate to the enclosure was padlocked, and within was a silent and ungrazed sanctuary of green. Javier climbed the gate, then Juan, and they jumped into the lush grass. Like shadows, black peccaries moved away from the far side of the pond. Midway to the windmill, knee-deep in grass, a deliberate and unequivocal rattle struck them like a current of electricity. Rooted to the ground, statues in the glade, they listened to the warning fill the enclosure. Pulse hammering, breath shallow and constricted, neither could see the snake or locate the sound. When it stopped, the silence was absolute and alarming.

They stood paralyzed for a moment, then Javier lifted his cedar stick and tapped the ground before him. When there was no response, he continued to try the grass until sure there was no immediate danger of being struck. They moved forward two steps, prodded the grass, and continued the procedure until they reached the windmill. Still shaking, they washed their hands and faces, ran water over their heads, filled the jug, and left the enclosure.

Hastened by the thought of the road, goaded by their nearness to complete exhaustion, they plodded on. The heat broke at five and there was a light breeze, but by then each step forward was punishment, and Javier's eye was red and swollen. At the top of every crest, they thought they would see the highway. Each time they saw more brush.

The sun set and they stopped. Javier opened a can of sardines, which they ate with the last of the crackers, and sipping the water like expensive whiskey, they sat in the dusk and smoked a cigarette. Juan stood up to kick out a spot to sleep and looked north. "*Qué es eso?*" he asked, and pointed toward a red blinking light.

"What?" Javier asked with vague interest.

"There's a light."

Javier raised himself to his knees and sighted north through his good eye. "Carrizo! It must be the radio antenna at Carrizo. Come on," he said, getting to his feet, "we're almost there."

The red light winked at them as they walked, telling them how far they had to go and how slowly they had traveled. At the top of a hill they could see a set of white headlights flash intermittently through the brush as a vehicle moved east to west. The next time they saw headlights they could hear the faint, mournful whine of a truck approaching and then receding in the night. The two brothers came to a pasture where the underbrush had been cleared and they walked quickly toward the road. At a fence, outside the possible sweep of headlights, they sat down on the ground to watch the pavement. "What do you think?" Javier asked. "If we ask for a ride, we might be in San Antonio tonight." He savored the idea. "Or *la emigración* might catch us."

"And if we don't ask for a ride?" Juan asked.

"Then we walk another seven days. More, if we have to work for food."

Juan looked straight ahead at the road and didn't answer.

"There are always risks," Javier decided and started for the fence.

The first car caught them in its headlights—Javier with his swollen eye, and black baseball cap; Juan with his white hat—and speeded up. A pickup passed and then a large Oldsmobile sedan hit its brakes as soon as they appeared in the light. They picked up their bags and ran toward the red taillights. A man on the passenger side leaned out and shouted in a friendly voice, "*Vámanos a San Antonio.*"

Javier and Juan stopped running.

"*¿A dónde van?*" the man called, "*¿Quieren un* ride?" Where you going? Want a ride?

Silence.

And then, "*¿Van a San Antonio?*" he asked again.

Silence.

And then, "*¿Son de México?*" Are you from Mexico?

"*Sí,*" Javier answered, knowing that it was too late. "*Somos de México.*"

"*Bueno, vámanos a México,*" the man said and got out. "*Somos de la emigración.*"

Within two hours, the car erased what it had taken Javier and Juan three days and nights to do and they were back at the border. The next morning they were processed, and in the afternoon they were put on a bus with other illegal aliens and driven across the bridge to be let out in Nuevo Laredo. Between the two of them, they had five dollars that Javier had held back for an emergency and a couple of cans of food. They stood for a minute watching the people stream back and forth across the bridge, and then Javier turned and started west, retracing their steps to the railroad trestle, over the embankment and through the brush, until he came to a stop beneath a large oak next to the river. "Here we rest," he said, and set his bags down.

"Then what?" Juan asked.

"Start again."

For once not impassive, Juan allowed a flicker of surprise to cross his face. "How?" he asked.

"That we'll think about while we rest," Javier said, and squatted down to watch the river. "But we'll make it." He looked up at Juan. "Do you know why?"

Juan shook his head.

"*La necesidad nos obliga,*" Javier said.

Necessity obliges.

Javier and Juan arrived in San Antonio thirteen days later on Sunday morning; on Monday Javier went back to his roofing job, and Juan began as a carpenter's helper on Wednesday.

LIVESTOCK

Cattle Watering in Lake

Joseph G. McCoy

Joseph G. McCoy (1837–1915) published his *Historic Sketches of the Cattle Trade of the West and Southwest* in 1874. McCoy's purpose in publishing the work, he says in the preface to that first edition, was "to convey in simple, unpretentious language, practical and correct information upon the opening, development, and present status of the live stock trade of the Great New West." The work is of particular historical importance because of the fact that McCoy was a leading figure in the cattle trade of which he speaks. As the first mayor of Abilene, Kansas—where one of his first official acts was to appoint James Butler "Wild Bill" Hickok to the position of town marshal—McCoy was instrumental in establishing that town as a principal shipping point for Texas cattle. He later worked to organize successful cattle markets in Newton and Wichita, Kansas, and in Saint Louis and Chicago.

The selection that follows describes one aspect of the cattle drive that has appealed to B-grade western filmmakers for some time. Hollywood has never been particularly hesitant to embellish when it comes to the cowboy. Such lack of similitude is important if we accept the notion that the moviegoing audience tends to accept as true whatever is portrayed on the screen that is beyond its collective experience. Larry McMurtry has pointed out, for example, the phenomenon of what he calls the "trotting cattle syndrome"—wherein "the moviegoer usually sees cattle being driven across the screen at a pace so rapid that even the wiriest Longhorn could not have sustained it the length of Hollywood Boulevard without collapsing."

On the Trail

WE left the herd fairly started upon the trail for the northern market. Of these trails there are several: one leading to Baxter Springs and Chetopa; another called the "Old Shawnee trail," leaving Red river and running eastward, crossing the Arkansas not far above Fort Gibson, thence bending westward up the Arkansas river. But the principal trail now traveled is more direct and is known as "Chisholm trail," so named from a semicivilized Indian who is said to have traveled it first. It is more direct, has more prairie, less timber, more small streams and less large ones, and altogether better grass and fewer flies (no civilized Indian tax or wild Indian disturbances) than any other route yet driven over, and is also much shorter in distance because direct from Red river to Kansas. Twenty-five to thirty-five days is the usual time required to bring a drove from Red river to the southern line of Kansas, a distance of between two hundred and fifty and three hundred miles, and an excellent country to drive over. So many cattle have been driven over the trail in the last few years that a broad highway is tread out, looking much like a national highway; so plain, a fool could not fail to keep in it.

One remarkable feature is observable as being worthy of note, and that is how completely the herd becomes broken to follow the trail. Certain cattle will take the lead, and others will select certain places in the line, and certain ones bring up the rear; and the same cattle can be seen at their post, marching along like a column of soldiers, every day during the entire journey, unless they become lame, when they will fall back to the rear. A herd of one thousand cattle will stretch out from one to two miles whilst traveling on the trail, and is a very beautiful sight, inspiring the drover with enthusiasm akin to that enkindled in the breast of the military hero by the sight of marching columns of men. Certain cowboys are appointed to ride beside the leaders and so control the herd, whilst others ride beside and behind, keeping everything in its place and moving on, the camp wagon and caviyard bringing up the rear.

When an ordinary creek or small river is reached, the leaders are usually easily induced to go in; and although it may be swimming, yet they scarce hesitate, but plunge through to the northern shore and continue the journey, the balance of the herd following as fast as they arrive. Often, however, at large rivers, when swollen by floods, difficulty is experienced in getting over; especially is this the case when the herd gets massed together. Then they become unwieldy and are hard to induce to take the water. Sometimes days are spent, and much damage to the condition of the herd done, in getting across a single stream. But if the herd is well broken and properly managed, this difficulty is not often experienced. As soon as the leaders can be induced to take to the water and strike out for the opposite shore, the balance will follow with but little trouble. Often the drover can induce the leaders to follow him into and across the river by riding ahead of them into the water and, if need be, swimming his horse in the lead to the opposite shore, whilst the entire herd follow much in the same order that it travels on the trail. It sometimes occurs that the herd will become unmanageable and frightened after entering the water and refuse to strike out to either shore, but gather around their leaders and

swim in a circle round and round, very similar to milling on the ground
when frightened. The aspect is that of a mass of heads and horns, the
bodies being out of sight in the water, and it is not uncommon to lose
numbers by drowning. When the herd gets to milling in the water, to
break this mill and induce the leaders to launch out for the shore, the
drover swims his cow pony into the center of the mill and, if possible,
frightens the mass of struggling, whirling cattle into separation. Not
infrequently the drover is unhorsed and compelled to swim for his life,
often taking a swimming steer by the tail and thus be safely and speed-
ily towed to the shore. Swimming herds of cattle across swollen rivers
is not listed as one of the pleasurable events in the drover's trip to the
northern market. It is the scarcity of large rivers that constitutes one of
the most powerful arguments in favor of the Chisholm trail. Nevertheless it is not entirely free from this objection, especially during rainy
seasons. When the herd is over the stream the next job is to get the

camp wagon over. This is done by drawing it near the water's edge and, after detaching the oxen and swimming them over, a number of picket ropes are tied together (sufficient to reach across the river) and attached to the wagon, which is then pushed into the water and drawn to the opposite shore; whereupon the team is attached and the wagon drawn onto solid ground.

Few occupations are more cheerful, lively, and pleasant than of the cowboy on a fine day or night; but when the storm comes, then is his manhood and often his skill and bravery put to test. When the night is inky dark and the lurid lightning flashes its zigzag course athwart the heavens, and the coarse thunder jars the earth, the winds moan fresh and lively over the prairie, the electric balls dance from tip to tip of the cattle's horns—then the position of the cowboy on duty is trying, far more than romantic. When the storm breaks over his head, the least occurrence unusual, such as the breaking of a dry weed or stick, or a sudden and near flash of lightning, will start the herd as if by magic, all at an instant, upon a wild rush, and woe to the horse or man or camp that may be in their path. The only possible show for safety is to mount and ride with them until you can get outside the stampeding column. It is customary to train cattle to listen to the noise of the herder, who sings in a voice more sonorous than musical a lullaby consisting of a few short monosyllables. A stranger to the business of stock driving will scarce credit the statement that the wildest herd will not run, so long as they can hear distinctly the voice of the herder above the din of the storm.

But if by any mishap the herd gets off on a real stampede, it is by bold, dashing, reckless riding in the darkest of nights, and by adroit, skillful management that it is checked and brought under control. The moment the herd is off, the cowboy turns his horse at full speed down the retreating column and seeks to get up beside the leaders, which he does not attempt to stop suddenly, for such an effort would be futile, but turns them to the left or right hand and gradually curves them into a circle, the circumference of which is narrowed down as fast as possible until the whole herd is rushing wildly round and round on as small a piece of ground as possible for them to occupy. Then the cowboy begins his lullaby note in a loud voice, which has a great effect in quieting the herd. When all is still and the herd well over its scare, they are returned to their bed ground, or held where stopped until daylight.

Often a herd becomes scattered and run in different directions, in which case the labor is great to collect them; some will run a distance of twenty or thirty miles before stopping and turning out to rest, after which they will travel on at a rapid rate. Many times great loss in numbers and condition is sustained by a single stampede; and a herd, when once the habit of running is formed, will do but little good in thrift—if they do not become poor and bony and get the appearance of greyhounds. And the habit, once contracted, is next to impossible to break up and get the cattle to be quiet and thrifty, save by putting them in small herds or fenced pastures, and this will not always remedy the evil or break up the habit.

During rainy, stormy seasons herds of cattle are apt to form the habit of stampeding every cloudy or stormy night. And although they may have long been off of the trail, held on good grazing ground, yet they are very liable to form the habit of running. It is generally the case that less than a score, often less than a half dozen, of old, wild, long-legged beeves do the mischief by getting a chronic fright, from which they never do recover; nor are they ever afterwards satisfied unless they are on the run. They would rather run than eat, any time, no matter how empty of food they may be. Stampeding becomes a mania with them, and day or night they seem to be looking for or studying up a pretext to set off on a forty-mile jaunt. How well one stampeder gets to know every other stampeder in the herd is astonishing, and they may be seen close together at all times, as if counselling how to raise Cain and get off on a burst of speed. The moment anything happens that may startle the herd, no matter how little, every chronic stampeder in the herd sets off at full speed, hooking and goring every steer before or upon either side of him. It does seem as if they had become possessed of several such devils as stampeded the swine into the sea in ancient Judea. It is actual economy to shoot down, if you cannot otherwise dispose of, a squad of these vicious stampeders. And often the prudent herder will order a single car cut out, and ship off every stampeder he may have in his herd; not that he expects to get anything of much account for them, for they are generally very poor and lean, but simply to abate them and their pernicious example and influence on the balance of the herd. The way the cowboy takes sublime pleasure in prodding a lot of stampeders into a car and sending them off, he cares not where, is beyond expression and beggars description. You should hear him pronounce his parting blessing on the brutes as the engine moves off with the car in which they are confined. The expression would not create an exalted opinion of the cowboy's piety. For he could tell you of the unnumbered sleepless hours they have cost him, and how many times they have caused him to leave his couch of sweet slumber, mount his horse, and ride through darkness and storm to overtake and bring back the herd from following the racy stampeders; and now that they are gone, words fail to tell his joyous delight.

Drovers consider that the cattle do themselves great injury by running round in a circle, which is termed, in cowboy parlance, "milling," and it can only be stayed by standing at a distance and hallooing or singing to them. The writer has many times sat upon the fence of a shipping yard and sang to an enclosed herd whilst a train would be rushing by. And it is surprising how quiet the herd will be so long as they can hear the human voice; but if they fail to hear it above the din of the train, a rush is made, and the yards bursted asunder unless very strong. Singing hymns to Texan steers is the peculiar forte of a genuine cowboy, but the spirit of true piety does not abound in the sentiment. We have read of singing psalms to dead horses, but singing to a lot of Texan steers is an act of piety that few beside a western drover are capable of. But 'tis said that "music hath charms that soothe the savage breast," or words to that effect, and why not "soothe" a stampeding Texan steer? We pause, repeating, "Why not?"

John Graves

John Graves was born and raised in Fort Worth, Texas. Educated at
Rice and Columbia universities, he presently lives on his four-hundred-
acre stock farm near Glen Rose in north central Texas. Graves has been
contributing stories and articles to magazines since the publication of his
first story in the *New Yorker* in 1947. His first book, the highly acclaimed
Goodbye To A River (1960), won the Collins Award of the Texas Institute
of Letters. Graves's other works include *The Water Hustlers* (1971), a
book on conservation for the Department of the Interior and the Sierra
Club, and *Hard Scrabble: Observations on a Patch of Land* (1974). The
essay that follows has been published in *From a Limestone Ledge* (1980),
which is a collection of Graves's regular contributions to *Texas Monthly*
magazine that serves as a continuation—*"footnotes,"* Graves has said—of
the ruminations and observations on country living begun in *Hard
Scrabble*.

Nineteen Cows

STANDARD agricultural publications and the farm-ranch pages of our
Sunday newspapers tend to be condescending toward small-scale cattle
raisers, as indeed they are toward small-scale anybody else in this age
of agribusiness, or agri-bigness as someone has called it. Only the
other day I ran across a slighting reference, in an interview with a
Texas A&M professor who was touting the recycling of used Baggies
into feedlot rations or something on that order, to "people that have
nineteen cows." It stung a bit, for I usually have only a few more cows
than that myself—rarely in excess of about thirty-five, with a bull and
varying numbers of attendant offspring from year to year. But it didn't
sting very much, because no learned Aggie could possibly wax more
brilliantly caustic about my relationship to bovines than I have waxed
about it myself when a bad winter or a drouthy summer has made
tending them an onerous daily concern, or when the market for calves,
as frequently, is so miserable that any owner who can count on his
fingers can see clearly that they're costing him more to raise than
there's any chance of recouping when he sells them as his land's major product.

And yet, despite occasional resolves to get rid of the whole herd
and to let the land revert to brushy wildlife habitat where I might stroll
unconcerned bearing gun or fieldglass or just a set of appreciative feel-

ings toward nature in her magnificence, such as it is around here, I'm
still saddled with my quota of these large and fairly stupid beasts about
a decade and a half after buying the eight weanling Angus heifers that
were the mothers and grandmothers of my present bunch. Nor does it
seem too likely that I'll break loose from them unless I manage to break
loose from the land itself, a possibility that I think about fondly from
time to time when country life grows cluttered and demanding. For
the cattle, unnumerous and marginally economic though they may be,
constitute the place's reason for being, in a way. It has been "improved" with them in mind. Together with some goats and a couple of
horses they make it a "stock farm," a designation that usually serves to
convince the mercenary outside world, including the Internal Revenue
Service, that I'm not hopelessly impractical in my possession of the
better part of a square mile of rough country most of which is suitable
for nothing but herbivores and wild things.

Another trouble is that for foggy and complex reasons I like cows,
stupid or not, and like the simple, only occasionally arduous, annual
routine of working with them. Beef cattle take care of themselves during a good part of a normal year if given enough pasture to graze—what
constitutes "enough" varying quite a bit from region to region. In my
neighborhood the carrying capacity of average unimproved grassland is
usually stated as about twenty acres per animal unit: i.e., one grown
cow with or without a calf, or equivalent numbers or fractions of other
beasts depending on size and appetite. Elsewhere the requisite acreage
may be considerably less or a great deal more, according to rainfall and
the richness of the land. Whatever it is, if you stay within it, most years
your cattle will be all right with only a little labor on your part. If you
don't you'll run out of grass, have to buy and haul in a lot of feed, and
get to watch your denuded topsoil escape as silt or dust under rains and
winds, but of course you'll be in good historic company. Overstocking
has long been the rule in most of the West and elsewhere, and it still is
among some operators. Of one rancher in Bosque County just south of
me, they used to say that every morning he'd go to a slope in his
pasture and lie down on his belly, and if by looking up toward the
hilltop and the sky he could see a sprig of anything growing, he'd go
out and buy another ten cows.

Much of the work with cattle lies in making sure they've got
enough to eat during the hard parts of the year, chiefly winter, and that

what they eat has all they need in it. This means storing up hay in spring and summer for the dead months and hauling it to them in a pickup when needed, sowing wheat or oats or rye on patches of arable land in fall for green high-protein grazing while regular grasses are dormant, and buying supplements and processed feed for use when rains fail or extreme cold keeps the green stuff from growing. Dry summers mean some extra feeding too. Otherwise, except for such general rancherly activities as doctoring occasional injuries and ailments, keeping an eye on first-calf heifers in case they need obstetrical help, segregating the younger ones against rape before their time, spraying or dusting the herd against flies, and fighting back brush in pastures to keep it from crowding out grass, the main work has to do with the production and nurture and management of calves, which are your stock farm's primary crop and the chief source of such cash profit, if any, as you will enjoy from it.

In the days when the horrific screw-worm was bad in Texas one of its favorite points of attack was the navels of newborn calves, where an infection could quickly prove fatal. Sensible owners themselves therefore tried to restrict calving to winter and early spring before the flies that bred these gnawing maggots appeared—which, gestation being a little over nine months, meant running a bull with the cows from about February until midsummer and then taking him away to dwell lovelessly in solitude or with some steers or horses. Nowadays, with the problem largely eliminated by annual releases of sterile male flies along the border and in northern Mexico, some of us still more or less follow the old schedule either because we're hidebound or because we pessimistically expect the flies to bypass the control program one of these years and come down in swarms again. Others avail themselves of new freedom by arranging to calve in spring and early summer when grasses are usually lush and cows' production of milk is highest.

Most range calves manage to get born without trouble at whatever time of year, and if they have good mothers grow healthily to the age of four or five months before you need to worry much about doing anything to them, though some graziers put out creep feeders to promote growth—roofed bins full of rich stuff that the calves can reach but larger stock can't. But at some point they need to be "worked," a process which I've found sometimes inflicts a bit of trauma on visiting non-enthusiasts but which, despite a component of casual brutality, is for cowmen a rather exhilarating task that has in it not only a lot of fine dust and bellowing and kicking and uproar but also the solid satisfaction of bringing order out of chaos. The main operations are inoculation of the calves against two or three common diseases (more in humid regions), marking them with a brand and/or earmarks and/or numbered eartags, worming where intestinal worms are a problem, dehorning horned breeds if you dislike horns, and castrating the males.

Except on some big ranches and among people who just like cowboying, few calves these days are worked in the old colorful way with ropers on horseback and other people who throw the beasts and hold them down while still others utilize knives and syringes and branding irons. Skilled help in this as in other realms is short, so instead, nearly all small operators and most big ones do the job with a minimum of assistants by driving or tolling the herd into a set of pens, separating the calves, and shunting them through alleys and chutes to some device that catches them and holds them more or less firmly. This can be a simple headgate that grabs the neck or, more efficiently and expensively, a squeeze chute that clamps on the whole creature or a "calf cradle" that not only clamps but then swings up and presents him to the attentions of his nurturers like, in the poet's phrase, a patient etherized upon a table. Except that anesthesia is not a part of the process.

Anthropomorphism being what it is, castration is the part that fascinates and bothers unaccustomed spectators most, especially male ones. It needs to be done in part because the market usually pays better for steers than for bulls, though many will argue with you that there is no difference in their meat. But the chief reason for it is convenience in handling cattle. Steers are docile, they can be put into a pasture with big nubile heifers without fear that the latter will be bred too young, and above all they lack the sexual smolder that sends even young bulls on patrol along fencelines, looking for a way out and often finding it.

On very young calves castration can be accomplished with practically no shock to either subject or witnesses by using a tool that places a heavy tight rubber band around the upper part of the scrotum, which subsequently atrophies and falls off. But in older animals this poses some danger of tetanus, and they have to be done with the ancient and very efficient knife or some other cutting instrument, or with bloodless emasculators like the Burdizzo, a heavy set of compound-leverage pincers that crush the spermatic cord without breaking skin. This implement was invented many years ago by an old Italian vet, whose name it bears and whom it made rich, and is still manufactured painstakingly in Milan for use throughout the world's warm regions where fresh wounds are subject to quick infection and to parasites. The instructions that come with it bear the doctor's mustached, starch-collared likeness and a rather hilarious photograph of a calf that must have been tranquilized to the gills, since he is shown submitting to the operation without a surge or a kick or, as far as can be told, a bellow of indignation. . . . Here in the Southwest the Burdizzo had its heyday when the screw-worms were having theirs, but even now a good many people, myself among them, still like it for its cleanness and lessened shock effect, though it's more trouble than a knife and can hardly be called humane.

Having worked your calves, the main thing you do with them is sell them at weaning age, six months or so, maybe a bit earlier or later according to rises and falls in the market and the state of your own pastures for sustaining some extra eaters over a period of time. After perhaps setting aside a steer to keep for fattening and slaughter and a few good heifers to raise as replacements for cows that need to be culled, you load the rest of the calves into a trailer and haul them to a weekly auction at some county seat not far away or maybe, if prices are rumored to be better there, to a city sale like the one on Fort Worth's North Side.

To confess a weakness, I find culling cows harder than almost anything to do with cattle except the worst kind of bloody obstetrics. With a small herd you come to know your animals as individuals and even if you don't view them sentimentally you have favorites among them and a relationship with the whole bunch based on what they have done for you and the longstanding responsibility you've exercised toward them. Hence it weighs a bit on the conscience when one of them has to go the hamburger route, which is where most cull cows do go, because she's started having sorry calves or no calves at all, and it weighs still more when drouth or a hard winter strikes, or cash is requisite, or the herd simply grows too large for the land you've got, and you have to cut back by selling several and need to decide which ones. Records help if you keep them, scribbled notebook pages that detail cows' lineage, birth, quirks, achievements, and imperfections, much in the manner of military service record books or a nosy government's dossiers on its citizens. If, for instance, a bright, large-eyed, trusting, shapely little cow named Pet, who will take feed cubes from your hand and will suffer her ears to be scratched, has been producing tiny calves that never get very big and are prone to things like warts, and an ill-tempered, ungainly, suspicious creature known only as Number thirty-nine has been rearing one after another a succession of large, thrifty sons and daughters, the records will show it and you know what you have to do. Pet goes, even if the innocent confusion you think to read in her face, as she's hustled through the ring to the music of cracking whips and shouts and the auctioneer's amplified gabble, does cause twinges in your breast.

Not that cold reason always prevails, even with tougher types than me. I once saw an ancient scrub brindle rack of bones, with one horn up and the other down, in the sleek Beefmaster herd of a rancher reputed to be hardnosed and practical, and asked what she was do-ing there.

"Oh, Rosie," he said with a shake of his grizzled head, evading the question. "Seventeen years old."

"But why?"

"Guess I like her," he answered with finality and I did not press, for it is unwise to tread on hard people's softnesses.

There are lots of us miniature ranchers across the continent. The scorn expressed by that expert Aggie and by others like him is not at all disinterested but sprouts, I think, from an uneasiness that afflicts agri-business types when they're brought eyeball to eyeball with the fact that a goodly percentage of the cattle marketed in the nation these days comes out of small to middlesized herds more or less like mine. This uneasiness afflicts others too, including old-line ranchers, who rather bitterly circulate among themselves such statistical gems as the one that ninety percent of the cattle in the fabulous feedlots of the Texas Panhandle come from the herds of people who own ten cows or less. This figure is hostile hyperbole, but the real ones are impressive enough. A Texas agricultural census shows that in 1974 people with fewer than fifty calving beef cows owned eighteen percent of well over five million such cows in the state, and people with fewer than one hundred cows—still relative small-timers in economic terms—owned thirty-eight percent.

What probably bothers our friend the Aggie most is that we're unpredictable, that the unexpectedly large or small numbers of beasts that whim or panic causes us to trailer to sales from year to year are a large factor in the market and can mean the loss or gain of millions by feedlots and commodity speculators and other would-be beneficiaries, according to whether they have second-guessed us well or badly. And what understandably gravels real ranchers is that after decades of hardship based on generally poor cattle prices, inflation, rising land and inheritance taxes, and whatnot, they are losing much of what little control they had over their own product to a rabble of johnny-come-latelies. This irritation is heightened by a deterioration of old ranching standards, especially a loss of prestige by the stalwart British breeds of cattle and a new demand for crossbred stuff which is favored by the feedlots, and therefore by the whole market, because its "hybrid vigor" enables it to gain weight faster at less cost—even if, as some ranchers claim and I tend to believe, the meat is not quite so good.

"People like you are just messing things up," one rancher said amiably to me a few years back, when the dimensions of all this were growing visible. His ancestral land was measured in quite a few square-mile sections instead of acres and stocked with several hundred big handsome whitefaces whose careful improvement, through selective breeding and the introduction of bulls from new bloodlines, had begun in his grandfather's time. "You can't make a living out of a little herd like that, and nothing that you do with them is ever done quite right. But there are so damn many of you that you're interfering with the way things are supposed to be. The other day I shipped a truckload of nice prime calves to Fort Worth, and I got six or eight cents a pound less for them than the buyers were bidding for little bunches of raunchy speckled stuff raised by weekend amateurs in the Blacklands and East Texas and Arkansas and God knows where else."

"I've got Angus," I said a bit defensively. "I didn't invent hybrid vigor either."

"Scrub vigor," he said with contempt. But the last time I saw him, a year or so ago, he spoke with enthusiasm about the crossbred calves he was getting from running Charolais bulls with his Hereford cows. Things change, and on the list of proud traditional ranching's troubles we stock-farm types are only a single item—another and more hurtful one being agribusiness itself and the sophisticated activities of "cattlemen" more at home with pocket calculators than saddles and with steer futures hedging than the identification of range grasses.

There is nothing new about owning a few beef cows, especially in places like Texas where social cachet of a sort has always attached to their possession and the ability to jaw about them. But the emergence of smallish grazing operations as a major sort of land use, from the upper-middle Atlantic coast down through and across the South and in parts of the Midwest as well, has taken place mainly since World War II, I believe, for various reasons of which the strongest are not social and may not even be economic. In part it grew out of the agricultural desolation of the Thirties, when farming was a dead end, and out of government emphasis since that time on taking marginal and tired or wornout country out of cultivation and sowing it to improved permanent grasses to let it rest and to stop erosion. In high-rainfall areas with deep soil, properly managed and fertilized grassland of this sort can be astoundingly productive of beef. Not uncommonly it will sustain a cow on every two or three acres or so, though in time, as world hunger swells, most places with such potential will likely be put back into crops. In less rich terrain, including places like my beat-up patch of rocky hills, the land's carrying capacity is skimpier, but on the other hand grazing is about all it's good for these days anyhow.

One element in beef cattle's appeal is the fact, already intimated, that they represent a lot less work than farming or horticulture, taking care of their own needs much of the time if given half a chance. This has weight with many owners who want their land to pay its way, but who make their main living in towns and cities, and on weekends either don't have time for agriculture or possess an immunity to the sentimental pull of plow and harrow. During market upsurges cattle can also bring in a fair amount of money, and such is human nature that upsurge prices are what cattlemen like to view as the norm, just as farmers are in love with the boom-based reference point of "parity." We are still in an upsurge just now, but unfortunately these joyous intervals have seldom lasted long, for when they begin large numbers of erstwhile spectators jump in, buy overpriced breeding stock of whatever description with borrowed money, throw them onto leased pasture, and flood the market with calves as promptly as biology permits, driving prices back down again. Thus a sleek, staggering, moony-eyed, newborn bullcalf, which your doting mind's eye sees as being worth, say, three hundred dollars or more as a weaned steer a few months later, may turn out to bring half that sum, a crucial difference considering steady inflation and the feed and hay and other things you will have invested in his mama during the long months of pregnancy and nursing. Sad to say, hardship ensues, whether small-scale or large and whether to high flyers or to the rest of us.

Nothing illustrates better the main reason, the irrational one, for the nineteen-cow phenomenon than the fact that so many of us stay with cattle despite such setbacks. We like the damned things, and our real motivation has little to do with money or labor but I suppose must be called romantic. Possibly the pull of the legendary Old West has something to do with it, for in the arteries of the purest romantics among us cowboy blood pumps hot and strong. Big hats and sharp-toed boots are common attire in regions where forty years ago their wearers would have been laughed back into brogans and farmer-style caps, and on full many a hundred-and-sixty-acre spread, on Saturdays, lariats of nylon hiss through the air and traildrivers born too late for the trail whoop yee-haw as they pound along on horseback behind high-tailed fleeing kine, making them wild as deer.

But the majority of us, Old Westerners at heart or no, do things with less flamboyance, mainly because this is easier on both the cattle and us. Some are highly progressive and thoughtful about the matter of management, perhaps lately graduated from some evening-college course in animal husbandry and loaded with data on the protein content of various feeds, artificial insemination, calf "gainability," and pregnancy testing. Others, maybe most, have read a few books and watched the way other folks do things and get along on that, and still others cling to casual methods, right or wrong, picked up in rural youth. A few happy-go-luckies engage in hardly any management at all, letting the beasts run nearly wild within their boundary fences to multiply or die and every once in a while, by one means or another, gathering up calves and selling them. And another contingent, gamblers at heart, keep no breeding stock but buy steers and heifers small and sell them large, at a profit if they're lucky.

Thus, clearly, unless a nineteen-cowman's proclivities get him slantwise with some local SPCA chapter or cause him to lose so much money that he goes broke, there is wide flexibility as to how much he needs to know and what he does with his cattle. There is also a rich variety of breeds from which he may choose—the old Herefords and

Shorthorns and Anguses, Brahmans and genetically stabilized Brahman crosses like Branguses and Santa Gertrudis and Beefmasters, modish newer "exotics" such as Charolais and Simmentals and Chianinas and Limousins, and quite a few other sorts ranging from Devons and Highlands to tiny Dexters. And in a day when "hybrid vigor" is a magic phrase, unstabilized crosses of every sort abound, whether planned with care by breeders who know what they're after in terms of shape and size, or achieved less studiously by someone who just dumps a bunch of varied cows into a pasture with some sort of bull and occasionally comes up with results that would appear to have been flown in by jet cargo plane from Masai-land. The ancient and tough and wily Longhorn has its partisans, and some owners even edge away from the genus *Bos* into things like buffaloes and Beefaloes and exotic game animals. And each and every kind of creature that I've named and a good many that I haven't possess distinctive qualities of physique and psyche which some human beings will admire and swear by and others will just swear at.

Small-scale beginners are often advised that they will do best to specialize in costly purebred registered beasts of whatever ilk, since the calves will be salable at premium prices, as heifers or bulls, to other breeders—who, the theory implies, will come flocking around checkbooks in hand without even being asked. This can be true enough in time if the beginner in question knows or quickly learns a good bit about genetics and conformation and artificial insemination and such things, maybe wins some prizes at livestock shows to build his herd's reputation, and builds his own by scrupulous attention to records and frank dealing with buyers. But not all of us are that fond of intricate record keeping, fuss and feathers, and the very special perfectionism and politics of the show ring, and there are some other difficulties with purebreds as well, especially in the rough country where some of us run our herds. Living on one end of your place you often find it hard to know precisely what's going on at the other ends, and hard also to keep fences in perfect repair at places where they cross streams and gullies. One visit from a neighbor's offbreed bull can wreck a purebred operation's purity for a year and reduce the calf crop's value to whatever a country auction ring determines it to be, and the young bulls you're keeping for sale to those eager buyers can wander too, messing up lineage records.

Hence registered stock is not for everyone, and most of us settle for something less expensive and less prestigious like my "grade" Anguses, maybe keeping purebred bulls with them year after year so that quality steadily improves even if pedigree doesn't. We find them good to look at, though increasingly with time we are nagged by an impulse to get a bull of another color and produce some of those bouncing, hybridly vigorous mongrels that consistently bring up to a dime or fifteen cents a pound more at sales than good calves of straight British breed. Even if we don't like their looks. . . .

Having made a little money on cattle in certain years and lost some of it back in others, having worried over an uneconomic small herd through drouths and bad winters with an intensity that would have been more wisely saved for life's main problems, having been kicked, butted, stomped, and run up corral fences countless times by Number Thirty-nine and others of like temperament, having pounded large quantities of time down a rat hole over the years in the maintenance of this grudging place for bovine use, and having liked just about all of it at least in retrospect, I am still fond of cows and of tending them and am sometimes puzzled, along with other devotees, to find that everyone everywhere doesn't feel the same way. My original eight heifers have all now gone down the long trail to McDonald's, the last of them just this year at a quite advanced age, but I remember them well by looks and traits and names—Roy's Mother, Nutty Johnson, White Tits, Big Navel, and the others—and take simpleminded pleasure in recognizing among members of the present group some cast of eye, some set of neck, some belligerence or timidity, some tone of bellow that traces back to one of those founding mothers.

I can't even work up any shame about the fact that such things matter to me, nor do I really much care what it was that caused them to matter to me in the first place, whether the romance of the West, or osmotic absorption in youth of the basic Texas myth of ranches and ranching, or a memory derived from the collective unconscious of some Neolithic herding time when human life was pretty carefree. And while I still may manage to break loose from cows one of these years, I know already that if I do I won't regret having expended time and energy on them. Because it seems they are something I needed to know about, and in a day when knowledge that you don't need comes washing in on your brain in waves like surf, it is good to have a little that you do.

I'm not talking about practical needs, any more than most other cow people are even when they think otherwise. Few of them, at any rate, have trouble in getting the point of an aged joke, maybe Neolithic itself, that is reshaped and recirculated from time to time. In one version it tells of a leathery West Texan who has fought all his life for a minimal living on a few sections of caliche and stones, but has now been blessed with a couple of million dollars of unexpected oil money. When queried as to what he intends to do he reflects for a moment and says, "No, I ain't heading for Las Vegas and all them naked floozies. I ain't going to buy me no Cadillacs either. I figure to do something different."

"You do?" say his questioners.

"Hell, yes," he says. "What I figure to do is just ranch and ranch and ranch and ranch, till every damn last cent of that money is all used up."

Al Reinert

Little is known about Al Reinert other than that he is rumored to live in the vicinity of Houston, Texas, and that he employs a pleasant-sounding answering service.

The End of the Trail

FRANTICALLY squealing and mooing, as if somehow aware of their destination, two cows and four calves lurch and bounce through an August Monday morning in the trailer towed by J. B. Haisler's half-ton Chevy pickup. The cows are ten and twelve years old. The calves are about five months, and none has ever before left the cozy 230 acres of pasture that now lie fifty traumatic miles behind them. The calves have been ready for market only a few weeks now, but today is the first Monday he's had a chance to take them. Still, J. B. Haisler feels sure it's a lucky day. It had rained most of the last week, the first heavy rain all summer, and it was his experience that "things just seems to perk up a bit after a good rain."

A tall, spare man whose plain, broad features have ripened during his seventy years, J. B. Haisler long ago learned to accommodate his life to nature's whims. Born on a bottomland farm near the Brazos River, he has moved several times over the years but never away from the land or beyond his means. Riding in the cab of the pickup with his son and partner, Melvin, he gazes out the window and smiles as they drive into Fort Worth.

For more than forty years J. B. Haisler has been coming here to sell his hogs, mules, dried-up dairy cows, and foundered horses, and, for the past twenty years, his beef cattle. His herd back in Denton consists of one mostly Angus bull, unblooded but dependable, together with a few dozen Hereford cows and whatever progeny they might produce, and currently totals 85, minus the 6 in the trailer. He belongs to no great union or movement, no agricultural organization or federation more imposing than the Denton County Livestock Association. He doesn't think of himself as a stockman, or as a cattleman, and certainly not as a rancher; in his own straightforward mind, J. B. Haisler is simply a farmer.

He is not much of a market strategist. He does subscribe to the

Weekly Livestock Reporter and he listens for the market summaries on the radio, yet somehow his four or five annual trips always seem prompted less by the going price than by pressing needs: debts, children's upcoming birthdays, visits from in-laws, or pure convenience. A year ago at this time J. B. Haisler sold his calves on a down market for 35 cents a pound and couldn't pay his expenses on them. So, like most of his neighbors, he held back as many head as he could this year, feeding them on grain as long as he could, but the market didn't start climbing until after Christmas and the winter brought the worst weather in years. In February his not-quite-yearling heifers brought only 45 cents a pound, his steers a dime more, and by then they were too light for him to recoup his losses.

Today, as they roll into Fort Worth, exiting the highway into the city's old North Side, J. B. Haisler is mightily hoping his calves will make 70 cents a pound, and maybe even better. The calves, meanwhile, bleat and sprawl helplessly as the trailer rattles over the cracked and twisted North Side roads—meandering, bewildering, meeting abruptly in six-way intersections—roadways that bore cattle for half a century before there was a need for asphalt or stop signs.

Cattle have been lumbering through here since the 1860s. Back then, they were longhorns, bad-tempered and lately branded, as tough as the buffalo whose range they had inherited, free for the rounding up on the South Texas plains. They brought $3 each at Fort Worth, where the big trail herds gathered on the grassy, sheltered, and easily forded northern banks of Clear Fork, the third stream forming the Trinity River. The fort had once been the westernmost post in the U.S. Army, facing the alien prairie and restraining the Comanches with its one thunderous howitzer. That was before the cattle started coming and inspired a town.

Bedded down and quickly fattened for the journey, the cattle were then urged further northward by adventurous boys and addled, visionary men who drove them, mapless, toward St. Louis, Sedalia, Abilene, Wichita: toward the railroads threading back to the industrialized East, where a longhorn steer brought $40 in 1876, the year the railroad finally reached Fort Worth. Four million cattle had passed through town by then, in less than a decade, and six thousand people had a reason to live there.

The rails still pass through the North Side, often rusty nowadays, grass sprouting between rotting ties. The tracks cut across the dilapidated roads, passing over or below them, iron and asphalt bending to meet on the near banks of Clear Fork, like aged veins and arteries joined at the heart of an old way of life. J. B. Haisler stares quietly out at the fallow rails and derelict roads, the disheveled buildings of north Fort Worth, and he shakes his head. He can remember when this place was booming, exciting, downright fabulous, back when he was a strapping young farmer from Seymour, Texas, who came here to sell his first cow for $5.

That was during the Depression when a man didn't get much for his animals, but, as J. B. Haisler recalls it, "you didn't need a whole lotta money to raise a family back then." He glances over at his son— one of three children he has raised and seen through college—and he wonders how a young man can make it farming these days, with everything so muddled and expensive. The little man can't make it, he figures, unless his wife takes a job, bringing in wages instead of children, and J. B. Haisler firmly believes that "you ain't really farmin' if you ain't raisin' children, too."

Then he looks back out at the shabby North Side, its futile thoroughfares lined with empty stores, until he begins to feel old himself. He can already see a few miles ahead the gutted wreck of the old Swift meat-packing plant, abandoned now for nearly a decade, crumbling slowly as its valuable antique bricks are stolen. Six tall stories of double-walled, close-fitted bricks, and sturdy as a tomb, the huge, ruined slaughterhouse dominates the view of the fabled Fort Worth stockyards.

But then, like a boyhood memory, comes the sound, at once mournful and petulant, of the mingled cries of yearling steers and failed milk cows, newly weaned calves and faltering bulls: the evocative dirge of the cattle pens. In a moment the smell arrives, too, a pleasingly familiar smell to a farmer's nose—an odor as earthy and constant as himself. Smiling again, J. B. Haisler is convinced that today is a lucky day.

He turns the pickup down the backstreets leading to the rear of the cattle pens, where the docking chutes are busy this Monday with men unloading small herds of eight or nine, rarely more than fifteen or twenty, head. A thin haze of rust-colored dust envelops the chutes, sweeping aloft in the hot summer air to drift above the pens like a sanguine fog. The pens are a riotous warren of corrals and stalls with clapboard alleyways passing among them, forming a wooden maze from the docking chutes to the auction barn. Each of the several hundred pens is furnished with a water trough and a bale or two of hay; each is built of rough cedar planks and floored with bricks. Virtually the whole of the stockyards is floored with these bricks: old-fashioned, hand-blocked, kiln-fired clay bricks, hard as stone.

Bricks were cheap when the Fort Worth stockyards were built, shortly after the railroad arrived, and nothing less could withstand all the hooves that rumbled through, bound for the mammoth packing plants of Kansas City and Chicago. For thirty years this was the major harbor on the Southwestern plains, the busiest junction of trail and train, the greatest of the cowtowns. By the end of the nineteenth century it *was* Cowtown, christened by cowboys and consecrated by their cows. Together they came here from as far away as Arizona or Old Mexico, coming each summer in numbers unsurpassed before or since to camp in the hills above Clear Fork and wait for room in the holding pens.

The bricks trap heat in the summer, especially in August when those 105-degree thermal waves come in off the simmering prairies. In the restless pens the body heat of the animals pushes the temperature even higher, stoking their frenzy and baking the air. In the old days, when the yards boomed and the pens were busy, strong men working here dropped from heat prostration, their jeans streaked white by the salt of evaporated sweat. A working saddle horse would lather up in less than an hour without so much as cantering, and the yardboys tending the pens needed three mounts each to spell a day.

Leon Ralls was a yardboy then, 45 years ago, at the age of fourteen. At sixteen he was the prodigy of the yards, dealing in mules and hogs with men twice his age; at nineteen he brokered his first cow on the Cowtown market. Those were the "private treaty" days, when a freelance stock trader would shake hands with a seller and a buyer who had never met each other, yet would go into debt on the strength of the trader's integrity. Following the Second World War, Leon Ralls came home from the Navy and, with his brother, started one of the 31 by then duly registered and regulated commission agencies on the Fort Worth Livestock Exchange: at that time, the Wall Street of the cattle business.

There are six commissioned agents left today and Leon Ralls is one of them. A small, pale, amiable man, he has the parched and sinewy look of desert mesquite but his alert eyes are soft and calm blue. By eight o'clock this Monday morning he has already broken into a sweat as he darts around the pens and back and forth to the docking chutes, where the cattle are being unloaded. Some of these farmers and ranchers have been his clients for thirty years and he greets them still with the same deliberate handshake, swapping rumors and taciturn pleasantries. From each he collects a pink receipt of ownership, which he stuffs unread in his coverall pocket, keeping tally in his head. Quickly assessing each small herd—judging their individual worth on the current market—he sorts them into auction lots of three or more that maximize their value, earning his fixed fee on the strength of his judgment. It is said in the cattle business that no one can tell more about a cow at a glance than a stockyard trader, such is the art of their profession.

Standing at the chutes with a small feedlot owner from North Texas, Ralls is appraising the man's cargo of a dozen crossbred Brahman bulls, all full-grown two-year-olds. Brought to maturity on the feedlot, gorged on milo and protein pellets, they are somewhat flabbier than Ralls would prefer. Minus a few bargain roasts, mature bull meat goes entirely into sausages, frozen hamburger, and cold cuts. It is ground up with cereals and crushed ice for speedy curing (called "water-added" in the package ingredients) a process that loses more weight as the fat content of the meat increases. Hence the buyers for packing plants will pay better prices for firmer, leaner animals. The only other buyers of mature bulls are short-term bull raisers. They can graze the fatter ones a couple of months to lean them out, then try to sell them to the packers for more than what they paid: thus, their profit, as in capital gains, is made on the market spread, and they bid on the market as much as on the animal.

In about two minutes, Leon Ralls has inspected the bulls and reckoned his options. His safest bet, the tight-market strategy, is simply to auction them in three lots—the fat ones, the lean ones, and the rest—assuring strong bids among each group of buyers at least once. But Ralls, with a rodeo gleam in his eye, instead bets a hunch and divides the bulls into four lots of three, the fattest paired with the leanest, the lots weighted equally and inclined toward flabbiness. He is betting that the bull raisers, properly tempted, will gamble on the rising market to bid up the packers on all four lots, and so inflate the price a bit.

Tumbled from their trailers and down the chutes, the bulls are abruptly separated, marked on their flanks, jostled and poked. In what must seem to them a pandemonium of insults, they are then rudely harried down the lanes by shouting, whooping yardboys mounted on noisy little motor scooters and equipped with electric cattle prods. Operating the gates like pinball flippers, they finesse the animals from alley to alley, between corrals and through the maze to whatever pen Leon Ralls has assigned them. Shunted into their appointed blind alleys the bulls mill around in circles, carom off fences, then finally settle down to join the others in some loud and resonant complaining.

Any cow that isn't eating is puzzled by its own existence: having evolved for thousands of generations by the grace of man, cattle have a tendency to be suspicious when they aren't being fed. They grow restive, make each other nervous, stomp and fume. In the sweltering morning air the dust rises slowly above them and spreads downwind. Spreading more invisibly but further is the smell, the raw and powerful compound aromas of fresh straw, animal sweat, scooter exhaust, adrenaline fevers, stale urine, hay, and the several scents of cattle manure—the oddly pleasant odor of grass-fed dung, the gaseous stench from feedlot bowels, the pungent diarrhea of newly weaned, panicky calves—all of it baking on the hot, dry bricks. Reaching still beyond the smell is the baleful sound, tremendous and urgent, like an amplified moan, more than a wail but less than a prayer. In the dim universe of a cow this is purgatory, that place where virtues are weighed against flaws, the awful interlude between the meadow and the slaughterhouse.

These are not show cattle, those haughty champions pictured in the agriculture sections of Sunday papers, spoiled on mineral supplements and acres of grama grass. These are rather the unwashed masses of common cattle, scrambled of breed and motley in appearance, unregistered, lackluster, and now disowned. Cast into their respective lots, milling and squalling, they range in age from three months to twenty years and include both sexes and the neuters of both. They are mangy, smelly, surly, lice-infested, too lean or too fat, often lame, and always abysmally stupid. Dumber than mules and lazier than dogs,

they could never survive on their own: this is what gives men the right
to ill-use them. They are not altogether docile and predictable, however, for somewhere out among them is the one-ton crossbred Brahman bull, black with brindle flanks, that today will make a cripple of
old Leon Ralls.

The stockyards really started booming after the turn of the century when the capitalists arrived. The newly simplified scheme of refrigeration promised to eliminate the cost and hazard of transporting
beef on the hoof, but first the meat-packing plants had to move closer
to the hooves. And so canny old Gustavus Swift and his dapper com-
petitor, young J. Ogden Armour, son of the founder of Armour & Company, journeyed down by private train to scout Fort Worth. The town
fathers, who were merchants by trade and peddlers by nature, predic-
tably endeavored to hard-sell the dignitaries on their growing city: lav-
ish receptions were held, proclamations made, Stetsons presented.
But then old Gus Swift, white-haired and yellow-bearded, a wily ty-
rant, gruffly remarked that Dallas had a bigger river and nicer trees.

The mortified boosters reacted with a prostrate offer of free land
and water, a tax haven, and whatever cash it took to build a slaughterhouse, all in the forlorn hope that one of the moguls might be lured
away from Dallas. With becoming dignity, both accepted the offer immediately and returned to Kansas City and Chicago, leaving their at-
torneys to deal with the jubilant storekeepers. In 1903 Swift and Armour opened gigantic, extravagant packing plants right across from
each other at the foot of Exchange Street, conveniently adjacent to the
greatest terminal market in the history of men and cattle. By the
1920s, two million head of cattle were sold and killed each year in the
Fort Worth stockyards, plus a million hogs and 500,000 sheep.

Even the horse and mule barns were fireproof concrete and Pitts-
burgh steel and floored with bricks like everything else. They were
built for $300,000 and described at the time as "among the finest sales
stables in the world." And these, of course, were for slaughterhouse
horses—spavined, lame, stove-in—200,000 of them a year.

At 5:30 every morning the shift whistle blew at the Swift plant, a
fierce metallic shriek that stirred the neighborhood and raised from
the other end of Exchange Street a melancholy, guttural echo. Harried
along by yardhands, the cattle and hogs, balky and churlish, would

start moving down the quarter-mile road, while the gentler sheep followed blissfully after a Judas goat. For most of four decades the enormous plants ran at capacity six days a week and, whenever they could make crews for the killing rooms, on Sundays as well. They were run, for the most part, on immigrant labor, Eastern European newcomers who worked hard, didn't talk back, and never met any cowboys—except perhaps in the bars at night, where they all went looking for trouble.

The North Side became notorious for its quick-fisted bars and edgy pleasures; it was where you went looking for the best illegal liquor or the highest poker stakes, for swing bands, dice games, bank robbers, bronc riders, streetwalkers, all kinds of bet takers, for the home of Bob Wills or the hideout of Bonnie and Clyde. By the mid-thirties the stockyards area had acquired the hell-bent nature and bad reputation of people who live in the vicinity of death, waking each morning to its shrill and demanding whistle. Smelling blood in their sleep, they arose with adrenaline already pumping, and they lived very hard in an old-fashioned style.

"In the old days, people they come here from all over Texas," sighs J. B. Haisler. "Some'd come in from Oklahoma, Louisiana, New Mexico even. Wasn't many places you could sell your animals back then, not if you needed real money for 'em.

"Pens was a whole lot bigger then, too. Sometimes it looked like most of the cattle in the world was here, carryin' on like crazy. Was hard to think what you had was worth much in the middle of all that. They didn't have no auction then, either. You'd meet up with the agents and the buyers out by the pens, settle your business right there."

Like all luxuries, Depression beef was a buyer's market and the only buyers that mattered were the purchasing teams from Swift and Armour, who fanned out over the yards, sparing no effort to outflank each other, but always stopping short of paying more. "People be runnin' all 'round out there," recalls J. B. Haisler with a distant grin. "They'd be all talkin' up a fuss, yellin'. Animals hollerin' ever'where. You didn't hardly know what you got till you went to the office to get your check."

Leon Ralls has a wry memory of laughing—but then most of Exchange Street laughed—when the first scattered local auctions, which would change the cattle industry forever and doom Fort Worth's monopoly, were organized after the war. The prices were a shade lower than in Fort Worth at first; nevertheless, they caught on quickly in places like Amarillo, San Angelo, Nacogdoches. Changes on the land were becoming obvious, imperative, inevitable. Advances in food technology—refrigeration and processing—compelled yet another dispersal of the meat-packing plants, while postwar America was also developing a new taste for corn-fed beef.

There is an axiom in the cattle business that it's always cheaper in the long run—since cattle are such awesome gluttons—to take them to their feed, instead of the reverse. Thus, Panhandle feedlots came into being when Americans began to want the kind of well-marbled, juicy, and tender meat that only a super-rich diet can develop, even on an animal as lazy as a cow. As the demand increased, the feedlot owners proved willing and able to outspend the packers for the prime young steers they intended to feed.

Breeding and feeding became sciences more than labors; new equipment became an investment and a tax write-off at the same time, instead of just an expense; the cattle business became complex, fragmented, specialized. Buyers proliferated in the cattle market, but not in Fort Worth.

Swift and Armour fought against it right to the end, but an auction barn was opened in the Fort Worth stockyards in 1960. Tucked belatedly into a corner behind the grandiose Exchange Building, built of ordinary cinderblocks to resemble one giant cinderblock—square, drab, unpainted—the auction barn is the cheapest and ugliest building in the entire stockyards, and, nowadays, the only one that can pay the rent. The regular Monday auction still gets underway at nine o'clock, promptly, reliably, and stubbornly.

By a quarter till, the yardboys are moving the cattle in the turbulent pens, running or scooting from gate to gate, opening one, closing another, almost like valves. The worst thing that can happen in the pens—Leon Ralls has lectured the yardboys often—is to lose the identity of the cattle, to mix up the lots, since that is the trader's sole means of influencing the auction. Concentrating thus on the brightly colored ear tags, instead of on the animals, the yardboys cull and maneuver them carefully, deftly, mechanically.

Sensing movement, the anxious cattle grow more unruly, moan louder. They fidget and complain, pace about, stomp and kick and crowd one another, panic, stampede in place. None of them aware of anything but noise and paranoia, they run sheerly for the sake of flee-ing, crashing into fences that sometimes swing open suddenly to de-flect a few into different pens or along new alleys. Heads down and straight ahead at all times, turning as required, the cattle lumber through the maze like boxcars in a freight yard: screeching and collid-ing, witless and manipulated. In due course and in an orderly manner they will all wind up before a huge green door, closed at the moment, waiting for Leon Ralls to signal it to be opened and for the auctioneer to call their numbers:

"All right now, boys, this next lot fourteen got some old retired milkers, six fine old Holstein dairy cows comin' up here now let's say good mornin' to the ladies, lot fourteen this is I say good mornin' ladies. . . ."

The big, green electric door jerks open, a steel gate slams behind them, a buggy whip pops overhead, and the six flustered ladies jump forward, completing their escape from the holding pens to the auction arena. Leon Ralls is awaiting them in a wide dirt semicircle holding a long, wooden staff such as men have used to herd cattle since they first found a reason to. After a last quick look he speaks to the auctioneer, who speaks into his microphone:

"Okay we're gonna pick it up at thutty-five for these ladies, lot fourteen this is an' we've got thutty-five, I say thutty-five, five-quahtah, I see five-naff, now five-naff, six it is, hey now six-a-quahtah, quahtah, quahtah. . . ."

Rising back away from the low-railed auction ring are twenty-odd tiers of frayed and battered theater seats, some five hundred in all. About two hundred are occupied this Monday by stark-looking men with angular faces and leathery hands, smelly boots, and tan straw Resistol hats. Many have bought Styrofoam cups of bad concession cof-fee, drunk it off quickly, and are now slowly refilling the cups with amber tobacco spit; others merely spit on the floor. About fifty of the men are buyers and the rest are smiling: they've all heard by now that barely 1,500 head of cattle were brought to auction this morning—the fewest in a year and less than half the summer average—assuring the sellers of premium prices.

Sitting halfway up in the bleachers, J. B. Haisler chuckles to him-self. It's because of the rain, he figures. You can never tell how a rain will affect the market. During the arid summer, farmers had been selling off their calfless cows and weak steers in order to stretch the brown grass for their stock herds and money cattle and because they were encouraged by the steadily rising market. Now, with the promise of greener pastures, most have chosen greedily to hold back everything, to fatten their cattle a while on free grass. Had the rain been lighter or the drouth longer, had the market been shaky, they might just as easily have decided otherwise.

Quietly pleased with his good fortune, J. B. Haisler sits back and watches the awkward Holsteins lurch around the arena. Bred since the Middle Ages for their milk and their stationary habits, dairy cattle, wide-hipped and swaybacked, are pathetic creatures when they try to run. As the six old cows wheeze about, their full sacks jiggle and bobble, which evokes a scowl from an ex-dairyman like J. B. Haisler. "It's them milkin' machines does it," he mutters. "Got those suction cups on 'em. Some folks hook 'em up and then forgets to come back 'n' *un*hook 'em. Ruins the bags where you can't do nothin' *but* sell 'em."

The ruined ladies are sold at $38.50 a hundred pounds—about $400 each—to a small local meat packer for low-grade hamburger, probably dog food. The packing house is the last reward of every calf born in America, irrespective of breed, sex, career, or term of service, but the packers no longer dominate the cattle market. In today's specialized, cost-effective cattle business it isn't unusual—in some parts it's normal—for a farmer to sell his weaned calves to a grass-rich rancher who pastures them until their quadruple stomachs can handle the protein saturation of the feedlots, whence they will be sold again to cattlemen who "shape" or "tone" them before finally selling them, sometime in their third year, to a slaughterhouse. At the Fort Worth auction on an average Monday, less than one buyer in eight is a packer.

The wonder is that any of them come here, to an irrelevant railhead hundreds of miles from the irrigated Panhandle Plains where the feedlots sprawl (Amarillo's auction is four times larger than Fort Worth's these days) and not much closer to the major breeders of South and Central Texas. Armour & Company shut its Fort Worth plant in 1962 in favor of smaller plants in handier places, while tight old Gus Swift's giant slaughterhouse ran a few years longer on obsolete equipment and low wages—paid to blacks and Chicanos—before it too was closed and razed. They will tell you around the stockyards that the ruins smoldered for three years afterwards, the smoke rising like dark steam from the heap of blood-red bricks, but that's the kind of talk you get around the Fort Worth stockyards.

Some of the men around here will tell you proudly that they were present in the stockyards Coliseum just up the street—the birthplace of indoor rodeo—the first time anyone ever rode Five-Minutes-to-Midnight. Forty years later none of them remembers the cowboy's name, but with rheumy eyes they can still see that legendary coal-black, cartwheeling horse. Some few others can recall Bonnie Parker holed up in the corner room of the old Right Hotel, waiting for Clyde, when she shot the first country fool who took her for a hooker. She then proceeded to party all week, and no one would report her.

Most of their memories are more prosaic but equally vivid, bound to this place by the same long, gritty tradition. There isn't a man in the auction barn who can't recall in sharp detail his first trip to Fort Worth, remembering clearly the first cow he sold here and for how much, and usually where the money went. This *is* Cowtown, after all, always has been, and, because they are men who respect endurance and value roots, their coming here seems natural, unremarkable, even practical. The drive to Fort Worth is a ritual older than they are, which is reason enough to make it worthwhile.

Creatures of habit but pilgrims in spirit, these are headstrong, durable men who have outlived their time and refused to admit it. They aren't modern white-collar cattlemen, profit-minded and management-trained; they're rather, grimy, workaday cowmen who tend to distrust marketplaces generally but feel comfortable here. Fort Worth remains a major terminal market for cattle—among the nation's ten busiest—because they can't believe it isn't, and by faithfully delivering their cattle for auction they make it one. Set in their ways and proud of it, they sit up in the bleachers of the auction barn and talk earnestly about the weather, rubbing their hands and nudging each other, as nervous as penny gamblers. With stern squinty eyes they stare down into the ring, where a mob of young heifers is surging back and forth, bawling and shrinking en masse from the tap, tap, tap of Leon Ralls' wooden staff.

It is the largest lot of the day, 34 heifers recently taken off grass, all at least one year old and 700-plus pounds apiece. A hundred days in a feedlot will put another 300 pounds on each and Ralls has sorted them accordingly. The feedlot buyers would much prefer young steers, which can gain 30 percent more weight on the same diet, so they don't ordinarily haggle over heifers. Selling them all together is the quickest way to dispose of them and shouldn't affect their price.

"Got fo'ty-two, fo'ty-two, two-naff yet two-naff, three! Now three, that's fo-ty-three, three, three-naff. . . ."

Using gestures as spare as their words, the men in the bleachers lift an eyebrow or a lone finger, nod or shrug imperceptibly to indicate their bids. The bidding occurs invisibly to everyone but the bidders themselves, the auctioneer, who sings out prices from his pulpit behind the ring, and Leon Ralls, who stands just below him surrounded by heifers. His back is against the shield, a shoulder-high protective screen built out from the auctioneer's platform and resembling the *barrera* in a bullfight arena. Despite the ten-ton crowd of milling hooves around him, Ralls doesn't bother to get behind the shield. Sweeping his staff in a low quadrant before him, knowing the hysterical heifers would sooner trample each other than challenge it, he doesn't even look at them; he's too busy watching the bidders.

"Now I'm seein' fo'ty-seven, fo'ty-seven, c'mon give me seven-a-quahtah, quahtah, I see seven-a-quahtah. . . ."

A month ago these same heifers would have sold at 40 cents a pound, but today, with so few cattle at auction, the bidding approaches choice steer prices. Obligated to long-term contracts and costly overhead, facing a market they expect to continue rising, the feedlot buyers are forced to shop for whatever is available. Ralls also notices a few bids coming from large-scale breeders who, apparently reading the market likewise, want the heifers for breeding stock. Spotting the trend, Ralls keeps the animals running even when the bidding lags, allowing the buyers to look and worry some more. Following his lead, the auctioneer ad-libs melodious nonsense to cover the gaps and sustain the momentum of the price advance. Not until the price reaches 50 cents does Ralls signal his acceptance.

Sitting among the nonbidders, J. B. Haisler slaps his boney knee and hoots. "Wheew boy, fifty cents and they ain't a calf in the lot," he says, poking the man next to him. "Last year you'd of got maybe two bits on a bunch of heifers." He leans forward rubbing his hands together, a smile easing across his plain, weathered face. "Not a calf in the whole bunch!" Weaned calves are a cowman's most profitable item, and J. B. Haisler hasn't seen a calf yet today that he thought was as good as his. "I knew this was gonna be a lucky day," he declares, then sits back wearing the small, warm grin of an honest man ready to claim his reward.

Down on the arena floor, Leon Ralls has slipped behind the shield to flip through his lot cards while three big crossbred bulls charge around the ring, all hot and bothered and mad, seeing red everywhere. Their bovine anger is as absolute and simple as their fear, the same blindness in another color, and it quickly reverts to fear the moment Ralls steps away from the shield after passing their card to the auctioneer. Firmly tapping his staff on the ground, he is instantly their master, a man herding cattle.

All three bulls, squat, blocky, and cream-colored, are of Charolais stock with about an eighth part Brahman, revealed by their high, humped backs and floppy ears. The Brahman blood usually makes them somewhat feisty, but Ralls knows they've just come off the feedlot so he isn't too concerned. Cattle in a feedlot do nothing but eat, sleep, and defecate, bloating themselves for a year or more on an endless blessing of "hot feed," a potent blend of whole grains, shelled corn, and protein pellets. Texas cattle are fed more grain and less corn than Northern cattle—it's the reason for their meatier flavor—but a feedlot anywhere is a cow's nirvana. Fed into a constant stupor, they grow not merely accustomed, but oblivious, to noise and commotion, narrow confinement, and people who goad them. Thunder and lightning won't even rile them so long as they're eating. Tranquilized by gratification, they come to maturity with soft, tender muscles and dull senses, sluggish instincts and indolent ways.

Turned out of paradise only this morning, the bulls are too demoralized to be quarrelsome. Ralls waves his staff at them and jabs them, now and then whacking one across the haunches, and they just wail and bolt like yearling heifers, bewildered and hungry. The bulls in fact are so thoroughly cowed that Ralls hardly pays them any mind, watching his audience instead and following the bids. This is the first of the four slightly overweight lots he sorted earlier, and his strategy of playing the packers against the bull raisers works better than he could have expected. In the end, the bulls are sold to a packer, but not before the ranchers have pushed the price to 48 cents a pound—generous for cannery animals, which usually dress out to less than 50 per cent of their live weight.

Moving quickly to keep up the auction tempo, Ralls ducks behind the shield again as the green door opens and the next lot of bulls charges madly into the arena. All have the flop ears and trademark humps of crossbred Brahmans—maybe one-quarter Brahmans—each weighs nearly a ton and has blunt, stubby, foot-long horns. Two of the bulls have the brunet coloring of Hereford stock while the other is an Angus cross, black with brindle flanks, but the Brahman blood is what gives force and passion to their anger.

"Don't much like them Brahmers," drawls J. B. Haisler, squinting down from the bleachers. "People say they's real hardy, grow real fast, but I don't care. They's mean. Jes' plain *mean*. I don't want no kinda cattle I can't let my grandchildren be 'round. I don't think they like people."

Named for the highest caste in the Hindu religion, Brahmans are the sacred cattle of India, holy animals incarnated differently but no less specially than men, the same life spirit in another form. Tough and adaptable, they were brought to Texas a century ago and they took easily to the hot Southern plains of the old Cattle Kingdom. Thin-skinned and hairless, they never travel north—even an eighth-part Brahman rarely goes as far as Colorado—but are kept in warmer country, where they grow faster, healthier, and stronger than any other breed of cattle with less care and feeding. They out-breed the others, too. Their blood can be diluted 31 parts to one and the back will still be humped, the ears will still flop, the Brahman spirit will predominate.

They have, however, responded poorly to being profaned, to say nothing of being eaten. Exalted partly for their gentleness in India, Brahmans in the Americas have become famous for their meanness. Even hard-bitten dry-land ranchers dislike the breed, introducing the blood to their herds only in cautious amounts several times removed from pure Brahman stock, and only from competitive necessity. Brahmans are the bulls that rodeo cowboys try to ride—for about eight seconds if they can—and the breed that, more than any other, recalls the character of the rangy old Texas longhorn.

The crossbred bulls in the arena haven't got a full set of Brahman genes among them, of course, and it shows. Snorting as they rush across the ring to avoid Ralls' jabbing staff, the bulls pile up together at the end of every pass, spin around fiercely, paw the ground for a moment, then flee back in the other direction, keeping just beyond reach of the stick. Bred for submission and fed into dependence, their anger dissolves into panic even when they're cornered. Ralls stands calmly at ring center, tapping his staff almost absentmindedly, not even worried enough to watch them. Thus, he is probably the only person in the auction barn who doesn't see the black, mottled bull stop abruptly in the middle of the ring, as if seized by an inspiration, turn with its head lowered to face the trader full-on, grunt once, and charge instantly.

As the bull lunges from ten feet away, Leon Ralls drops his staff and leaps for the shield, scrambling up it. He is a spry and wiry man, and only his age prevents him from escaping. He is five feet up the wall, nearly over it, when the bull hits him in one smooth, solid movement that never wavered from the moment of decision. The blow is so sharp that both bones of Ralls' left leg snap loudly, breaking cleanly. As he tumbles to the ground, fighting to crawl behind the shield, yard-boys spring from the gates to harry the bull off, but the animal makes no effort to charge again. Tossing its head and bellowing, it struts twice around the ring and runs out the open gate to the weighing station.

J. B. Haisler takes it all in rather impassively. "Jes' like a Brah-mer," he observes finally, conclusively. The men in the auction barn all lean back and stretch, hitch one leg across the other, spit in their cups or onto the floor, and watch patiently as Leon Ralls is carried out of the ring. The trader is placed in a folding chair just outside the arena rail, his leg propped awkwardly, then he signals for the three bulls to be brought back. A pair of yardhands—posted discreetly behind the shield—assume the task of running cattle and Ralls proceeds with the auction while he waits for the ambulance.

Displaying no trace of its recent bravado, the brindle-flanked bull and its two lot-mates resume their flight around the ring, quailing before the yardhands' tapping staffs, behaving again like normal cattle. Up in the bleachers, apparently unmoved by the outburst of bovine temper, the men look on with the same rapt attention as before, solemn as judges in an election year. The bidding starts up anew and rises swiftly to the price of the previous lot of bulls and these, too, are sold for hamburger. Wasting no time, Ralls calls for the next lot, shuffling hurriedly through his cards, waving signals to the auctioneer and keeping things moving.

By the time the ambulance arrives, Ralls has sold a dozen more lots and his face is ashen, his lips blue. The attendants give him oxygen and cut away his pants leg, pack the swollen limb in a plastic inflatable cast, then he stubbornly pushes them back and calls for more cattle.

The attendants roll in a bed and stand around perplexed while Ralls directs a few more sales: one of J. B. Haisler's cows turns up in a lot sold at 38 cents, almost a nickel more than he had hoped for. Twice more the medics offer the oxygen mask and attempt to argue, but Ralls just ignores them, as does virtually everyone else. The men in this building are as hard to distract as they are to impress. When he's finally loaded on the bed and wheeled out, Ralls is nearly in shock, but another agent takes over and the auction never slackens, so no one notices. These are single-minded men, here in Cowtown to buy and sell cattle, attentive to their purpose and not very curious.

J. B. Haisler's calves are sold shortly after noon in a lot with a few other calves, all indistinguishable from his in appearance but inferior in his opinion. They are bought by a Panhandle feedlot buyer for 76 cents a pound, top price for the whole summer, equal to $650 per calf, the best price J. B. Haisler has ever gotten for his calves. Quietly grinning, he and his son Melvin go down to the office to collect their check, then they walk outside to the parking lot. It is early afternoon by now. Most of the cattle have been sold, and most of the farmers are starting to drift outside, heading for home. There isn't much to keep them here any longer.

The Haislers climb into their pickup and drive off down Exchange Street, rattling over the bricks, turning past the fabled stockyards Coliseum—once the Westminster Abbey of the Cattle Kingdom—past the barns, now mostly unoccupied, and crossing abandoned railroad tracks. The road bends erratically, unpredictably through the North Side, passing by the shuttered bars and bankrupt stores of the old rowdy neighborhood. Downtown Fort Worth moved upwind fifty years ago, across the river to the south, and the downtown banks all redlined the North Side in the fifties, stifling its development, as if trying to forget it.

Just before reaching the highway that leads back to Denton, J. B. Haisler rolls down his window and looks back again toward the stockyards. All he can see for certain is the crumbling, dark red shadow of Gus Swift's slaughterhouse, but faintly, *very* faintly, he thinks he can see the dust swirling above the cattle pens; he can even smell the pens, and if he listens closely, devotedly, he can still hear the wailing cattle. And he smiles. Once again, he tells himself, it's been a lucky day in Cowtown.

CEREMONIES

D. H. Lawrence

D. H. Lawrence was born on September 11, 1885, in Eastwood, Nottinghamshire, England. Although he lived and wrote in various parts of the world during his lifetime—England, Australia, Italy, and Mexico among them—Lawrence was especially fond of New Mexico. "The moment I saw the brilliant, proud morning shine high up over the deserts of Santa Fe, something stood still in my soul. . . . In the magnificent fierce morning of New Mexico one sprang awake, a new part of the soul woke up suddenly and the old world gave way to a new" (*Phoenix: The Posthumous Papers of D. H. Lawrence*, p. 142). Lawrence had first visited the area in 1922 at the urging of Mabel Dodge Luhan (whom Lawrence called a "culture-carrier" who enjoyed the role of patroness), a wealthy New York woman who had come to Taos, fallen in love with the Indians, married a Taos Pueblo man, and turned her home into a European-style salon in an attempt to gather around her a colony of writers and artists. In August, 1924, the Luhans took Lawrence and his wife, Frieda, to see the Hopi Snake Dance in Arizona. During a stopover in Santa Fe on their return trip, Lawrence wrote a piece ridiculing the ceremony—not so much the Hopi, but rather the whites who had gone to see the spectacle. Mabel railed against Lawrence for producing a "mere realistic recital . . . [with] no vision, no insight, no appreciation of any kind."

The following essay, first published in 1927 in *Mornings in Mexico*, is the result of Lawrence's second effort. Mabel eventually gave Lawrence a ranch in the mountains north of Taos where he and Frieda lived for a short time. Four years after his death in Italy in 1930, Lawrence's body was exhumed and cremated and returned to the ranch, where his ashes are enshrined in a small chapel.

The Hopi Snake Dance

THE Hopi country is in Arizona, next the Navajo country, and some seventy miles north of the Santa Fé railroad. The Hopis are Pueblo Indians, village Indians, so their reservation is not large. It consists of a square track of greyish, unappetising desert, out of which rise three tall arid mesas, broken off in ragged, pallid rock. On the top of the mesas perch the ragged, broken, greyish pueblos, identical with the mesas on which they stand.

The nearest village, Walpi, stands in half-ruin high, high on a narrow rock-top where no leaf of life ever was tender. It is all grey, utterly dry, utterly pallid, stone and dust, and very narrow. Below it all the stark light of the dry Arizona sun.

Walpi is called the "first mesa." And it is at the far edge of Walpi you see the withered beaks and claws and bones of sacrificed eagles, in a rock-cleft under the sky. They sacrifice an eagle each year, on the brink, by rolling him out and crushing him so as to shed no blood. Then they drop his remains down the dry cleft in the promontory's farthest grey tip.

The trail winds on, utterly bumpy and horrible, for thirty miles, past the second mesa, where Chimopova is, on to the third mesa. And on the Sunday afternoon of August 17th, black automobile after automobile lurched and crawled across the grey desert, where low, grey, sage-scrub was coming to pallid yellow. Black hood followed crawling after black hood, like a funeral cortège. The motor-cars, with all the tourists, wending their way to the third and farthest mesa, thirty miles across this dismal desert where an odd water-windmill spun, and odd patches of corn blew in the strong desert wind, like dark-green women with fringed shawls blowing and fluttering, not far from the foot of the great, grey, up-piled mesa.

The snake dance (I am told) is held once a year, on each of the three mesas in succession. This year of grace 1924 it was to be held in Hotevilla, the last village on the farthest western tip of the third mesa.

On and on bumped the cars. The lonely second mesa lay in the distance. On and on, to the ragged ghost of the third mesa.

The third mesa has two main villages, Oraibi, which is on the near edge, and Hotevilla, on the far. Up scrambles the car, on all its four legs, like a black-beetle straddling past the schoolhouse and store down below, up the bare rock and over the changeless boulders, with a surge and a sickening lurch to the sky-brim, where stands the rather foolish church. Just beyond, dry, grey, ruined, and apparently abandoned, Oraibi, its few ragged stone huts. All these cars come all this way, and apparently nobody at home.

You climb still, up the shoulder of rock, a few more miles, across the lofty, wind-swept mesa, and so you come to Hotevilla, where the dance is, and where already hundreds of motor-cars are herded in an official camping-ground, among the piñon bushes.

Hotevilla is a tiny little village of grey little houses, raggedly built with undressed stone and mud around a little oblong plaza, and partly in ruins. One of the chief two-storey houses on the small square is a ruin, with big square window-holes.

It is a parched, grey country of snakes and eagles, pitched up against the sky. And a few dark-faced, short, thickly built Indians have their few peach trees among the sand, their beans and squashes on the naked sand under the sky, their springs of brackish water.

Three thousand people came to see the little snake dance this year, over miles of desert and bumps. Three thousand, of all sorts, cultured people from New York, Californians, onward-pressing tourists, cowboys, Navajo Indians, even negroes; fathers, mothers, children, of all ages, colours, sizes of stoutness, dimensions of curiosity.

What had they come for? Mostly to see men hold *live rattlesnakes* in their mouths. *I never did see a rattlesnake, and I'm crazy to see one!* cried a girl with bobbed hair.

There you have it. People trail hundreds of miles, avidly, to see this circus-performance of men handling live rattlesnakes that may bite them any minute—even do bite them. Some show, that!

There is the other aspect, of the ritual dance. One may look on from the angle of culture, as one looks on while Anna Pavlova dances with the Russian Ballet.

Or there is still another point of view, the religious. Before the snake dance begins, on the Monday, and the spectators are packed thick on the ground round the square, and in the window-holes, and on all the roofs, all sorts of people greedy with curiosity, a little speech is made to them all, asking the audience to be silent and respectful, as this is a sacred religious ceremonial of the Hopi Indians, and not a public entertainment. Therefore, please, no clapping or cheering or applause, but remember you are, as it were, in a church.

The audience accepts the implied rebuke in good faith, and looks round with a grin at the "church." But it is a good-humoured, very decent crowd, ready to respect any sort of feelings. And the Indian with his "religion" is a sort of public pet.

From the cultured point of view, the Hopi snake dance is almost nothing, not much more than a circus turn, or the games that children play in the street. It has none of the impressive beauty of the Corn Dance at Santo Domingo, for example. The big pueblos of Zuni, Santo Domingo, Taos have a cultured instinct which is not revealed in the Hopi snake dance. The last is grotesque rather than beautiful, and rather uncouth in its touch of horror. Hence the thrill, and the crowd.

As a cultured spectacle, it is a circus turn: men actually dancing round with snakes, poisonous snakes, dangling from their mouths.

And as a religious ceremonial: well, you can either be politely tolerant like the crowd to the Hopis; or you must have some spark of understanding of the sort of religion implied.

"Oh, the Indians," I heard a woman say, "they believe we are all brothers, the snakes are the Indians' brothers, and the Indians are the snakes' brothers. The Indians would never hurt the snakes, they won't hurt an animal. So the snakes won't bite the Indians. They are all brothers, and none of them hurt anybody."

This sounds very nice, only more Hindoo than Hopi. The dance itself does not convey much sense of fraternal communion. It is not in the least like St. Francis preaching to the birds.

The animistic religion, as we call it, is not the religion of the Spirit. A religion of spirits, yes. But not of Spirit. There is no One Spirit. There is no One God. There is no Creator. There is strictly no God at all: because all is alive. In our conception of religion there exists God and His Creation: two things. We are creatures of God, therefore we pray to God as the Father, the Saviour, the Maker.

But strictly, in the religion of aboriginal America, there is no Father, and no Maker. There is the great living source of life: say the Sun of existence: to which you can no more pray than you can pray to Electricity. And emerging from this Sun are the great potencies, the invincible influences which make shine and warmth and rain. From these great interrelated potencies of rain and heat and thunder emerge the seeds of life itself, corn, and creatures like snakes. And beyond these, men, persons. But all emerge separately. There is no oneness, no sympathetic identifying oneself with the rest. The law of isolation is heavy on every creature.

Now the Sun, the rain, the shine, the thunder, they are alive. But they are not persons or people. They are alive. They are manifestations of living activity. But they are not personal Gods.

Everything lives. Thunder lives, and rain lives, and sunshine lives. But not in the personal sense.

How is man to get himself into relation with the vast living convulsions of rain and thunder and sun, which are conscious and alive and potent, but like vastest of beasts, inscrutable and incomprehensible. How is man to get himself into relations with these, the vastest of cosmic beasts?

It is the problem of the ages of man. Our religion says the cosmos is Matter, to be conquered by the Spirit of Man. The yogi, the fakir, the saint try conquest by abnegation and by psychic powers. The real conquest of the cosmos is made by science.

The American-Indian sees no division into Spirit and Matter, God and not-God. Everything is alive, though not personally so. Thunder is neither Thor nor Zeus. Thunder is the vast living thunder asserting itself like some incomprehensible monster, or some huge reptile-bird of the pristine cosmos.

How to conquer the dragon-mouthed thunder! How to capture the feathered rain!

We make reservoirs, and irrigation ditches and artesian wells. We make lightning conductors, and build vast electric plants. We say it is a matter of science, energy, force.

But the Indian says No! It all lives. We must approach it fairly, with profound respect, but also with desperate courage. Because man must conquer the cosmic monsters of living thunder and live rain. The rain that slides down from its source, and ebbs back subtly, with a strange energy generated between its coming and going, an energy which, even to our science, is of life: this, man has to conquer. The serpent-striped, feathery Rain.

We made the conquest by dams and reservoirs and windmills. The Indian, like the old Egyptian, seeks to make the conquest from the mystic will within him, pitted against the Cosmic Dragon.

We must remember, to the animistic vision there is no perfect God behind us, who created us from his knowledge, and foreordained all things. No such God. Behind lies only the terrific, terrible, crude Source, the mystic Sun, the well-head of all things. From this mystic Sun emanate the Dragons, Rain, Wind, Thunder, Shine, Light. The Potencies or Powers. These bring forth Earth, then reptiles, birds, and fishes.

The Potencies are not Gods. They are Dragons. The Sun of Creation itself is a dragon most terrible, vast, and most powerful, yet even so, less in being than we. The only gods on earth are men. For gods, like man, do not exist beforehand. They are created and evolved gradually, with aeons of effort, out of the fire and smelting of life. They are the highest thing created, smelted between the furnace of the Life-Sun, and beaten on the anvil of the rain, with hammers of thunder and bellows of rushing wind. The cosmos is a great furnace, a dragon's den, where the heroes and demi-gods, men, forge themselves into being. It is a vast and violent matrix, where souls form like diamonds in earth, under extreme pressure.

So that gods are the outcome, not the origin. And the best gods that have resulted, so far, are men. But gods frail as flowers; which have also the godliness of things that have won perfection out of the terrific dragon-clutch of the cosmos. Men are frail as flowers. Man is as a flower, rain can kill him or succour him, heat can flick him with a bright tail, and destroy him: or, on the other hand, it can softly call him into existence, out of the egg of chaos. Man is delicate as a flower, godly beyond flowers, and his lordship is a ticklish business.

He has to conquer, and hold his own, and again conquer all the time. Conquer the powers of the cosmos. To us, science is our religion of conquest. Hence through science, we are the conquerors and resultant gods of our earth. But to the Indian, the so-called mechanical processes do not exist. All lives. And the conquest is made by the means of the living will.

This is the religion of all aboriginal America, Peruvian, Aztec, Athabascan: perhaps the aboriginal religion of all the world. In Mexico, men fell into horror of the crude, pristine gods, the dragons. But to the pueblo Indian, the most terrible dragon is still somewhat gentle-hearted.

This brings us back to the Hopi. He has the hardest task, the stubbornest destiny. Some inward fate drove him to the top of these parched mesas, all rocks and eagles, sand and snakes, and wind and sun and alkali. These he had to conquer. Not merely, as we should put it, the natural conditions of the place. But the mysterious life-spirit that reigned there. The eagle and the snake.

It is a destiny as well as another. The destiny of the animistic soul of man, instead of our destiny of Mind and Spirit. We have undertaken the scientific conquest of forces, of natural conditions. It has been comparatively easy, and we are victors. Look at our black motor-cars like beetles working up the rock-face at Oraibi. Look at our three thousand tourists gathered to gaze at the twenty lonely men who dance in the tribe's snake dance!

The Hopi sought the conquest by means of the mystic, living will that is in man, pitted against the living will of the dragon-cosmos. The Egyptians long ago made a partial conquest by the same means. We have made a partial conquest by other means. Our corn doesn't fail us: we have no seven years' famine, and apparently need never have. But the other thing fails us, the strange inward sun of life; the pellucid monster of the rain never shows us his stripes. To us, heaven switches on daylight, or turns on the shower-bath. We little gods are gods of the machine only. It is our highest. Our cosmos is a great engine. And we die of ennui. A subtle dragon stings us in the midst of plenty. *Quos vult perdere Deus, dementat prius*.

On the Sunday evening is a first little dance in the plaza at Hotevilla, called the Antelope dance. There is the hot, sandy, oblong little place, with a tuft of green cotton-wood boughs stuck like a plume at the south end, and on the floor at the foot of the green, a little lid of a trap door. They say the snakes are under there.

They say that the twelve officiating men of the snake clan of the tribe have for nine days been hunting snakes in the rocks. They have been performing the mysteries for nine days, in the kiva, and for two days they have fasted completely. All these days they have tended the snakes, washed them with repeated lustrations, soothed them, and exchanged spirits with them. The spirit of man soothing and seeking and making interchange with the spirits of the snakes. For the snakes are more rudimentary, nearer to the great convulsive powers. Nearer to the nameless Sun, more knowing in the slanting tracks of the rain, the pattering of the invisible feet of the rain-monster from the sky. The snakes are man's next emissaries to the rain-gods. The snakes lie nearer to the source of potency, the dark, lurking, intense sun at the center of the earth. For to the cultured animist, and the pueblo Indian is such, the earth's dark centre holds its dark sun, our source of isolated being, round which our world coils its folds like a great snake. The snake is nearer the dark sun, and cunning of it.

They say—people say—that rattlesnakes are not travellers. They haunt the same spots on earth, and die there. It is said also that the snake-priests (so-called) of the Hopi, probably capture the same snakes year after year.

Be that as it may. At sundown before the real dance, there is the little dance called the Antelope dance. We stand and wait on a house-roof. Behind us is tethered an eagle; rather dishevelled he sits on the coping, and looks at us in unutterable resentment. See him, and see how much "brotherhood" the Indian feels with animals—at best the silent tolerance that acknowledges dangerous difference. We wait without event. There are no drums, no announcements. Suddenly into the plaza, with rude, intense movements, hurries a little file of men. They are smeared all with grey and black, and are naked save for little kilts embroidered like the sacred dance-kilts in other pueblos, red and green and black on a white fibre-cloth. The fox-skins hang behind. The feet of the dancers are pure ash-grey. Their hair is long.

The first is a heavy old man with heavy, long, wild grey hair and heavy fringe. He plods intensely forward, in the silence, followed in a sort of circle by the other grey-smeared, long-haired, naked, concentrated men. The oldest men are first: the last is a short-haired boy of fourteen or fifteen. There are only eight men—the so-called antelope priests. They pace round in a circle, rudely, absorbedly, till the first heavy, intense old man with his massive grey hair flowing, comes to the lid on the ground, near the tuft of kiva-boughs. He rapidly shakes from the hollow of his right hand a little white meal on the lid, stamps heavily, with naked right foot, on the meal, so the wood resounds, and paces heavily forward. Each man, to the boy, shakes meal, stamps, paces absorbedly on in the circle, comes to the lid again, shakes meal, stamps, paces absorbedly on, comes a third time to the lid, or trap door, and this time spits on the lid, stamps, and goes on. And this time the eight men file away behind the lid, between it and the tuft of green boughs. And there they stand in a line, their backs to the kiva-tuft of green; silent, absorbed, bowing a little to the ground.

Suddenly paces with rude haste another file of men. They are naked, and smeared with red "medicine," with big black lozenges of smeared paint on their backs. Their wild heavy hair hangs loose, the old, heavy, grey-haired men go first, then the middle-aged, then the young men, then last, two short-haired, slim boys, schoolboys. The hair of the young men is growing after school, and is bobbed round.

The grown men are all heavily built, rather short, with heavy but shapely flesh, and rather straight sides. They have not the archaic slim waists of the Taos Indians. They have an archaic squareness, and a sensuous heaviness. Their very hair is black, massive, heavy. These are the so-called snake-priests, men of the snake clan. And to-night, they are eleven in number.

They pace rapidly round, with that heavy wild silence of concentration characteristic of them, and cast meal and stamp upon the lid, cast meal and stamp in the second round, come round and spit and stamp in the third. For to the savage, the animist, to spit may be a kind of blessing, a communion, a sort of embrace.

The eleven snake-priests form silently in a row, facing the eight grey-smeared antelope-priests across the little lid, and bowing forward a little, to earth. Then the antelope-priests, bending forward, begin a low, sombre chant, or call, that sounds wordless, only a deep, low-toned, secret Ay-a! Ay-a! Ay-a! And they bend from right to left, giving two shakes to the little, flat, white rattle in their left hand, at each shake, and stamping the right foot in heavy rhythm. In their right hand, that held the meal, is grasped a little skin bag, perhaps also containing meal.

They lean from right to left, two seed-like shakes of the rattle each time and the heavy rhythmic stamp of the foot, and the low, sombre, secretive chant-call each time. It is a strange low sound, such as we never hear, and it reveals how deep, how deep the men are in the mystery they are practising, how sunk deep below our world, to the world of snakes, and dark ways in the earth, where are the roots of corn, and where the little rivers of unchannelled, uncreated life-passion run like dark, trickling lightning, to the roots of the corn and to the feet and loins of men, from the earth's innermost dark sun. They are calling in the deep, almost silent snake-language, to the snakes and the rays of dark emission from the earth's inward "Sun."

At this moment, a silence falls on the whole crowd of listeners. It is that famous darkness and silence of Egypt, the touch of the other mystery. The deep concentration of the "priests" conquers, for a few seconds, our white-faced flippancy, and we hear only the deep Háh-ha! Háh-ha! speaking to snakes and the earth's inner core.

This lasts a minute or two. Then the antelope-priests stand bowed and still, and the snake-priests take up the swaying and the deep chant, that sometimes is so low, it is like a mutter underground, in-audible. The rhythm is crude, the swaying unison is all uneven. Cul-turally, there is nothing. If it were not for that mystic, dark-sacred concentration.

Several times in turn, the two rows of daubed, long-haired, in-sunk men facing one another take up the swaying and the chant. Then that too is finished. There is a break in the formation. A young snake-priest takes up something that may be a corn-cob—perhaps an antelope-priest hands it to him—and comes forward, with an old, heavy, but still shapely snake-priest behind him dusting his shoulders with the feathers, eagle-feathers presumably, which are the Indians' hollow prayer-sticks. With the heavy, stamping hop they move round in the previous circle, the young priest holding the cob curiously, and the old priest prancing strangely at the young priest's back, in a sort of incantation, and brushing the heavy young shoulders delicately with the prayer-feathers. It is the God-vibration that enters us from behind, and is transmitted to the hands, from the hands to the corn-cob. Several young priests emerge, with the bowed heads and the cob in their hands and the heavy older priests hanging over them behind. They tread round the rough curve and come back to the kiva, take perhaps another cob, and tread round again.

That is all. In ten or fifteen minutes it is over. The two files file rapidly and silently away. A brief, primitive performance.

The crowd disperses. They were not many people. There were no venomous snakes on exhibition, so the mass had nothing to come for. And therefore the curious immersed intensity of the priests was able to conquer the white crowd.

By afternoon of the next day the three thousand people had massed in the little plaza, secured themselves places on the roofs and in the window-spaces, everywhere, till the small pueblo seemed built of people instead of stones. All sorts of people, hundreds and hundreds of white women, all in breeches like half-men, hundreds and hundreds of men who had been driving motor-cars, then many Navajos, the women in their full, long skirts and tight velvet bodices, the men rather lanky, long-waisted, real nomads. In the hot sun and the wind which blows the sand every day, every day in volumes round the corners, the three thousand tourists sat for hours, waiting for the show. The Indian policeman cleared the central oblong, in front of the kiva. The front rows of onlookers sat thick on the ground. And at last, rather early, because of the masses awaiting them, suddenly, silently, in the same rude haste, the antelope-priests filed absorbedly in, and made the rounds over the lid, as before. To-day, the eight antelope-priests were very grey. Their feet ashed pure grey, like suede soft boots: and their lower jaw was pure suede grey, while the rest of the face was blackish. With the pale-grey jaw, they looked like corpse-faces with swathing-bands. And all their bodies ash-grey smeared, with smears of black, and a black cloth to-day at the loins.

They made their rounds, and took their silent position behind the lid, with backs to the green tuft: an unearthly grey row of men with little skin bags in their hands. They were the lords of shadow, the intermediate twilight, the place of after-life and before-life, where house the winds of change. Lords of the mysterious, fleeting power of change.

Suddenly, with abrupt silence, in paced the snake-priests, headed by the same heavy man with solid grey hair like iron. To-day they were twelve men, from the old one, down to the slight, short-haired, erect boy of fourteen. Twelve men, two for each of the six worlds, or quarters: east, north, south, west, above, and below. And to-day they were in a queer ecstasy. Their faces were black, showing the whites of the eyes. And they wore small black loin-aprons. They were the hot living men of the darkness, lords of the earth's inner rays, the black sun of the earth's vital core, from which dart the speckled snakes, like beams.

Round they went, in rapid, uneven, silent absorption, the three rounds. Then in a row they faced the eight ash-grey men, across the lid. All kept their heads bowed towards the earth, except the young boys.

Then, in the intense, secret, muttering chant the grey men began their leaning from right to left, shaking the hand, one-two, one-two, and bowing the body each time from right to left, left to right, above the lid in the ground, under which were the snakes. And their low, deep, mysterious voices spoke to the spirits under the earth, not to men above the earth.

But the crowd was on tenterhooks for the snakes, and could hardly wait for the mummery to cease. There was an atmosphere of inattention and impatience. But the chant and the swaying passed from the grey men to the black-faced men, and back again, several times.

This was finished. The formation of the lines broke up. There was a slight crowding to the centre, round the lid. The old antelope-priest (so-called) was stooping. And before the crowd could realize anything else a young priest emerged, bowing reverently, with the neck of a pale, delicate rattlesnake held between his teeth, the little, naïve, bird-like head of the rattlesnake quite still, near the black cheek, and the long, pale, yellowish, spangled body of the snake dangling like some thick, beautiful cord. On passed the black-faced young priest, with the wondering snake dangling from his mouth, pacing in the original circle, while behind him, leaping almost on his shoulders, was the

oldest heavy priest, dusting the young man's shoulders with the feather-prayersticks, in an intense, earnest anxiety of concentration such as I have only seen in the old Indian men during a religious dance.

Came another young black-faced man out of the confusion, with another snake dangling and writhing a little from his mouth, and an elder priest dusting him from behind with the feathers: and then another, and another: till it was all confusion, probably, of six, and then four young priests with snakes dangling from their mouths, going round, apparently, three times in a circle. At the end of the third round the young priest stooped and delicately laid his snake on the earth, waving him away, away, as it were, into the world. He must not wriggle back to the kiva bush.

And after wondering a moment, the pale, delicate snake steered away with a rattlesnake's beautiful movement, rippling and looping, with the small, sensitive head lifted like antennae, across the sand to the massed audience squatting solid on the ground around. Like soft, watery lightning went the wondering snake at the crowd. As he came nearer, the people began to shrink aside, half-mesmerised. But they betrayed no exaggerated fear. And as the little snake drew very near, up rushed one of the two black-faced young priests who held the snake-stick, poised a moment over the snake, in the prayer-concentration of reverence which is at the same time conquest, and snatched the pale, long creature delicately from the ground, waving him in a swoop over the heads of the seated crowd, then delicately smoothing down the length of the snake with his left hand, stroking and smoothing and soothing the long, pale, bird-like thing; and returning with it to the kiva, handed it to one of the grey-jawed antelope-priests.

Meanwhile, all the time, the other young priests were emerging with a snake dangling from their mouths. The boy had finished his rounds. He launched his rattlesnake on the ground, like a ship, and like a ship away it steered. In a moment, after it went one of those two young black-faced priests who carried snake-sticks and were the snake catchers. As it neared the crowd, very close, he caught it up and waved it dramatically, his eyes glaring strangely out of his black face. And in the interim that youngest boy had been given a long, handsome bull-snake, by the priest at the hole under the kiva boughs. The bull-snake is not poisonous. It is a constrictor. This one was six feet long, with a sumptuous pattern. It waved its pale belly, and pulled its neck out of the boy's mouth. With two hands he put it back. It pulled itself once more free. And again he got it back, and managed to hold it. And then, as he went round in his looping circle, it coiled its handsome folds twice round his knee. He stooped, quietly, and as quietly as if he were untying his garter, he unloosed the folds. And all the time, an old priest was intently brushing the boy's thin straight shoulders with the feathers. And all the time, the snakes seemed strangely gentle, naïve, wondering, and almost willing, almost in harmony with the men. Which of course was the sacred aim. While the boy's expression remained quite still and simple, as it were candid, in a candor where he and the snake should be in unison. The only dancers who showed signs of being wrought-up were the two young snake-catchers, and one of these, particularly, seemed in a state of actor-like uplift, rather ostentatious. But the old priests had that immersed, religious intentness which is like a spell, something from another world.

The young boy launched his bull-snake. It wanted to go back to the kiva. The snake-catcher drove it gently forward. Away it went, towards the crowd, and at the last minute was caught up into the air. Then this snake was handed to an old man sitting on the ground in the audience, in the front row. He was the old Hopi of the Snake clan.

Snake after snake had been carried round in the circles, dangling by the neck from the mouths of one young priest or another, and writhing and swaying slowly, with the small, delicate snake-head held as if wondering and listening. There had been some very large rattlesnakes, unusually large, two or three handsome bull-snakes, and some racers, whipsnakes. All had been launched, after their circuits in the mouth, all had been caught up by the young priests with the snake-sticks, one or two had been handed to old snake-clan men in the audience, who sat holding them in their arms as men hold a kitten. The most of the snakes, however, had been handed to the grey antelope-men who stood in the row, with their backs to the kiva bush. Till some of these ash-smeared men held armfuls of snakes, hanging over their arms like wet washing. Some of the snakes twisted and knotted round one another, showing pale bellies.

Yet most of them hung very still and docile. Docile, almost sympathetic, so that one was struck only by their clean, slim length of snake nudity, their beauty, like soft, quiescent lightning. They were so clean, because they had been washed and anointed and lustrated by the priests, in the days they had been in the kiva.

At last all the snakes had been mouth-carried in the circuits, and had made their little outrunning excursion to the crowd, and had been handed back to the priests in the rear. And now the Indian policemen, Hopi and Navajo, began to clear away the crowd that sat on the ground, five or six rows deep, around the small plaza. The snakes were all going to be set free on the ground. We must clear away.

We recoiled to the further end of the plaza. There, two Hopi women were scattering white cornmeal on the sandy ground. And thither came the two snake-catchers, almost at once, with their arms full of snakes. And before we who stood had realized it, the snakes were all writhing and squirming on the ground, in the white dust of meal, a couple of yards from our feet. Then immediately, before they could writhe clear of each other and steer away, they were gently, swiftly snatched up again, and with their arms full of snakes, the two young priests went running out of the plaza.

We followed slowly, wondering, towards the western, or north-western edge of the mesa. There the mesa dropped steeply, and a broad trail wound down to the vast hollow of desert brimmed up with strong evening light, up out of which jutted a perspective of sharp rock and further mesas and distant sharp mountains: the great, hollow, rock-wilderness space of that part of Arizona, submerged in light.

Away down the trail, small, dark, naked, rapid figures with arms held close, went the two young men, running swiftly down to the hollow level, and diminishing, running across the hollow towards more stark rocks of the other side. Two small, rapid, intent, dwindling little human figures. The tiny, dark sparks of men. Such specks of gods.

They disappeared, no bigger than stones, behind rocks in shadow. They had gone, it was said, to lay down the snakes before a rock called the snake-shrine, and let them all go free. Free to carry the message and thanks to the dragon-gods who can give and withhold. To carry the human spirit, the human breath, the human prayer, the human gratitude, the human command which had been breathed upon them in the mouths of the priests, transferred into them from those feather-prayer-sticks which the old wise men swept upon the shoulders of the young, snake-bearing men, to carry this back, into the vaster, dimmer, inchoate regions where the monsters of rain and wind alternated in beneficence and wrath. Carry the human prayer and will-power into the holes of the winds, down into the octopus heart of the rain-source. Carry the corn-meal which the women had scattered, back to that terrific, dread, and causeful dark sun which is at the earth's core, that which sends us corn out of the earth's nearness, sends us food or death, according to our strength of vital purpose, our power of sensitive will, our courage.

It is battle, a wrestling all the time. The Sun, the nameless Sun, source of all things, which we call sun because the other name is too fearful, this, this vast dark protoplasmic sun from which issues all that feeds our life, this original One is all the time willing and unwilling. Systole, diastole, it pulses its willingness and its unwillingness that we should live and move on, from being to being, manhood to further manhood. Man, small, vulnerable man, the farthest adventurer from the dark heart of the first of suns, into the cosmos of creation. Man, the last god won into existence. And all the time, he is sustained and threatened, menaced and sustained from the Source, the innermost sun-dragon. And all the time, he must submit and he must conquer. Submit to the strange beneficence from the Source, whose ways are past finding out. And conquer the strange malevolence of the Source, which is past comprehension also.

For the great dragons from which we draw our vitality are all the time willing and unwilling that we should have being. Hence only the heroes snatch manhood, little by little, from the strange den of the Cosmos.

Man, little man, with his consciousness and his will, must both submit to the great origin-powers of his life, and conquer them. Conquered by man who has overcome his fears, the snakes must go back into the earth with his messages of tenderness, or request, and of power. They go back as rays of love to the dark heart of the first of suns. But they go back also as arrows shot clean by man's sapience and courage, into the resistant, malevolent heart of the earth's oldest, stubborn core. In the core of the fist of suns, whence man draws his vitality, lies poison as bitter as the rattlesnake's. This poison man must overcome, he must be master of its issue. Because from the first of suns come travelling the rays that make men strong and glad and gods who can range between the known and the unknown. Rays that quiver out of the earth as serpents do, naked with vitality. But each ray charged with poison for the unwary, the irreverent, and the cowardly. Awareness, wariness, is the first virtue in primitive man's morality. And his awareness must travel back and forth, back and forth, from the darkest origins out to the brightest edifices of creation.

And amid all its crudity, and the sensationalism which comes chiefly out of the crowd's desire for thrills, one cannot help pausing in reverence before the delicate, anointed bravery of the snake-priests (so-called), with the snakes.

They say the Hopis have a marvellous secret cure for snake-bites. They say the bitten are given an emetic drink, after the dance, by the old women, and that they must lie on the edge of the cliff and vomit, vomit, vomit. I saw none of this. The two snake-men who ran down into the shadow came soon running up again, running all the while, and steering off at a tangent, ran up the mesa once more, but beyond a deep, impassable cleft. And there, when they had come up to our level, we saw them across the cleft distance washing, brown and naked, in a pool; washing off the paint, the medicine, the ecstasy, to come back into daily life and eat food. Because for two days they had eaten nothing, it was said. And for nine days they had been immersed in the mystery of snakes, and fasting in some measure.

Men who have lived many years among the Indians say they do not believe the Hopi have any secret cure. Sometimes priests do die of bites, it is said. But a rattlesnake secretes his poison slowly. Each time he strikes he loses his venom, until if he strikes several times, he has very little wherewithal to poison a man. Not enough, not half enough to kill. His glands must be very full charged with poison, as they are when he emerges from winter-sleep, before he can kill a man outright. And even then, he must strike near some artery.

Therefore, during the nine days of the kiva, when the snakes are bathed and lustrated, perhaps they strike their poison away into some inanimate object. And surely they are soothed and calmed with such things as the priests, after centuries of experience, know how to administer to them.

We dam the Nile and take the railway across America. The Hopi smooths the rattlesnake and carries him in his mouth, to send him back into the dark places of the earth, an emissary to the inner powers.

To each sort of man his own achievement, his own victory, his own conquest. To the Hopi, the origins are dark and dual, cruelty is coiled in the very beginnings of all things, and circle after circle creation emerges towards a flickering, revealed Godhead. With Man as the godhead so far achieved, waveringly and for ever incomplete, in this world.

To us and to the Orientals, the Godhead was perfect to start with, and man makes but a mechanical excursion into a created and ordained universe, an excursion of mechanical achievement, and of yearning for the return to the perfect Godhead of the beginning.

To us, God was in the beginning, Paradise and the Golden Age have been long lost, and all we can do is to win back.

To the Hopi, God is not yet, and the Golden Age lies far ahead. Out of the dragon's den of the cosmos, we have wrested only the beginnings of our being, the rudiments of our godhead.

Between the two visions lies the gulf of mutual negations. But ours was the quickest way, so we are conquerors for the moment.

The American aborigines are radically, innately religious. The fabric of their life is religion. But their religion is animistic, their sources are dark and impersonal, their conflict with their "gods" is slow, and unceasing.

This is true of the settled pueblo Indians and the wandering Navajo, the ancient Maya, and the surviving Aztec. They are all involved at every moment, in their old, struggling religion.

Until they break in a kind of hopelessness under our cheerful, triumphant success. Which is what is rapidly happening. The young Indians who have been to school for many years are losing their religion, becoming discontented, bored, and rootless. An Indian with his own religion inside him *cannot* be bored. The flow of the mystery is too intense all the time, too intense, even, for him to adjust himself to circumstances which really are mechanical. Hence his failure. So he, in his great religious struggle for the Godhead of man, falls back beaten. The Personal God who ordained a mechanical cosmos gave the victory to his sons, a mechanical triumph.

Soon after the dance is over, the Navajo begin to ride down the Western trail, into the light. Their women, with velvet bodices and full, full skirts, silver and turquoise tinkling thick on their breasts, sit back on their horses and ride down the steep slope, looking wonderingly around from their pleasant, broad, nomadic, Mongolian faces. And the men, long, loose, thin, long-waisted, with tall hats on their brows and low-sunk silver belts on their hips, come down to water their horses at the spring. We say they look wild. But they have the remoteness of their religion, their animistic vision, in their eyes, they can't see as we see. And they cannot accept us. They stare at us as the coyotes stare at us: the gulf of mutual negation between us.

So in groups, in pairs, singly, they ride silently down into the lower strata of light, the aboriginal Americans riding into their shut-in reservations. While the white Americans hurry back to their motorcars, and soon the air buzzes with starting engines, like the biggest of rattlesnakes buzzing.

Earle R. Forrest

In the preface to his book *Missions and Pueblos of the Old Southwest*, Earle R. Forrest says that his interest in what he calls the "old Spanish Southwest" of New Mexico and Arizona began at the turn of the century when as a young cowboy in search of adventure, he hired on with cow outfits and rode the cattle ranges of the area. While Forrest is concerned mainly with the history of the missions and pueblos, as the title suggests, he has included a chapter on the highly secretive Penitente sect of northern New Mexico and southern Colorado.

The Penitentes, a secret lay order, were originally the Third Order of St. Francis, organized in Italy. From Italy they spread to Spain and from there to Mexico and then up to the Southwest. The order was adopted by people in remote areas of northern New Mexico who were without priests. Later the Church outlawed the sect, and anyone found to be a Penitente was excommunicated.

Frank Waters, a portion of whose work appears elsewhere in this volume, maintains that he has observed an entire Good Friday ceremony, including a crucifixion as is hereafter described. Furthermore, he has incorporated some of those rites into his novel *People Of The Valley*, published in 1941. There are those who maintain that the Penitente Brotherhood practices its bizarre ceremony in remote villages of northern New Mexico even to this day.

The essay that follows was published in 1929.

The Penitentes of New Mexico

As you travel over central and northern New Mexico, visiting the ancient missions and pueblos, you will see hundreds of wayside crosses, some large, many small, scattered over hill and vale and rocky gorge in that desert land. In some remote, almost inaccessible corner of the wilderness you may suddenly find one, as though an effort had been made to conceal it from the eye of man for all time; and far away on the summit of a hill you will see another clearly outlined against the evening sky, flooded in the golden light of the setting sun, just as another cross stood on Calvary at the close of another day long centuries ago. Then again you will find them at the side of the road, all with a little pile of stones around the base; and occasionally you will see one with a name and a date. All bore inscriptions once; but the desert sun and winter snows of the passing years soon weather them off. Each one tells a silent story of a bloody religious tragedy, of self-inflicted torture and suffering, the like of which no man has ever known since that other

tragedy on Calvary long ago. Each one of those white crosses, bathed in the life-blood of some human being unable to survive the most fearful and agonizing suffering since the days of the Spanish Inquisition, marks the spot where his soul has found a refuge and rest from religious fanaticism.

It is impossible to believe that such things still exist in the United States at the present time unless you have been in the land of the Penitentes. Every visitor to New Mexico has heard of them, more like a myth than grim reality, and when travelling through the Penitente country their moradas and wayside crosses are pointed out here and there; but very few travellers have ever witnessed the crucifixion with its Cristo, cross bearers, and whipping brothers, who beat their own naked backs with cactus whips until, not infrequently, their very life blood is spattered over the desert sands along the line of the march.

These rites are held annually, in some sections several times a year; but the most important occur during the Lenten season, reaching a climax on Good Friday. This strange ceremony has been called the American passion play; but in religious frenzy it surpasses the famous Passion play of Oberammergau. That members of the cult are actually crucified even today in remote sections of the Penitente country is a well known fact in New Mexico.

The Penitente brothers, the official name of the sect, are found in Sandoval, San Miguel, Mora, Taos, Colfax, Rio Arriba, and Valencia counties, New Mexico, and in southern Colorado. The traveler from the east will see the first Penitente cross outlined against the blue sky on the summit of Starvation peak, a few miles west of Las Vegas on the old trail to Santa Fé. In a lonely arroyo twenty miles southwest of the capital is a morada with its accompanying cross high on a nearby hill; and as you go north from Santa Fé to Taos the wayside crosses and moradas increase in number.

Each community of Penitente brothers has a morada, or meeting house. This is built of adobe now, but some of the older ones in remote sections were of stone. These have nearly all disappeared. The old-time morada was without windows, the only opening being the one doorway with a small cross on the roof above the entrance. These are slowly being replaced by the more modern buildings having one or two small windows, and some are without the cross, especially when near the road. The reason for this change is not generally known, but with the advent of the automobile and more tourists it is probable that the brotherhood does not wish the meeting places to attract attention. The morada and the church are two distinct buildings, the former being the meeting place of the Penitente brothers, while the latter is the house of general worship.

The brotherhood of each morada is governed by ten officers, known as Los Hermanos de Luz, or the Brothers of Light. The leader, called the Hermano Mayor, or Chief brother, is the ruler and his word is law. He not only guides the ceremonies, but settles all disputes among the Penitentes of his colony and frequently between the members and outsiders. The other officers are the Warden, Helper, Nurse, Teacher of the novices, Secretary, Pricker, One Who Prays, and Piper.

The principal ceremony takes place during Lent, but another is held on All Saints' Day. Self whipping is practiced during these periods as well as at funerals of members of their families. During the Lenten season the devotions flame to fever heat, culminating with the procession to the cross and the crucifixion on Good Friday.

One of the most weird sounds imaginable is the wild shriek of the Piper's reed flute. Carried on the night air to the farthest corners of the desert, it is the signal for the Penitente tortures to start; and it strikes terror to many a brave heart who hears the wail. Each night during Lent the brothers meet in the morada for prayer and instruction; and every Friday night until the last a procession of self-whippers marches from the meeting-house to the Calvario cross at the end of the path.

The traveler who is hardy enough to brave the cold and terrors of the night is rewarded after a long wait with as strange a sight as mortal man ever witnessed. As the door of the morada opens the Piper comes forth, followed by five brothers clad only in white muslin trousers, each carrying a whip made of Spanish bayonet fibers with a knot of cholla cactus spines on the end. In the rear is the Hermano Mayor, while one or two others carry lanterns, and another guides the whippers.

With the Piper in the lead, the brothers form in line, singing a doleful chant which adds to the solemnity of the scene. Moving slowly, a step at a time as though in dread of the ordeal before them each of the whippers swings the terrible lash, first over one shoulder and then over the other, and with a swish and a dull thud it lands on the naked back, inflicting a terrible wound, each time cutting deep into raw flesh. If one of the brothers should falter, or cringe before the torturous lash he is brought back to his self-inflicting punishment by the Guide who cuts into the quivering flesh with a black-snake whip. When the cross is reached the five flagellants prostrate themselves before it as the others chant a hymn; and at its conclusion they all return to the morada.

Very few outsiders have ever witnessed the mysterious ceremonies in the morada; but those who have been permitted to enter its sacred portal tell a fearful tale of self-inflicted torture with the whip, and walking with bare feet on paths of cholla cactus.

On Ash Wednesday the "Christ" is selected by drawing lots; and during Lent the final preparations are made for the American Passion play. Good Friday is the greatest day of the year for the Penitentes. As the first light of the rising sun dawns over the Sangre de Cristo range to the east, the door of the morada opens and the Penitente brothers come forth for the last ceremony; for some of them it may be the last on earth. It is more than passing strange that these mountains which border the heart of Penitente land on the east should have been named Sangre de Cristo by the Spanish padres of old for this means in English the "blood of Christ."

The procession forms with the Piper at the head, followed by the Cristo staggering under the weight of a huge cross, and several others bearing lighter crosses. Slowly it moves towards the Calvario. In the rear are the whippers, naked to the waist and shivering with the cold; but this is soon forgotten in the agony of the self-inflicted tortures of the cactus whip. On each side are armed men who keep back the curious or any who might attempt to interfere, while kodak fiends are absolutely barred.

The weight of the cross borne by the Cristo is so great that he stumbles frequently and would fall prostrate more than once and probably receive serious injuries under his burden if some brother did not aid him. When the permanent cross at Calvario is reached a circle is formed with fourteen crosses; and around this the Penitentes march, stopping for a prayer at each cross, which represents one of the fourteen stations.

The time for the crucifixion has arrived but the Cristo does not show the least sign of fear as he watches the preparations. When all is ready he is stretched out on the cross he carried, and his arms and legs are bound so tight that the flesh turns blue. The cross is slowly raised with its human burden, and all is silent, except perhaps for the sobs of his mother or his wife. Surely no truer representation of the crucifixion of Our Lord was ever staged in all the world. His body slowly turns purple with cold and lack of circulation. At last the Chief Brother gives a signal, and the poor Cristo is taken down—unconscious, perhaps dead, and carried back to the morada.

If he lives, well and good; but if he does not survive the terrible ordeal he is buried secretly before the dawn of another day; and his boots or shoes, placed on the doorstep of his home, are the only word his relatives ever receive of his fate. It is simply a message that the unfortunate Cristo has gone on a long journey. The location of his grave is unknown to the family until a year later when one of those small wayside crosses so common in that section of New Mexico is erected over the sepulcher. It may be in some secluded spot; it may be at the side of the road; and at the foot of the cross each passing friend places a stone which soon becomes a pile known as the descanso.

Nor do the whippers always survive their fearful self-inflicted tortures; for it is not uncommon for one or more to die from exhaustion or infection brought on by their wounds and suffering. When this occurs they too are taken from the morada at midnight and buried secretly; and the next morning their relatives find their shoes outside of the door. I was told that when a Penitente dies from suffering caused by either crucifixion or whipping he is buried in an upright position in the grave, but I was unable to verify the statement from authoritative sources.

The last service of Lent takes place on the night of Good Friday. Just before darkness has fallen the weird notes of the Piper's flute pierce the night air—a summons to the people, and the entire Mexican population, men, women and children, turns out. A procession forms at the morada and marches to the little catholic church, where the service known among the Penitentes as tinieblas is held in utter darkness. The Penitente translation of this tinieblas service is "earthquake"; and they evidently look upon it as a culmination of the actual occurrence on Cavalry after the crucifixion of Christ.

The Penitentes of the Southwest are descended from the Flagellantes that swept Europe in the Middle Ages. This sect appeared first in Italy in 1210, and with amazing rapidity the strange rites spread during the next fifty years until thousands of devotees were seen in processions throughout all Italy, carrying banners and crosses and lashing themselves with leather whips. The Flagellante movement grew with the passing centuries until it had spread throughout all southern Europe; but the date it was carried across the sea to the New World is not definitely known. However, it seems to be the general belief that the present sect is descended from the laymen's organization known as the Third Order of Saint Francis, and during the Spanish regime practically everyone of any consequence in New Mexico was a member. The expulsion of the Franciscans from New Mexico after the Mexican revolution left the Third Order without regular government, and the theory is that it drifted into the present Penitente organization.

However, the fact that the Penitentes existed before the revolution is shown by an ancient document in the cathedral of Saint Francis at Santa Fé. Under date of September 17, 1794, mention is made of the

"Venerable Third Order of Penitente," which, it states, was founded in the two villages of Santa Fé and Santa Cruz, and "has been in existence since the earliest years of the Conquest."

People who have never been in the Penitente country believe that the sect is dying out, but this is not the case. In the region north of Santa Fé are many moradas where whipping processions take place every year, and a crucifixion is not infrequent. Alcalde is entirely a Penitente settlement, and they are so strong in the Taos and Abiquiu sections that they have a strong influence on politics. With the advent of the automobile tourist the decline has set in, and in a few years public performances will be rare. In former times only a few outsiders ever penetrated the Penitente country during the Lenten season; but now the automobile brings them in by the hundred. The condition at Alcalde in 1926 is only a fair example of what may be expected at every morada in a very short time. On account of being near to Santa Fé many machines were parked around the morada with headlights turned on the building the entire night preceding Good Friday. As a result the brothers remained within; and there was no procession to the cross at daybreak.

DIVERSIONS

Larry McMurtry

Larry McMurtry was born June 3, 1936, in Wichita Falls, Texas. The son and grandson of Texas cattlemen, he grew up in Archer City, took degrees at North Texas State and Rice universities, and studied further at Stanford. McMurtry has taught at Rice, Texas Christian University, George Mason College, and American University. His first three novels— all published before he was thirty years old—were translated into film: *Horseman, Pass By* (1961) as the award-winning *Hud*; *Leaving Cheyenne* (1963) as *Lovin' Molly*; and *The Last Picture Show* (1966), for which McMurtry shared the screenwriting credit with director Peter Bogdanovich. His other novels include *Moving On* (1970), *All My Friends Are Going to be Strangers* (1972), *Terms of Endearment* (1975), *Somebody's Darling* (1978), and *Cadillac Jack* (1982). McMurtry is also a book reviewer and film critic. He currently divides his time between Washington, D.C., where he operates a rare book store in the Georgetown area, and the McMurtry home outside Archer City. The following is from his collection *In a Narrow Grave: Essays on Texas* (1968).

The Old Soldier's Joy

ATHENS is a medium-sized East Texas county-seat town, located some seventy miles southeast of Dallas. It lies between the Neches and the Trinity, in country that is not too heavily wooded. In May, when the Old Fiddler's Reunion is held, the country is green and clean-smelling, with a little pine in the smell.

I arrived around nine in the morning, early enough that the air was still cool. At the red light by the southeast corner of the courthouse square I stuck my head out of the car window, expecting to hear the screech of country fiddles. Instead, I heard a vastly amplified city-billy voice singing "Don't Let the Stars Get in Your Eyes" (don't let the moon break your haw-art . . .), a sound so loud and so quintessentially downhome that I was momentarily paralyzed with emotion, or something, and had to be honked into a parking place.

On the east side of the courthouse there was a big pine-lumber platform, upon which the fiddling and string-band contests would be held. The platform was occupied just then by a Mr. Red Rogers and his band, a group that seemed committed exclusively to the music of Bob Wills. I had not driven all the way from Ft. Worth to hear such a decadent strain of hillbilly, so I hurried off to look for old fiddlers.

When the substantial barrier of the courthouse was between me

and Mr. Rogers' music I felt better about things and stopped to survey
the scene. A small, quietly lyrical group was gathered nearby, and on
the extreme periphery of it stood the first old fiddler I was to talk with:
Mr. Clarence McGraw of West Los Angeles, California. The group
proper consisted of two fiddlers (one of them Mr. McGraw's brother),
one guitar player, one policeman, and two totally committed listeners.
The fiddlers and the guitar player were playing "Cripple Creek," and
the listeners gave the music their gravest attention. Mr. Clarence was
fiddling too, but not "Cripple Creek." He was off to one side, fiddling
angrily to himself. He looked exceptionally clean and vigorous for a
man his age, or any age. His grey khakis were brand clean and strongly
starched. He kept one eye on his brother, who had a curious way of
tucking his fiddle under his solar plexus, rather than under his chin. I
had a notebook in my hand, and when he noticed it he immediately
began to fiddle in my direction.

"You're a reporter for the paper, ain't you?" he asked, and then
quickly turned aside and scratched out a few disgusted measures to
himself.

Before I had time to deny it, he was on the attack.

"What I'd like to know is how a feller goes about gettin' an
account of this here fiddlin'," he said. "This here's about got me
whupped."

"How so?" I asked.

"I come here last year and fiddled," he said. "By god when I got
home I wrote three separate letters back, askin' them to send me an
account of how she all come out. I never got nothin'. Not a damn fare-
thee-well. You ask me, this here's the ass of nowhere."

About that time the group finished "Cripple Creek" and quietly
began to break up. The policeman made mild protests.

"Hey," he said. "Y'all play that 'Under the Double Eagle.' Y'all
ain't played that yet."

But the group demurred and went their way. The McGraw brothers got into an inconclusive argument over who would use which
fiddle-bow in the contests to come. Mr. Clarence was bitterly self-
deprecatory and said it made no difference, he could fiddle about as
well without a bow. His brother, a quiet man, seemed inclined to let
him try.

When the McGraws left I decided to look for the man in charge of the contests, so as to know what was happening when. A farmer was sitting a few feet away on the courthouse steps, resting himself beneath the long morning shadow of the courthouse and the smaller but more portable shadow of an old felt hat that in its day had soaked up a lot of head sweat and dust and Rose hair oil. When I asked him about the contests he was thrown slightly off balance.

"Why they're liable to start any time," he said sadly. "Pretty soon, I 'spect. Ole Bob Hall's the man to ask about that, he'll have the papers on it. Just go up and ask him, first time you catch a chanct. Bob won't care."

I thanked him and said I would, but I didn't. Though I found the man he was talking about, I never could quite catch the chanct.

By ten o'clock there were swarms of fiddlers about, and not all of them old. Indeed, the most popular fiddler present that day was a local youngster named Texas Shorty, a fiddle-playing *arriviste* if there ever was one. He was in his mid-twenties, short and stocky, and dressed in the artificial-pearl-button and near-gabardine of a minor hillbilly entertainer—the sort who, ages ago, would have drawn only the faintest crackle of applause from Horace Height's applause meter.

I listened to him awhile and his fiddling seemed as passionless and repetitive as the tinkle from a moderately well-made music box. While he fiddled, a female relative circulated through the crowd, selling glossy pictures of him and letting it be known that he would autograph them. I would have thought a career of Saturday-night shitkicking at the Big D Jamboree would have been the summit of Shorty's ambition, but apparently I am no judge of fiddling. I found out later that he had just returned from a tour of England—a tour sponsored by the State Department. The news cooled me a bit on the New Frontier, but before the day was over I was forced to admit that Shorty did have *something*. What he had was tenacity: all day long he fiddled steadily, now here, now there, but always fiddling. "Sally Goodin'" was all he knew on earth and all he needed to know. When I left at nine that night he was up on the big platform, sawing sturdily away.

After the McGraw group broke up I wandered back around to the platform side of the courthouse, looking at faces in the crowd. There was a curious group of teen-age pseudo-thugs: they wore identical cheap straw hats and had them pulled so far down over their eyes that they had to walk leaning backwards in order to see. And there was the youngest and least confident sailor I've ever seen. He had on a white uniform and stood around all day wishing he could go home and take it off before someone challenged him to a fight. The country people were there too. Old timers sat on the courthouse steps, chewing tobacco. Now and then one would rise and hobble painfully over to some bush, spit his tobacco juice into it, and hobble back. Infants lay on spread-out quilts under the trees, sucking their blue-plastic bottles while their grandmothers or little sisters sat by and shooed the flies.

Around 11 o'clock Mr. Rogers and his fellows ceased trying to scale the heights of Bob Wills and the old fiddler's contest started. Happily, it was soon over. Only about twenty old men were entered, and each fiddled only two short numbers. By noon they had all put their fiddles away and retired to shade trees or the homes of relatives. I was glad. The contest was like *Paradise Lost*: no one could have wished it longer.

As they stepped up, one by one, to fiddle, the old men reminded me of the superannuated ministers one sees in the congregations of southern churches. On special Sundays like Christmas and Easter the old Brother may be asked as a matter of courtesy to stand up and say a prayer or lead a benediction. Now and then one will get up and do the job briskly and sit down, but more often the old preacher will rise shakily, tremble, work his jaws a little, quaver out a beginning, perhaps forget what comes next, cry a little, desperately improvise a line or two, and, to the infinite relief of all, ashamedly slump down, more than ever aware that he has become too old to cut the mustard.

So it was with the old fiddlers. One or two sawed their way vigorously through "Turkey in the Straw" or "The Arkansas Traveller," but most didn't. Most quavered. A local man named Bunyard won the contest, and Mr. Clarence's brother came in third. Mr. Clarence's fiddling I missed. I went across the street to get a Coke and stopped to listen to a vulgar woman of high community standing who was sitting in front of the platform in a pre-parked Cadillac. She was talking loudly about the Burton-Taylor romance—the gist of her remarks was that Elizabeth Taylor ought to be spayed, else the menfolk of the entire Western world would soon be reduced to a state of slavering idiocy. When I got back to the platform Mr. Clarence was just coming down, and I asked him how he had done.

"Pitiful," he said. "My arm was too stiff on that first piece. I got to talkin' and never took enough warm-ups."

On the platform Uncle John Murdock of Rusk, Texas, was fiddling gallantly away at "The Old Soldier's Joy." He had not taken enough warm-ups either, or perhaps had taken too many. He was eighty-four years old and had roses painted on his fiddle.

Around lunchtime the old fiddlers were replaced by the Light-crust Doughboys, a hillbilly band of some renown. I remembered hearing them on the radio in the late forties. The personnel had probably changed, but as I remembered it they sang good energetic hillbilly, and I was prepared to like them. Their pink vests were something of a deterrent, however, and their humour (i.e. "Don't-go-around-with-another-man's-wife-unless-you-can-go-two-rounds-with-her-husband") was another. Their music moved steadily pop-ward until it was nudging Glenn Miller, at which point I found that my nostalgia had been over-ridden.

While the Doughboys were whirling through "Cimarron, Roll On" I wandered off in search of authentic East Texans and found one right away in the curious, friendly person of Colonel Colin Douglas. Colonel Douglas' black beard was easily the equal of Allen Ginsberg's, and went well with his short-topped California motorcycle boots. He was a local ranch owner and a travelled and experienced man. He had been in pictures in the twenties, he said, but had left them for the oil business at about the time Clark Gable did the opposite. In a few minutes the Doughboys finished and abruptly yielded the platform to a politician, a (now-forgotten) gubernatorial candidate who had slipped in to take advantage of the free people. He had more force than the old fiddlers, but considerably less poignance. The world, he said, was divided into two warring ideologies: the freedom lovers and the atheists. That elemental distinction established, he went on to draw a subtle parallel between himself and Abraham Lincoln (his subtlety consisted in not mentioning the latter by name). He had been born in a one-room cabin on the wrong side of the tracks, and as a boy had gone to school with cardboard in his shoes. He elaborated on that point for awhile, shook a few hard-knuckled hands, eased himself into a white Cadillac, and vanished forever.

A local group got the platform and managed to hold it awhile, all of them singing as loudly as it is possible to sing through one's nose. Shortly, however, they were routed by the master of ceremonies, who announced that the young fiddler's contest was about to begin. That meant that Texas Shorty was going to fiddle over the loudspeaker, a prospect that for me held small appeal. It was a hot afternoon and I was half in the mood to go home, but when I stopped to gas up a filling station man warned me against leaving too soon. He assured me that the real Fiddler's Day action had not yet begun. By nightfall, he said, there would be several thousand people around the square. There would be street-dancing, whiskey drinking and wild, wild women.

I was impressed and said I'd hang around. To pass the time I set out in search of Miss Zilla B. Elledge and her sister, two women of artistic bent who lived in the woods near Athens. For years, legend had it, they had lived in an old ex-mansion in the pines, keeping what house they kept in one room and slowly stripping the others down and burning them for firewood. A year or so earlier they had reportedly burned the last of the mansion, after which they moved into the chickenhouse. All I really knew about them was that Zilla B. had sent my friend John Graves a Christmas card with a red pepper tied to it and a note saying: "This is good, eat it." That was enough to make a search seem worthwhile, but unhappily the search proved futile. Some whittlers at a little country grocery-store informed me that the girls were off in Mexico and were not due back until frost.

Disappointed, I drove to the nearby town of Corsicana and whiled away the afternoon in a second-run movie house. It was getting on toward the cool of the evening when I got back to Athens—the lawn and the streets were filling up with people, and the string band contest, my last and brightest hope, was just about to begin.

I went up on the platform to study the contest list, and the lineup of bands looked impressive. The Fiddle Swingsters were to kick things off, followed more or less in order by such groups as the Texas Ramblers, the Shawnee Wranglers, the Texas Blue Eagles, and the Twilight Serenaders. I crept across the stage and squeezed into a corner on the south side. A big red snare drum sat on one side of me, and the three contest judges sat on the other.

The judges were stalwart men indeed: all day they hardly left their chairs. One was fat and looked complacent and the other two were thinner and looked vacant. Their judging methods seemed highly instinctive: none of them seemed to make the slightest effort to score performances, or even to keep track of who was performing, yet win-

ners were announced almost immediately. While I was sitting near
them a lady pressed herself against the chickenwire screen and asked
Red Hayes, the nearest judge, if Texas Shorty was going to per-
form again.

"He's awful good, ain't he," the lady said.

"Yes ma'am," Red said. "He sure plays that fiddle."

"Next time he comes on ask him to play the 'Tennessee Waltz' for
me, will you? My sister's crippled with arthritis, she's been that way
ten years. We got her out here in the car and that's her favorite song."

"Lady, we can't take no requests," Red said. "I sure am sorry."

"Oh, you don't have to take none," she assured him. "Just tell
Shorty Mrs. Muldrow wanted him to play that for her sister. Shorty
won't mind. I've known Shorty's mother since she was a girl. We sure
are proud of him around here."

About that time the Texas Swingsters came on stage and began to
plug in their numerous electric instruments. From the cut of their
pink, sequined vests I supposed them to be Doughboy imitators and
got set to endure "Tuxedo Junction" on the Hawaiian guitar. Instead
they played three polkas, and the contest was off to a wailing start.

Before the first polka died away I ceased paying the musicians any
mind. I sat and looked off the platform at the people. The filling station
man had been right: the people were coming. The courthouse lawn
was solid full, and the street in front of the courthouse was filled to the
center esplanade and was packing tighter. Those farthest from the platform were still in the sunlight, but most of the crowd stood within the
cool widening shadow of the courthouse.

Looking down on all those shifting faces it was hard not to lapse
into generalization. I was looking down, not just on East Texas, but on
the South. The people below me were Southern: they had more in
common regionally with the people who might gather on the courthouse lawns of Georgia and Alabama than with the Texans who lived in
Lubbock, San Antonio, or El Paso. East Texans are moulded by the
South, West Texans by the West, and the two cultures are no longer
correspondent.

Below me was a fair sampling of the region's peasantry. It had not
been dramatically destroyed, not smitten with a sword; but it was
surely witnessing its own slow and ruinous depletion. In those people,

the sap was drying, the seed withering. As they moved about beneath the insulating, isolating twang of the Swingster's steel guitar the sense one got was of lethargy and defeat, of apathy, not tragedy. The compelling if sometimes wicked grandeur of Sutpen and Sartoris was past, a grandeur of myth, of fictive or historical dream: there is little of it left in the present-day South. One would have had a hard time finding in that crowd the kind of faces that Walker Evans and Dorothea Lange photographed three decades ago, when our peasantry was enduring a harsher and more tragic trial. The faces below looked softer and less sharp, and the hard, austere grace had mostly eroded away.

As I was bringing these gloomy speculations into focus, something good finally happened on the platform. A young man named Johnny Grimble came on stage with his quartet. They were four good-natured local boys in khakis, and they didn't have a voltage-powered instrument of any kind. Apparently they had already tuned up, because they lit right into a song called "Rubber Dolly." If they had had nothing but their energy they would still have been better than any group I had heard that day. But besides energy, they had the sense to sing songs that meant something to them, and they were not too citified to swing their elbows and pat their feet. When "Rubber Dolly" was over the leader stepped to the microphone and sang a ballad with sex in it. One line was repeated over and over:

She called me Baa-by, baa-by all night loong.

He had no great skill nor great concern with skill, but he had passion enough to transform a corny song and make it seem true. When he switched to

Have I told you lately that I love you . . .

the crowd responded to what was genuine and got quiet. The sun had dropped behind the courthouse. For the first time that day I felt I was hearing music that expressed the people around the platform, though more probably it was Johnny Grimble who expressed them. When he stepped back from the microphone the group swang into "Under the Double Eagle." I hoped that morning policeman was still around.

When the Grimble boys stepped down things deteriorated rapidly back to the level of the Swingsters. The next two bands had so many steel guitars that my ears began to ring, and I left the platform. It seemed a good time to see what breed of men and women had come in for the street dancing.

Certainly East Texas womanhood was showing me its painful worst. All day I had not noticed a pretty woman around the bandstand, nor could I spot one in the evening crowd. A few were of the long-legged, gawky variety, but the majority were short straggle-haired farm women with dumpy breasts, thin legs, and fat behinds. There were a lot of town women around, but except for stiff permanent waves and more make-up they looked like the country women.

While I was walking through the crowd they turned on the yellow bulbs that had been strung above the street to light the dancing. Their strong, almost urinous glare contrasted with the soft dusk and gave colors of grotesquerie to the whole assemblage. A bunch of flabby-armed, hugely pregnant women stood by the curb, talking about their pregnancies. There was a concession stand, and a little booth next to it where they sold cotton candy and pennants and monkeys on strings, foam rubber dice to dangle from rear-view mirrors, raccoon tails and Confederate flags. Passing the booth, I saw a little barefooted, sandy-haired East Texas boy in overalls, standing with his obviously stone-broke, whiskey-breathed father. The little boy was staring with his whole being at one of the cheap telescopes on sale for $1.98. The purity of his want was too much to look upon. When the man beckoned, the boy followed, but one felt that for years part of him would remain right there, wanting that telescope. Part of me has remained there too, for the moment hangs in my mind—a glimpse of the beginnings of destruction, his or mine or everyone's, in that real and terrible hunger for a trivial thing.

The older boys in the crowd cheered me somewhat. They were hungry for sex and were clustered around the teenage girls. Then I went into the courthouse to get a drink of water and ran into a family of idiots. I had been seeing one of them all day, a taciturn boy-man with a concave face and receded nose. One could have laid a rule from forehead to chin without touching either his lips or his nose. Suddenly, grouped on the steps like freaks from the old Tod Browning movie, were four more like him, one of them an old lady and one a pregnant girl who looked no older than fourteen. The crowd just wasn't working out for me.

On the platform a group called the Western All-Stars was having its try. They sported a female vocalist, a small, thin-legged girl in a grimy looking black skirt and a tasselled blouse.

I'm driftin' in-to deeep wa-ter . . .

she sang, a faint Kitty Wells timbre in her voice. The folk listening in silence—or were they the folk? Once the concept of folk carried with it an implicit relation to the soil: the folk lived on and worked the land. Now they are drifting, surely, but not toward deeper waters—toward the same suburbs and television swamps in which the cowboys were bogged.

That day I had driven from Ft. Worth to Dallas, through Dallas, and on to Athens. Of the hundred miles I travelled, fifty had been suburbia. I had driven along the new Stemmons Freeway and got the commuter's view of the Big D skyline, with the bright tincan facades of the skyscrapers flashing in the morning sun. They tapered upward, at that time, to the ultimate Southwestern phallus, the shaft with the light in its head above the Republic National Bank. The Flying Red Horse that had once reared unchallenged above all Texas was far below. I drove up Commerce Street, so aptly named, past Neiman-Marcus, its *ne plus* produce and *ultra* customers beautifully juxtaposed to the beerjoints, wine-bars and shoeshine parlors of South Ervay. I drove out Second Avenue, past the Fair Grounds, a Goodwill store, a D.A.V. store, twenty second-hand furniture stores, numerous used car lots, a Negro pictureshow, two junk-auto yards, forty hamburger stands, and the Kaufman Pike Drive-In. Behind me was where the folk had drifted, to Neiman's and Second Avenue, South Ervay and the Stemmons Freeway and the thirty miles of cottonpatch suburbia between Ft. Worth and Dallas. It was little wonder that the farms around Athens had a wilting look, even though the grass was green and the air the air of spring.

The last band I heard that night was the Twilight Serenaders, a group unique in two respects. First, in regard to instrumentation: they were far and away the most elaborately equipped group to appear, with over a dozen pieces and everything electric but the fiddle.

Second, and more remarkable, they had for a vocalist the one really lovely woman I saw that day.

She came on stage with her daughter, who was to accompany her. They sat just beyond the judges, at my end of the stage. She was to sing only one song, and sat very quietly, her hands folded in her lap, during the long half-hour it took the Serenaders to get their twelve instruments plugged in and tuned. I watched her from amid the empty instrument cases. She was in her early forties, still shapely and high-breasted, a calm, graceful, brownhaired woman. All day I had watched graceless bodies and resigned faces, but her face was not resigned, merely sorrowful. Her name was Obera Waters. Though she sat with a quiet, pleasant look on her face, what one noticed most in her was a combination of melancholy and weariness—the tired, composed weariness of someone who has lived a long while in the love of people whose capacities were smaller than her own.

When Mrs. Waters stood up to sing, I noticed that she was missing two lower front teeth. She sang "Standing in the Shadows," and sat back down. One of the musicians came over and squatted by me for a minute. He put up his electric banjo and took out an electric mandolin. Underneath the instrument was a little sheaf of song lyrics, typed on variety-store tablet paper and held together with a paperclip. The song on top was "I Am Weak but Thou Art Strong," a song that simply begs for mandolin accompaniment.

He plugged in the mandolin and the Serenaders began their elaborate tune-up—only this time it was too elaborate. The strain of all those instruments was finally too much for the circuits, and several fuses blew. The Serenaders were reduced to a few discordant tinkles. It took them twenty minutes to get the fuses replaced, and in the interim I learned that Texas Shorty was up next, with Red Rogers in the wings. The street dance seemed suddenly not worth waiting for, and I left. When I walked off the platform Mrs. Waters still sat calmly in the chair, her hands folded again and her face still lovely and tired.

In less than an hour I was back on Second Avenue. I crossed Dallas and stopped for a cheeseburger at a little beerjoint near the Circle. Sitting next to me at the counter was a good-natured guy in a green Dr. Pepper Bottling Co. uniform—he was a baseball fan, and lacked several more teeth than Mrs. Waters. A girl called to him from a booth and he grabbed his two bottles of Pearl and left.

If Dallas is good for nothing else, it is a useful divider. I had been in the South all day, but as I turned toward Ft. Worth I re-entered the West—for me, always a good feeling. Ahead, north to Canada and west to the Coast lay what to me is the most exciting stretch of land in America. Despite its rudeness, newness, rawness, it is not worn out, not yet filled, not yet exhausted.

If one loves the West it is sometimes deeply moving to drive along one of its rims and sense the great spread of country that lies before one: West Texas, New Mexico and Colorado, Wyoming, the Dakotas, Utah, Arizona, Montana and Idaho, Nevada, Oregon and Washington, and the long trough of California; with the names of rivers and cities and highways now binding the land like the old trails which once led to Oregon or Santa Fe—now it is Highway 40 and Highway 80 and Highway 66 that lead one from the Mississippi to the Pacific, to Cheyenne or to Denver, to Phoenix, El Paso, Los Angeles or San Francisco.

On the rims of the West—and perhaps, in America, only there—one can still know for a moment the frontier emotion, the loneliness and the excitement and the sense of an openness so vast that it still challenges—in Gatsbian phrase—our capacity for wonder.

I can summon no wonder for what lies between Dallas and Washington. The South is memories, memories—it cannot help believing that yesterday was better than tomorrow can possibly be. Some of the memories are extraordinarily well-packaged, it is true, but when a place has been reduced in its own estimation no amount of artful packaging can hide the gloom. I hope Mr. Clarence stays out there in West Los Angeles; his description of Athens, Texas, struck me as very apt. And when I think of Obera Waters, who is left there still, it is as a rare and weary reminder of a people's departing grace.

Kirk Purcell

Kirk Purcell was born September 24, 1950, in Big Spring, Texas. He grew up in Wichita Falls, Texas, and Alexandria, Virginia. After attending "half the colleges in the Western hemisphere," Purcell studied law at Baylor. He is currently a personal injury lawyer in Clear Lake City, Texas.

A Rodeo Memoir

> *Well, he's rosined his riggin'*
> *And laid back his wages;*
> *He's dead set on ridin' the big rodeo.*
> Billy Joe Shaver

> *I'd like to ride the rodeo*
> *but I've got Brahma fear.*
> Jimmy Buffet

IN the Spring of 1969 I was a draft-dodging, decidedly unacademic freshman at the University of Colorado who had recently fallen victim to literary epilepsy. Since my affliction was serious enough that I couldn't even hold a book, much less actually read one, without being overcome by a twitching fit, I decided to quit school and become a rodeo clown or "bullfighter." Not just a garden-variety rodeo clown, mind you, but a genuine, bona fide, authentic, card-carrying member of the Rodeo Cowboys Association (now the Professional Rodeo Cowboys Association), the National Football League of rodeo. I had to know if I had the heart to make it in the big time.

This would not be my first wading into the dung dirt of the rodeo arena. For the previous three years I had nursed the illusion that one day I would wear a gold belt buckle with the inscription "World's Champion Bull Rider." While living the illusion I had climbed down into the chute and nodded for the gate at rodeos from Archer City, Texas, to Madison Square Garden. Of the two hundred fifty or so bulls I had climbed aboard I had ridden probably only thirty or forty to the

eight-second buzzer announcing a qualified ride. My winnings might
have added up to seven hundred dollars.

During a week I spent at the Madison Square Garden Rodeo (in
the Sodom and Gomorrah of the East), a bull named Brutus threw me
out of the arena and almost into orbit at a moment when others of my
generation were getting high on a variety of non-prescription drugs at
a place called Woodstock. Once, after having been tap-danced upon by
an eighteen-hundred-pound Charolais bull, my right leg turned as
black and hard as the top of a baby grand piano and stayed that way for
the better part of a month. Finally, I had to admit to myself that I was
not destined to become rich and famous as a bull rider.

Having grown up as the son of a distinguished congressman, I
wanted with all I was to escape the yoke of being "the congressman's
son." More than anything, I yearned to distinguish myself in an arena
where the people had never heard of the congressman and his many
accomplishments. I wanted to rise by my own strengths or fall by my
own frailties. In those pre–Urban Cowboy days, there was nothing the
least bit hip or chic about being a rodeo clown. If anything, in the eyes
of most of my suburban contemporaries I had only been slumming
throughout my rodeo career. But in my eyes the challenge of rodeo
clowning was as romantically alluring as European borders were to
Napoleon.

I discovered you didn't just begin as a rodeo clown; you either was
one or you wasn't. Back then there were no training grounds—no sem-
inars, no courses, no workshops. Not even LaSalle Extension University of matchbook fame offered any guidance for any ambitious but
unlettered young American such as me.

The first benefactor to this ambition turned out to be a highly Republican businessman in Boulder, Colorado. Before I met Rex Walker I
had never known a Republican to commit an act of generosity toward
anyone. In the way of the monied, Walker could spot counterfeit at a
glance. But, also as the monied might, he sensed the urgings of out-
rageous ambition and in sympathy let it have its try. Walker, I soon
learned, had made an obscene pile of money in the "oil bidness" and
had recently bought Rocky Mountain Rodeo Company as a sideline.
He was an unabashed admirer of Senator John Tower of Texas. From
the moment he learned I was from Tower's home town of Wichita Falls,
I could do no wrong. I didn't mention that I came from a long line of

Democrats who had always thought Senator Tower was a fairly useless American.

I drove to Mr. Walker's office, introduced myself, and told him of my ambition to get my RCA clown card. He leaned back in his chair, took a deep drag of a long, nasty-looking black cigar, and stared at me for a while.

"Son, what are you majoring in over at the university?" he asked. I said I didn't have a major.

"Well, have they taught you how to read and write?" he asked, his voice gradually growing louder. I said they had.

"Then why in God's name would you want to be a rodeo clown?" he roared. "Have you got a death wish or am I blind? If you're tired of livin', just call up my good friend Richard Nixon and he'll ship your ass to Viet Nam where you can die like a man ought to. How did you get it in your head you wanted to be a rodeo clown? You got any experience?"

I quickly invented out of whole cloth a fictional career in amateur rodeos throughout Texas. I rambled on and on about all the rodeos I had worked and the bad bulls I had faced. After listening to my non-stop palaver for a while longer, Walker stood up and put both hands on his desk. "Son, that is pure-dee horseshit. You're no more big-time rodeo clown than Ho Chi Minh is. But I like a man who'll take a chance. I tell you what I'll do. I've got a cousin by the name of Pat Mantle. Pat runs the 7-11 Rodeo Company out of Craig, over on the western slope. It's an amateur outfit, but he's got some bulls that'll mash the shit out of you if you give 'em half a chance. Pat's got some rodeos coming up. I'll get you some jobs with him and if Pat says you're all right, then I'll let you work a couple of rodeos for me. If I like your work, I'll let you have all my rodeos next year. How does that sound to you?"

I said it sounded all right by me. Walker got on the phone to Pat Mantle and within a few minutes I had my first contract. At the end of the month, 7-11 Rodeo Company would be producing a high school rodeo at Canon City, Colorado, and the safety of the bull riders would be my responsibility. It would be a heavy load to tote. I knew it would be a cruel hoax on the cowboys contesting at Canon City to get my on-the-job training at their expense. I had to find a way to get some experience and I had to do it fast.

A hoodlum friend of mine mentioned that in two weeks Quail Dobbs would be working the Colorado State High School Finals Rodeo in the nearby town of Westminster. Quail had a reputation as one of the premier clowns in the RCA. He was from Coahoma, just a few miles from the West Texas village of Big Spring, where I was born.

During my bull-riding days I had seen Quail work several times and had been amazed that anyone so small and with such an unassuming manner could play so fast and loose with mortality. He had seemed too open and innocent to be cursed by those existential urgings that drive people to seek danger of the sort most certainly crippling and maybe terminal.

I also knew of Quail's reputation for modesty. He liked to brag that the peak of his high school football career had come when he played substitute halfback on the second string of the B team during practice. But his rodeo career had been otherwise. Although blessed with little physical ability, by sheer force of will and strength of heart Quail had already accomplished things in the rodeo world that were far beyond his true capacity. I just hoped I could convince him to give me a chance to work with him for a couple of days.

I spent the next two weeks gathering the tools of the clowning trade. The good folks at the Levi Strauss Company of San Francisco kindly sent me a new pair of baggy Levis with a fifty-four-inch waist and a twenty-six-inch inseam. I found a pair of bright red fireman's suspenders at the Salvation Army store. My mother gave me a red, white, and blue Vera scarf to wear around my neck. The manager of the University of Colorado football team gave me a pair of used football shoes. I bought a wig, some makeup, and a Kelly green top hat at a theatrical supplies store. The Ralston Purina people gave me several red and white checkerboard square shirts. I bought a shotgun and a rubber chicken at a pawn shop in the skid row area on Larimer Street in Denver. My wrestling coach at the university gave me an imitation leopard-skin sport coat formerly worn by Wahoo McDaniel, the New York Jets linebacker turned professional wrestler. Then I went to the Goodwill store and found an African pith hunting helmet that went well with the sport coat. My true love gave me a pair of red and white boxer shorts underwear covered with Valentines and portraits of Romeo and Juliet. They proved to be inspiring. Lastly, I bought a protective steel cup to slip into my jockstrap during the bull riding. The only other thing I needed was the courage to face the bulls, and I didn't know where I could buy that.

It bordered on the absurd to ask a man of Quail Dobbs's standing in the rodeo world for free clowning and bullfighting lessons. It would be comparable to strolling into Nureyev's dressing room about an hour before the curtain goes up and saying something like, "Rudolph, I been thinkin' 'bout bein' a rich, famous toe dancer myownself, and I'd be real proud if you'd show me a few steps and let me join you onstage for the second half of the show."

Driving the thirty miles from Boulder to Westminster, I mused on what I would do if Quail told me to take a slow walk to Tucumcari. Would I try to bribe him? Would I beg? Or would I simply climb the fence, jump into the arena, and offer myself to the bulls as though I were a deranged spectator in Hemingway's Pamplona?

Quail's camper was parked behind the bucking chutes, and he was working on his comedy car, Apollo 18⅓, when I pulled into the parking lot. I climbed out of my car, walked up to him, and stuck out my hand.

"My name's Kirk Purcell," I said. "I was born in Big Spring and I want to learn how to fight bulls. I'll stay out of your way if you'll just let me work with you."

He looked up from his work and gave me a look of profound indifference. "This is Walt Alsbaugh's rodeo," he said. "You go talk to him. It's all right with me if it's all right with him."

I found Walt Alsbaugh across the parking lot, unloading a truckload of bucking horses. He was so potbellied he looked like he was hauling a watermelon in his shirt. I said I wanted to learn how to fight bulls and told him what Quail had said. He rolled his eyes and thought about it for a minute. Then he stuck a giant wad of Red Man chewing tobacco in his cheek, hustled his balls, hitched up his pants, and thought about it some more.

Finally, he looked me in the eye and spoke. "Son, if you're simpleminded enough to want to walk out there and face those bad fightin' bulls and get yourself crippled, I guess I've got little enough sense to let you try. You just stay out of Quail's way and do what he says. He'll take care of you."

I was so happy I wanted to fall back, flap my arms, and strut like a peacock. "Yes, sir," I said, shaking his hand like a pump handle. "I'll sure do that. I'll stay out of his way and I'll do just what he says. Thank you, sir."

When I got back to Quail's camper with my warbag in hand, he was visibly surprised to learn that Alsbaugh had given his blessing to my foolhardy escapade. But Quail proved to be a man of his word. He quickly set about teaching me how to create a new face using red and white greasepaint and an eyebrow pencil. He showed me how to use the white makeup around my mouth and eyes to produce a look of bug-eyed wonderment. He used the eyebrow pencil to draw crow's-feet at the corners of my mouth and eyes. He showed me how to spread the red makeup into a flesh tone to make the bald pate of my wig blend into my forehead. Then he added a final touch of talcum powder to keep the greasepaint from smearing. In a wink I was transformed into a balding, disheveled, grey-haired relation of Red Skelton's Clem Kadiddlehopper.

The strange new aroma of greasepaint and talcum powder flooded my senses as I climbed out the back door of Quail's trailer into the dust of the parking lot. Cowboys and cowgirls were loosening up their horses, loping slowly around the arena as Ray Price's version of "The Wild Side of Life" drifted out over the grandstands. I strolled over to examine Walt Alsbaugh's renowned herd of bulls. As I stood looking at Droopy, the notorious red Brahman the top bull riders had selected as Bucking Bull of the Year for 1968, I began to reflect on all the famous clowns who had surely gone through this same ritual, perhaps looking into this same bull's eyes. Most of them are men you probably never heard of—George Doak, Wick Peth, Buck LeGrand, Kajun Kidd, Junior Meek, Tom Lucia, Tommy Sheffield, Larry McKinney—but, believe me, beloved, they are spoken of in tones of reverence among the inner circles of the professional bull riders. I found myself wondering how I would measure by comparison to the greats and near-greats when my turn came to face the bulls.

Then, a moment later, it occurred to me how bizarre it was to find myself, Son of Suburbia, in such a setting, having such thoughts. What strange force had brought me here? What did I have to prove to myself? What if I ended up paralyzed from the ears down? How would I know when I had passed or failed the test? Or did it really matter?

Quail brought me back to reality: "We've got three performances to work together. Don't worry about doing too much this first night. Just stand back and listen to me. I'll take care of the cowboys because that's what I'm getting paid for. Once the cowboy gets away safely, you're on your own. If you want to make a pass, make a pass. But don't take a hookin' just to impress me; I've seen fools get crippled before. And one last thing—look out for a black, droop-horned bull named Teddy. He'll camp on you if he gets you on the ground."

With those words of encouragement I stumbled into the arena. I began praying to Jesus, Allah, Buddha, and the Wild Man from Borneo, hoping not to miss anybody with any influence. I kept hoping the police would come and arrest me for some crime that had gone undetected until that fateful moment. But there was no salvation—I had to face the bulls.

Walt Alsbaugh climbed onto the platform behind chute number one. He turned toward the cowboys and bellowed, "Bull riders, git it on your mind." All of a sudden, I felt like the poor man's Gary Gilmore. I knew I was going to die; we just couldn't afford the bullets.

Then somebody walked up behind me and whispered, "Son, this is your big chance. I sure hope you've got your hammer cocked. You know, Teddy killed a boy last week. Broke his neck clean in two." I turned around and no one was there.

Somehow I managed to struggle through three performances without getting crippled or killed. In my mind's eye I was defying death almost every moment, but, in reality, I spent most of the time climbing the fence as though I were a bull rider who still had a right to be there. More than once, Quail had to call to me from the middle of the arena, "Hey, the rodeo ain't up there in the bleachers. It's out here in the deep water. Come on in, the water's fine."

But Quail more than made up for what I lacked. He showed me how to make a bull turn back and spin. On more than one occasion, he tiptoed to the inside of a fast-spinning bull to untie a cowboy who had hung up and been rendered helpless. And, most importantly, he showed me how much heart it took to fight bulls in the RCA.

At the second performance, Teddy had quickly bucked off a cowboy and then cleared the area in front of the chutes. He chased the pickup men and their horses to the far end of the arena. Most bullfighters in Quail's position would have been working from behind a barrel. But not Quail. Instead, he stood flat-footed in the middle of the arena and waited for the bull. The crowd got deathly quiet as Quail and Teddy eyed each other. Then Teddy got his bearings and made his charge, eyes wide open, horns trained on Quail.

With the bull only steps away, Quail began moving to his left,

measuring his steps, ready to make his pass. But Quail's calculations
were off. Teddy caught Quail under his right armpit and threw him
eight or ten feet. Quail landed on his side and struggled to regain his
footing before Teddy could hit him again. But Teddy was too fast. He
hit Quail in the small of his back and ground his face into the arena
dirt. He smoothed him out flat and ran smack-dab over him.

Quail had to be hurt. I ran toward him, thinking he might be
disoriented and want directions to the nearest gate. I knew that was
where I was headed. Teddy was at the other end of the arena, fixing to
arrange a two-hearse funeral.

When I got to Quail he struggled to his feet, looked at me, and
began adjusting his wig. "Are you all right?" I asked.

"Where's my hat?" he asked.

"Do what?" I asked.

"My hat," he said. "I was wearing a hat when I came in. Where'd
it go?"

I reached down and picked his hat off the ground and handed it to
him. He dusted it off and put it back on. Then he reached out and
pulled me to him. "You know why I need my hat?" he asked.

"No," I said. By now I was getting scared. I knew Teddy was going
to kill us if we waited a second longer.

"The reason I need my hat is because they're havin' a rodeo here
tonight and it's fixin' to start just as soon as I can find that bull. I always
wear my hat to a rodeo."

With that, Quail began hollering at Teddy and dancing and
shadow-boxing in the bull's direction. I knew severe brain damage
when I saw it. So I headed for the gate.

Quail was still dancing in the middle of the arena. Teddy was
bearing down on him, shifting from a fast trot to a lope to full throttle.
Quail didn't move left or right. He just stood his ground, dancing like a
manic Watusi. Then Quail began running straight *toward* Teddy. Quail
had taken perhaps four or five steps when Teddy lowered his head and
sighted his horns, ducked his head and made his final lunge. Just as he
did, Quail pushed off like a high hurdler, and all Teddy stabbed was the
cool night air. Quail had jumped over Teddy's head and horns. Not bad
for a man who stands about as tall as Mickey Rooney or Truman Capote.

The crowd went apeshit. Everybody was whooping and hollering
and whistling and stomping their feet. I was afraid the spectators were

going to tear down the bleachers. Teddy knew the score. He ducked out the catch-pen gate and headed for the showers. Quail tipped his hat to the crowd and strolled down the center of the arena, as modest as though he had just bogeyed the eighteenth hole at the Putt-Putt. I had a hero for life.

After apprenticing with Quail, I knew I had to get my RCA card and work all the rodeos I could. I needed a mule and a small grubstake. At the RCA convention at the Brown Palace Hotel in Denver, I met some of the other top clowns. Buck LeGrand of Sedan, Kansas, offered to sell me a miniature mule and a miniature trailer in which to haul it.

Buck said the trailer would cost $150 and the price of the mule depended on what kind of equipment I wanted. I had no idea what he meant by that. He explained that he had an economy model, one-eyed white mule that was $100 or a deluxe model, two-eyed white mule that was $125. Since I had no money and didn't have the vaguest notion where my grubstake would be coming from, I played it conservative and bought the economy model. I named him Eugene.

At first I worked a few college rodeos for Walt Alsbaugh. Then Jerome Robinson, Bryan McDonald, and Keith Pollet, three RCA bull riders who had become my friends and mentors, attested to my bull-fighting ability and helped me get my clown card. And Rex Walker agreed to give me the chance he had promised a few months earlier. I just hoped I was ready.

My RCA debut came in Dixon, Wyoming. I rode Eugene in the grand entry and did a couple of fill-in acts between the contest events, but I had hoped to save my energy and concentration for the bull riding. It's a good thing I did.

J. J. Moon was the first cowboy up. He had drawn Donald Duck, a big, stout, yellow, flat-horned bull that had been selected for the National Finals Rodeo the previous year. I had seen the Duck buck a few times before, and I knew he had gone unridden for at least three or four years. He was a living legend. If the Duck stayed true to his pattern, I knew he would jump out of the gate, turn back to the right, and jump and kick in a tight, drifting spin. He normally stayed there until the cowboy went into orbit, which usually wasn't long.

J. J. rode with his left hand, and, if he was to have a chance to get past the Duck, he knew he would have to lean to the inside of the spin, or "down in the well." Bucking off into the well, away from his riding hand, is the greatest danger a bull rider faces. When that happens, the cowboy's riding hand gets in a bind and he becomes a rag doll tied to the bull, vulnerable to feet and horns. J. J. stood a good chance of getting into a bad storm, and I knew this could be my first real test in front of the jury of professional cowboys.

I was right on both counts. J. J. looked good for the first three or four jumps, then the Duck took control. He jerked J. J. down onto his head right between the Duck's horns. When the Duck's head collided with J. J.'s, it sounded like a sledgehammer hitting a ripe watermelon. It looked as though J. J. had been knocked as cold as a wedge, and he began flopping around like Raggedy Andy tied to a whirlwind. I had to untie him before things got worse. My training took control. I stepped in and got my hand on the Duck's inside horn. He followed me out of the spin and turned back to the left. I stepped to the Duck's left shoulder and was safe on the inside of the spin as long as I could stay on my feet. J. J. was now laid out horizontally on the outside of the spin, whirling like a helicopter blade gone berserk. He was safe for the moment, if I could just untie him. I reached for his riding hand and made a blind grab for the tail of the bull rope. I got lucky and found it on the first try. It was J. J.'s rip cord. He came loose and fell in a heap, blood streaming from his nose and forehead. Amazingly, he got up and stumbled back to the chutes while Donald Duck trotted triumphantly around the arena.

Standing there, looking at J. J. leaning against the chute gate, I experienced a helpless feeling that was to haunt me throughout my clowning career. I knew I had done my best, and I knew the cowboys knew I had done all anyone could have. Still, it gnawed at me that I had been unable to save J. J. from injury, even though all the damage had been done before he hit the ground.

Nobody else got in a bad storm that day, but later in that same performance I got cocky and jumped a little black fighting bull named Porky. The crowd loved it. For the first time, I learned there's nothing like a little applause to make a man try something really foolish.

Sitting on the side of my trailer that afternoon, taking off my makeup, I was a satisfied man. Several of the cowboys came by, introduced themselves and bragged on my work. Since I knew professional rodeo cowboys to be a stoic breed, their reception was not something I had expected. But I was pleased; I knew I had passed the test and was among brothers.

Afterword

I got my RCA clown card in January, 1970. Eugene and I spent the next year or so traipsing back and forth across the heartland of America. I remember waking up in fleabag motels with names like Ed's Beds or the Wigwam Courts, feeling as though the Third Reich had spent the previous night goose-stepping up and down my spine. If I had taken an especially bad hooking, there were mornings when it was all I could do to crawl or stumble across the floor to the bathtub. On such days I spent the better part of the morning soaking in the tub and trying to convince myself I could stand up and walk back to the bed. Finally I would work up enough courage to go to the nearest greasy spoon for a cheeseburger or even a chicken-fried steak, if I was in a part of the country where one could find that delicacy.

I usually spent the afternoon feeding and watering Eugene and rigging up the fireworks on my feature act, the Acme Shrinking Machine. I always spent the final hour before the grand entry putting on my makeup, wrapping my left ankle, and taping whatever ribs I had most recently bruised or cracked. Then came the time to walk to the pens behind the bucking chutes for a one-sided conversation with the bulls I would be facing within a couple of hours. It was my way of psyching myself and overcoming the pain still lingering from the night before or the week before or, at times, even the month before.

Talking with the bulls prepared me for the awesome adrenaline rush that would start gushing full force at the moment the first bull exploded from the chute, marking the beginning of the real rodeo for me. Even today, standing behind the bucking chutes, hearing the clanging of the cowbell tied to the bull rope still brings on the same hybrid feeling of nausea and euphoria.

Today, in my law practice, I know a different sort of fear. When the judge gavels the courtroom to order, right before the jury selection begins, I often sit and wonder if I am up to the task at hand. Whether I am representing a working man or woman who has been injured or a fellow citizen who stands accused of crime, sitting at the counsel table, I can still hear Walt Alsbaugh's words come fogging through my head, "Bull riders, git it on your mind."

Gary Cartwright

Gary Cartwright was born August 10, 1934, in Dallas, Texas. His career has included work as a reporter, sports writer, and sports columnist with Dallas and Fort Worth newspapers; two novels, *The Hundred Yard War* (1968) and *Thin Ice* (1975); the screenplay for *J. W. Coop* (1973); and contributions to several popular magazines—*Esquire*, *Harper's*, *Saturday Review*, and *Rolling Stone* among them. He won the Texas Institute of Letters' Stanley Walker Award for Journalism in 1977 for "The Endless Odyssey of Patrick Henry Polk," published in *Texas Monthly*. In addition, his highly acclaimed *Blood Will Tell* (1979) is the documented account of the Fort Worth murder trial of millionaire T. Cullen Davis, charged with murdering his twelve-year-old daughter and his estranged wife's boyfriend. The following is Cartwright's less serious account of the annual Texas-Oklahoma football rivalry.

The Rites of Autumn

THERE is a seasonal turn to life, a time of rebirth, consecration, and sensation. Easterners, poets, and young lovers call it spring. The Bible calls it the Resurrection. Dallasites call it the Texas-OU Weekend. It is the harvest of a long hot summer's suffering, a time to celebrate madness. Somewhere there might be buried some reason for it, some root cause to the rivalry, but the reason is not sought because no excuse is needed. Lunacy is a powerful therapy that cuts across class, race, age, and gender.

Maybe you've experienced it, even if you've never been to Dallas in October. It begins in a hundred towns and villages at least a month before the unrelenting hordes sweep down on Dallas. It begins like a fever: an unaccountable tingle; a vague restlessness; a sweet apprehension. The drone of a sweltering afternoon is violated suddenly by the thump of a football in a vacant lot down the street. The wind shifts unexpectedly, rattling the trees, and for a split second you catch the smell of something baking. Kids with summer-swollen feet and new lunch boxes appear in the early morning. Trapped layers of heat shimmer from the sidewalk in front of Neiman-Marcus, distorting the reflection of the sleek, tanned woman who has paused to fancy herself on the 50 yard line at the Cotton Bowl in that stunning wool poncho. The coffee shop in the Southland Life Building that could barely meet its overhead in the dog days of summer buzzes now with crisp specula-

tion, and shoeshine boys pop their rags with new vigor and speak of point spreads. It is a time for fellowship, a time to show your colors. "Hey, coach," the prematurely graying man in the three-piece suit calls out from the parking lot, "we gonna kick some ass this year!" If young bones hold up; if last year's blue-chipper is all they say he is; if it doesn't rain too much, or too little.

On Thursday night and Friday morning in early October the exodus begins: the fever is about to peak. For a 200-mile radius, all the way north to Norman and all the way south to Austin, the freeways to Dallas sizzle with Cadillacs and Continentals of old loyalists, flushed and streaming ribbons of red or orange. A fresh crop of students, who so recently turned their new Capris toward these bedrocks of education, turns now toward Dallas, knowing that everything in between was temporary, a mere prelude to Texas-OU Weekend. At the stroke of Friday noon, in the exact geographical center of downtown Commerce Street, along the wide, crooked intersection between the Baker Hotel and the Adolphus, they will converge like two tribes on the eve of battle. A thousand auto horns will honk simultaneously and without interruption, signaling to the hundreds of others who are there out of stubborn curiosity, or because they have been trapped in the combustion, that the war council has begun; nothing else will be tolerated.

Every hotel, guest bedroom, and spare sofa in the Metroplex has been claimed for months. In the case of many of the merrymakers, there would be nowhere to go even if they wanted to, which no doubt many do. Until a few years ago Dallas police helped solve the hotel problem by throwing hundreds of revelers in the city slammer, but in recent Texas-OU Weekends a wall of riot-helmeted police has managed to preserve order and even a trace of decorum: since it would be nearly impossible for police paddy wagons to maneuver the bumper-to-bumper traffic, this is both practical and socially prudent. Ticket scalping is a problem, but nothing like it used to be. All 72,000 Cotton Bowl seats are long gone, a portion of them to students but the bulk to the old loyalists with powerful connections. The best way to get a ticket to the game is to read the obits. Here at the hub of the tribal camps on Commerce Street, tickets are a small concern. Texas-OU is not a game, it's a celebration masking as a conflict. Mardi Gras without Lent. Lauderdale without sand fleas. A parade without bands, floats, or twirlers. A parade where the judges wear riot helmets.

When the broiling October sun slips behind the skyscrapers and neon streaks the night, the tribes advance, but not on each other. It is not so much a promenade as a dance. Like satyrs in a concrete dell, they sway to the trumpeting of plastic horns, auto horns, whistles, proclamations, invectives. A speaker mounted to a van plays *Boomer Sooner*, and another speaker somewhere answers with *Texas Fight*. A dark-haired girl with a wide mouth shouts that Longhorns are large shit factories, and her counterpart in orange retorts that anyone who would claim to be a Sooner would also squat on a bull nettle. A crowd circles a plastic waste-basket, dipping paper cups of Purple Jesus, a potion consisting of many parts alcohol to one part grapejuice. Good-hearted strangers lean from hotel windows, lobbing cans of beer to grateful passersby. The bars and topless joints are doing business, but it's a revolving business, turning them in and out like a soup kitchen. Pickpockets, hookers, dope dealers, and free booters are typecast with the mob, trading commodities, and funny looks. Girls in T-shirts and tight sweaters spew each other with warm beer, then stagger arm in arm, laughing. A child hugs her mother's leg and tries to cry, but it's not easy with the man in the monkey suit dancing around her.

On the parking ramp outside the Statler Hilton a grizzly sour-dough in a soiled cowboy hat mounts his Model-T with the customized rear suspension, rearing it upon its hind wheels and riding it like a bucking horse. A transient steps off a Greyhound at the Commerce Street depot, blinks, and decides that purgatory, if indeed that is what he has encountered, isn't such a bad place. There will be some fights, a few of them serious, but a strange magnet of accord grips this crowd. They are not here to fight—the Cotton Bowl is for fighting—they are here to look and laugh and be seen. It's a place they've heard about, a citadel of anarchy and supercharged particles. It's a place to find a new love, or lose an old one. A place to make for yourself, a place to prove you've been.

The night goes fast, like black powder. They'll push and drink and love and fall down and do things they never dreamed, but it's okay. Somehow they know it's only a frame in time. Somewhere, there is a floor to sleep on. Somewhere, there is something else, something new, something better. Sometime before dawn they will go to their places and, except for a few roving bands looking for the Texas School Book Depository, the streets will be deserted trenches of rubble.

The broiling sun will reappear on Saturday, claiming the weak, testing the strong, shimmering and swimming over the dizzy jam of vehicles and pedestrians inching along every artery to Fair Park. The 72,000 football fans will be a vocal minority, but a minority, nevertheless. According to tradition, there will be a football game; but the bulk of the tribe will sleep through it, preferring that the outcome speak for itself. When the game has been decided, the victors will parade back down Commerce, honking horns and waving banners, and the losers will seek air-conditioned rooms and begin mixing drinks. By Saturday night the freeways will already be clogged, north and south. A righteous few will already be talking about next year, but the tribe will relive Friday night and maybe pray for Sunday morning. To hell with next year.

William C. Martin

William C. Martin was born on New Year's Eve, 1937, in San Antonio, Texas. He was educated at Abilene Christian College (B.A., 1958; M.A. 1960) and at Harvard University (Ph.D., 1969; B.D., 1973). His writing, much of which concerns popular religion and especially media evangelists, has appeared in popular magazines, including *Atlantic*, *Esquire*, *Harper's*, and *Texas Monthly*. Martin currently resides in Houston, where he teaches sociology at Rice University.

Growing Old at Willie Nelson's Picnic

I don't much like heat or dirt or loud noise or even being outdoors for long stretches at a time, but I do like picnics and special events and crowds and country music and Willie Nelson. So when Willie first announced he was organizing a three-day Fourth of July picnic featuring 36 hours of traditional and progressive country music, and expected 50,000 people to be there, I made up my mind to go, and I went. I thought you might like to hear about it.

The picnic was held in the 160-acre infield of the Texas World Speedway south of College Station, an inhospitable site attractive to promoters because it is highly resistant to gate-crashers but as barren of trees or other shade as it has been of auto races. Yet as I joined the crowd walking through two long tunnels to the infield, I sensed that we had come because we knew the stark landscape and three days of searing heat would inflict great suffering, and since our lives are so easy and our chances to test ourselves against the elements so few, we grimly determined to pursue a happiness of discomfort on this our nation's birthday.

At the top of the grade coming out of the tunnels, where we had felt the last coolness of the day, members of the volunteer medical staff handed out free salt tablets with the promise they would help us last two extra hours if we drank a lot of liquids. Most of the people walking in with me looked prepared to heed the advice on liquids, having estimated their needs at approximately one case of beer per person. I was impressed. Even at the American Legion picnics I went to when I was a boy, nobody would come close to drinking that much beer except oilfield workers and Catholics.

The crowd was not quite what I had expected. It was probably no larger than half the hoped-for 50,000, but what surprised me more was its composition. I had expected thousands of cosmic cowboys and assorted freaks, but I had also expected fairly large numbers of authentic rednecks, and I knew if I got uncomfortable with the freaks I could go sit with the kickers. I am not trying to pretend I grew up a redneck, because I didn't. We were town people. My daddy ran the feed store and was president of the school board, my mama was big in the PTA, and I knew when I was five years old that I was going to college. But I also knew a lot of rednecks and, if it came right down to it, I figured I might feel more at home with them than with long-haired hippie weirdos eating toadstools and smoking LSD.

There were some kickers there, all right. About six. The other 25,000 were freaks or freak-ish, all under 25. I began to realize that I stood out, because I was wearing an honest-to-goodness western shirt with pearl grippers and, at age 36, I was a Senior Citizen. Clearly, I was a stranger in a strange land. Since the closest I had ever been to an event like this was watching the first half of the Woodstock movie, I found a spot to set my cooler down and spent most of the Fourth just paying attention.

For those interested in fashion, it can be reported that the Gatsby look has not taken over everywhere. It's probably just as well, since white is not practical without a certain commitment to cleanliness. Still, observable regularities of dress indicated the young folk had indeed thought about what they were going to wear. The standard uniform for "dudes"—a useful designation for someone no longer a boy but not quite a man—consisted of jeans and sleeveless shirts. With rare exceptions, "chicks" wore shorts and halters. A lot of the dudes walked around with jockey shorts sticking out of the waist of their Levis. I used to have nightmares about showing up in public places in my underwear, but it didn't seem to bother them. Sometimes they had holes in their pants and you could tell they didn't even have on any underwear or, if they did, that it was all worn out and torn. What if they were in an accident? The police would take one look at their underwear and send them to the charity hospital.

If there was sameness in Levis and shorts and sleeveless shirts and halters, there was marvelous variety in cap and hat. There were derbies and dapper Panamas, porkpies and pith helmets, hard hats and Hombergs, mountaineer hats and Mexican sombreros, Navaho hats and Scottish tams, Budweiser hats and Lone Star visors, golf hats and tennis hats and fishing hats, fatigue caps and baseball caps and railroad caps, Dodge Truck and Yamaha Motorcycle and York Air Conditioning caps, International Harvester caps and Caterpillar caps just like the man wore in the cafe in *Easy Rider*, lumberyard caps and polka-dot paint caps, and caps advertising Lone Star Feed and Fertilizer, Equidyne Horse Pellets, and the Athens Livestock Commission. Those who had neglected to bring hats fashioned substitutes from T-shirts and jockey shorts, or by jamming a six-pack carton on their heads, or by combining a Budvisor with a Holiday Inn towel to create the look of an ersatz A-rab from the burning sands of Cairo, Illinois. Most common, of course, were beat-up western hats, with the brims flattened out or bent down in front to look mean. At kicker dance halls, skilled laborers try to look like ranchhands. Here, unemployed students were trying to look like rustlers. I understand the desire to dress up, but if I were picking a costume, I would choose a black and silver outfit and pretend I was a town tamer. My name would be Johnny Laredo.

After I got my bearings I began to pay closer attention to the music. I had been a bit apprehensive about how I would respond to three days of what has come to be called "progressive country," or, more recently, "redneck rock." I like country music because the tunes are easy to remember and I can understand the words. I don't like most rock music because it is too loud, and straining for the words seldom proves worth the effort. I just didn't see how country music was going to gain much from crossbreeding. I do like some rock, of course. I've got two Carole King albums and a Neil Diamond tape and I really enjoy the Living Strings version of "Hey Jude" and "Let It Be" on KYND ("All Music, All the Time"). I had liked a good bit of what I had heard of progressive country, especially Jerry Jeff Walker and Michael Murphey and the Nitty Gritty Dirt Band, and I had been told I would like Greezy Wheels and Freda and the Firedogs and several others, but I had never gone to hear them in person because they usually appear at places where people stand up and walk around and make a lot of noise. So, really, I was open, and I'm glad I was. I picked up some new enthusiasms.

One of the groups I enjoyed most was Jimmy Buffett and his Coral Reefer Band. Buffett started out with a song about wishing he had "a pencil-thin moustache, a two-toned Ricky Ricardo jacket, and an autographed picture of Andy Devine." It made me think about the time I got Lash LaRue's autograph—for all you older people who have wondered whatever happened to Lash, he did a night-club act in Juarez for awhile and is now a street preacher in Florida, bullwhipping for the Master. Buffett claimed the fellow who wrote "Pencil-thin Moustache" is named Marvin Gardens; I imagine he lives in a yellow house near the water works and pays $24 rent. When Jimmy rendered a lament for the fact that "They don't dance like Carmen Miranda anymore," I was about to decide I could come to like his work. Then he sang a number called "Why Don't We All Get Drunk and Screw?" which I found not only a sharp break with nostalgic themes, but a rather more direct sentiment than I like in my love songs. I really prefer something a bit more sensitive and delicate, like Snooky Lanson and Dorothy Collins singing "Lavender Blue—Dilly Dilly."

The sound system was excellent, performers were reasonably good about sticking to half-hour sets, and in the relatively short exchange time between groups we got to hear Kris Kristofferson records, which was fine with me since I think Kristofferson is the greatest living American next to Carl Yastrzemski. At the beginning of an act, or at any point when enthusiasm seemed to be waning, most of the performers could be counted on to say something like "Hot Damn! Aren't we having a good time at the Willie Nelson Picnic?" or "Who in the entire globe of the planet earth could ever put something on like this but Willie Nelson?" which inevitably drew automatic shouts and applause of the sort right-wing politicians trigger by calls for law and order or tent preachers get when they ask their flocks to say Amen if they love Jesus. Despite these periodic outbursts, however, the crowd paid no more than half-hearted attention during most of the acts. They knew the music was playing and moved their feet or hands or something, but treated it rather as if it were background music, except that it was hard to determine what it was background *to*. They really did very little except drink and smoke and stare.

There were exceptions, of course. When Augie Meyers and his Western Headband played, a dude with a benign but decidedly crazy look danced around off the beat, blowing a harmonica and kicking dirt on the folk around him. Even though he had lost a lot of his fine motor control and could never have handled the Samba, especially on the trickier steps like the Copa Cabana, he did have spirit, a quality that marked him from his peers. Directly in front of me three of the most taciturn young men I have seen in some time, including one who was a dead ringer for my Cousin Bolo (that's not his real name, of course; his real name is Little Walter), sat for ten hours passing beer and dope but no more than 50 words. Once, the one in the middle leaned over and threw up between his feet. A girl stepped over and rubbed his back with his wadded-up shirt and in a few minutes he straightened up and resumed his torporous attitude. As far as I could tell, his friends did not notice. Behind me, four boys about the age of my sons—thirteen and fourteen—managed to sustain a state of unbroken somnambulance by alternating between beer and marijuana. A couple of times, the youngest, who might have been no more than twelve, offered me a joint, for which I thanked him but no-thanked him. I'm pretty sure there is a law against taking dope from a twelve-year-old.

Picking one's way through a crowd of 25,000 people, sitting or lying next to one another like stricken pilgrims at the Ganges, is a delicate maneuver at best. For those whose sense of height and depth had been altered by marijuana, it became an assignment of mammoth proportion. I watched one boy make three unsuccessful attempts to lift his foot high enough to get over the edge of an army blanket lying flat on the ground. He finally gave up and took another route. But perhaps what was lost in precision of movement was regained in a greater capacity for informal adaptive measures. A chick clad in shorts and two bandanas tied loosely above her breasts, managed the task more effectively by offering people a hit off her Schlitz in return for safe passage. She will be a good wife for some nice young man. She's frugal, friendly, resourceful, and makes her own clothes.

On another occasion, a dude with a pleasant grassy look stumbled into the neighborhood and announced he felt a certain sexual tension, or words to that effect: "Anybody wants me, come on. I don't mean to be nasty, but come on. Right here." In a similar spirit of forthrightness, a wild-looking youth lurched into the vicinity and began to ask loudly, "Would anybody mind if I take a piss right here? Be honest." I admired his direct approach; I recognize that urination is just another bodily function and nothing to be ashamed of, and because I was a member of a minority group, I was somewhat reluctant to insist that his needs violated my sense of territoriality. Still, I was as relieved as he was not, when my younger neighbors suggested he move on. No more than twenty feet behind us, however, he found an accommodating group willing to step aside for him, and he took his ease for all to see. As a reciprocal gesture—and we know that reciprocity is essential to community—he offered us a good price on that which had so relaxed his inhibitions: "Anybody want any Quāaludes? Anybody want any reds?" His sense of enterprise encouraged me about his generation. As my father used to point out, being able to sell is the best job security a man can have. It's as good as a teaching certificate for a woman.

By late afternoon, the combination of sun, alcohol, and drugs had taken a terrible toll. The heat, though relieved slightly by a brief shower, was simply awful. I was uncomfortable, but managed to avoid collapse by continual intake of liquid. I don't know what the record is, but I was quite surprised to learn that it is possible to eliminate through the pores of one's skin the liquid from twelve cans of assorted beverages and a 70-cent sack of ice. No lie. Members of the medical staff circulated through the crowd, pushing salt pills and spraying Solarcaine on the lobstered backs of people who had gone to sleep or passed out. The medical center itself resembled a ward for the insane as kids jammed in for treatment. Many were badly burned and crying, others were upset and uncomfortable from the unhappy effects of mixing Quāaludes or other downers with alcohol, a few who had taken LSD worked with modeling clay and colored pens, and half a dozen kids had to be sent to the hospital after what a sadist had sold them as THC or given them as salt tablets turned out to be either rat poison or strychnine. A staff member who worked in the medical center all weekend said later, "It was really very sad. So many were having such a horrible time. They were hot and dirty and really, really sick, and wishing so much they had not come."

Of those who never made it to the medical center, hundreds slumped around in a red-eyed stupor, as if the life had gone out of them. They may have been watching *Fantasia* in a theater-of-the-mind that was twenty degrees cooler inside; on the outside, they looked hot, tired, and miserable. But they had told their friends they were coming and they would want to tell them they had had a good time, so it was necessary for them to stick it out.

Even after blessed night finally came and the temperature dropped into the bearable range, it was hard to strike and hold a truly festive mood. A little after ten P.M. Jerry Jeff Walker began a highly promising set, but was interrupted repeatedly by unscheduled fireworks and emergency medical announcements. Most of the fireworks were roman candles and cluster rockets, but a few less socially conscious persons threw large firecrackers into clumps of people, and one of the rockets zipped into the crowd and burned a spectator rather badly. The management declared there would be no more music until the fireworks stopped and the pyromaniacs eased off momentarily, but when the music started up again, so did the fireworks. Unnerving as they were, they added a nice touch when Jerry Jeff sang "Up Against the Wall, Redneck Mother." At precisely the moment that 25,000 people yelled "REDNECK!" the biggest and most spectacular rocket of the night burst into a sparkling cluster high over the stage. It was the sort of thing that happens in movies.

What followed was the sort of thing that happens in bad dreams. The medical staff had gotten a report that a woman somewhere in the crowd was in a coma from insulin shock and needed immediate attention if she were not to die. Trouble was, they didn't know just exactly where she was, so would we check out the unconscious chicks around us and see if any of them appeared to be in insulin shock and if we found one, would we please yell out while everybody else got quiet? Most of the crowd got quiet but a good many yelled out from different parts of the audience—for a joke, probably, but given the number of unconscious people strewn about, perhaps not—and one guy got a good laugh when he called out, "Anybody got any downers?" I wondered how many of those who laughed were diabetics, and I wondered at the capacity of my fellows to laugh when one of their number might be dying. But, as someone called out, we had come to hear music, not to look for sick chicks, and after a bit the show resumed. As it turned out, the delay and search had been unnecessary. The diabetic in question was not a girl but a boy named Val, and he had already been treated before the announcement was made, but the irritation of the crowd at having their concert interrupted by what appeared to be a hoax did not augur well for the survival chances of other medical emergencies.

In fact, the medical people did report some difficulty with the crowd, especially on the first two days. Rory Harper, one of the supervisors of the medical staff, said, "Occasionally, people even pushed the stretcher crews back and wouldn't let them through. Or we would be trying to treat somebody who had passed out and somebody would yell, 'Give her a couple of Quāaludes and she'll be all right.' They were either stoned or just didn't give a damn."

To climax the confusion, operations manager Tim O'Conner took the microphone to announce that a peculiar Texas law governing mass gatherings required that the show end promptly at eleven o'clock. Not only would the last four scheduled acts be cancelled, but Jerry Jeff would not be allowed to come back for an encore. As the young folk began yelling about rip-offs and suggesting that the law and its agents occupy themselves in acts of sexual self-gratification, I feared there might be some unpleasantness. But this was not a violent crowd and the height of the objection came when a young man stood on a beer chest and screamed frustratedly at O'Conner: "You're a fart!" It is possible to be irritated with a person so designated but one does not lynch him. Defeated, perhaps at some level relieved to have the ordeal ended without having to admit they were ready to quit, the crowd filed out peaceably.

It may be that anything worth doing is worth doing to excess, but as I eased my ravaged body into the soft bucket seats of my little red station wagon, I reckoned that the folks who schedule three-hour concerts in air-conditioned auditoriums have a basically sound idea. And as I drove past the tired, dirty kids bedding down in the Willie Nelson Approved Campsites next to the Speedway, I was pleased that because I have this good job teaching school and writing stories, I could afford to stay at the Ramada Inn. I caught the last part of *No Time for Sergeants* on the motel TV. I could have seen all of *China Gate* if I had wanted to.

On Friday, July 5th, I awoke at noon and enjoyed a delightful breakfast of pizza and iced tea, which I preferred to the Alice B. Toklas brownies and Kool-Aid I imagined the kids were eating out at the Speedway. I didn't go back to the picnic until about four o'clock, but that was early enough. I still managed to get in a full day's entertainment.

Despite what was probably greater heat—reports of 103 may have been exaggerated but indicated what folk thought of the weather—most people seemed to be suffering less than on the Fourth. Hundreds of umbrellas and makeshift sunshelters had been erected, creating the appearance of vacationers who had headed for the beach but missed. Apparently because most people took salt tablets and upped their liquid intake, the medical staff had far fewer cases of heat prostration. But in its place, they treated thousands of cuts that resulted when the threshing action of a grounds-cleaning machine left millions of small chunks and shards of glass lying in wait for romantically bare feet.

I roamed a good bit on the Fifth and found the much smaller crowd friendly and relaxed, even though the young folk kept confirming my sense of strangerhood by asking, "Are you having a good time, Sir?" and "What's happening, Daddy?" I wanted to point out to them that most of the performers they liked best were a lot closer to my age than theirs, and that my having never heard of the Lost Gonzo Band or the Neon Angels did not mean I had ridden into town on a head of cabbage. I wanted to tell them about the time I had breakfast at Cisco's Bakery in Austin with Willie Nelson and Tom T. Hall and Coach Darrell Royal, or about hearing Bill Monroe when Lester Flatt and Earl Scruggs were part of his Blue Grass Boys. I even considered telling them about the time I heard Gene Krupa and Charlie Parker on the same night, but I didn't want to have to explain who they were. Mostly, I just smiled and said, "Fine." But when the third person of the day asked me if I was a sheriff, I asked him whatever had made him think I might be. He said, "Well, it's your shirt." I asked him what was wrong with my shirt. It's a good shirt. My wife gave it to me for Christmas. "That's just it," he said. "It's too good. You need an old shirt." I don't go along with that. It seems to me that pretending I am poor isn't taking poverty seriously. Besides, I don't have any old shirts. I give them to the Goodwill and take it off my income tax.

While wandering around, I ran into several fine folk of maturity comparable to my own, but none delighted me more than Mr. and Mrs. Weldon Wilson from Wharton. Mr. Wilson, who had on grey trousers and a peach-colored shirt with the short sleeves rolled up a couple of turns and who wears his thin grey hair in a close trim, fixes TVs for Sears over at Bay City. He and Mrs. Wilson, who wore a navy blue shorts outfit with white socks and sneakers and had a chain fastened to her grey half-rim glasses so she wouldn't have to put them down when she took them off, were enjoying themselves. "The main reason I am here," he said, "is because I like country music. And I haven't seen any of the kids that I don't like. They are going to be running this world in the future and from what I have seen here, I think I'll enjoy living with them. I really do. A little girl asked me awhile ago why I was here. I asked her why she asked me that question and she said, 'Well, usually only kids come to these things. Do you enjoy it?' I said, 'Definitely!' She said, 'You don't think we're wrong?' I said, 'Definitely not! When I was your age I did things the older people thought I was wrong in doing.' And, you know, she just loved my neck. Anyone that would say that all these kids are out here for is to get doped up, there's something wrong with them. There might be some of it I don't agree with, but they've got their own lives to live and they are going to live them, one way or another. They'll have to pay for their mistakes, the same as you and I did, but I haven't seen them doing that much wrong yet."

Mrs. Wilson said, "Neither one of us has ever smoked marijuana or taken dope and we probably never will, but there is something that is funny to me. Out of all them I know that are smoking it, there is not but one I know that wasn't a cigarette smoker first. So smoking can lead to marijuana just like marijuana can lead to heroin. And, you know, if this had been the thing to have done when I was this age, I don't know that I wouldn't have tried it." Mr. Wilson wasn't sure about that. "I've got enough adrenalin in my body that I don't need anything to slow it down or speed it up. Anything they can use their smoking or their drugs to do, I can do the same thing naturally. Say, would you like a beer? We've got Coors."

Late Friday afternoon, the Nitty Gritty Dirt Band galvanized the audience into the form it would hold until well after midnight as hundreds, maybe thousands, of young people wedged themselves into a sweating, writhing, ecstatic mass of back-to-front bodies that stretched outward from the wide stage in a 50-yard-wide semicircle. As the Dirt Band raised the speed and volume of its excellent music, the crowd raised the intensity of its response. Five attractive chicks persuaded their dudes to lift them onto their shoulders that they might better see and perchance be seen. I thought about how much it would make my neck hurt to have a girl sit up on my shoulders like that and how I would resent not being able to put my hands in my pockets because I would have to hold her by the thighs to keep her from falling off, but the dudes seemed to bear up under their burdens rather well.

Eventually, inevitably, one of the girls untied her halter and threw it onto the stage. Within seconds, three of the remaining four had done likewise, to the delight of the gathered multitude. As they jiggled and swayed bare-breasted through several long numbers, the plight of the fifth girl became apparent and poignant. Less abundantly blessed than her sisters, she had not foreseen, as I am relatively certain they had, that matters might come to this. As the others grew more wanton by the bar, she tightened her lips and stiffened noticeably. She could not climb down without losing face, she could not disrobe without revealing less than she cared to. I remembered young teenaged boys, friends of mine mostly, who dreaded gym classes because of the showers that followed, and I hoped she would think of a graceful exit. She did not; but as she suffered, others prospered. A striking blonde girl, whom I suspect I would recognize if I were to see her at any point during the next twenty years, slowly but surely stole the show from the others. When Willie Nelson came out to finish up with the Dirt Band, he tossed her a fine straw hat which she set at what had to be the most provocative angle possible—people who wear clothes well have a knack for that sort of thing—then threw back her head, shouted "I love it!" and went into a magnificent shiver of the sort one seldom experiences alone. Her actions seemed to set up needs in others for similar release of tension. Several girls stripped buck-naked and tried to climb onto the stage. Most were beaten back by heartless security guards but one streaked briefly to the rear of the platform. God knows what happened to her back there with all those musicians.

As I watched this scene which did not remind me much of the dances at the Faculty Club, I thought of a sober colleague who recently confided that his secret fantasy was to be a rock star and to enjoy the adulation of hundreds of nubile young women. I remembered what Mark Twain had said about naked people having little influence in society. And I wondered what the odds were, given the fact that man has been on the earth for thousands, perhaps millions of years, that one would miss the sexual revolution by less than ten. I'm sure Weldon Wilson is right. They'll have to pay for their mistakes the same as he and I did. But I don't think he and I were ever offered such an impressive line of credit.

Actually, I face my missing the sexual revolution without much difficulty. I acknowledge there is a certain attractiveness to a firm, smooth, tan, lissome young body with well-fitted parts, but I have come to appreciate, perhaps even prefer, the sensual beauty of women in their mid- to late thirties, women whose eyes and smiles reflect experience not just with sex but with love, and whose softer bosoms and the gentle ring of stretch-marked waists that will not quite be contained inside their swimsuits or jeans give tangible evidence of time shared by man and child. I pondered the casualness of sexual display and of sex itself in this age group and thought that, for all its momentary allure, sex not undergirded by love, sex between people who seek their own pleasure rather than a true experience of mutuality, sex with a person one may hardly know, however attractive that person may be physically, could never be as meaningful and fulfilling as sex with a person to whom one has made a lifetime commitment and with whom one has shared the bad times as well as the good. Probably.

And I thought that if I had a hat like Willie Nelson's I would have put a tether on it before tossing it out to that blonde girl.

All the naked bodies and reveling and such during the peak of the Nitty Gritty set had led me to believe that we might, following parallels in nature, expect things to tail off for a spell, that folk would find seats and smile about what a nice time they were having, and respond a bit more passively to the efforts of the next group or two. Probably because I failed to take into account that most of them don't have jobs that demand much physical or mental effort—peeling avocados in health-food restaurants, sitting on the sidewalk selling jewelry, things like that—I had seriously underestimated the amount of reserve energy these young folk still possessed after two days of grooving in the sun. Here I was, trapped and unable to move, slumping under the years of gravity's relentless pull, feet aching despite special arch supports and Comfisoles, and realizing that they intended to stay there right up to the end, which obviously was not coming soon. A friendly, smiling dumpy-pretty sort of girl explained it was precisely this kind of experience that had attracted many to the picnic. "It's a stimulus, just like the dope and the music. It keeps you going. It's a weird high."

As I gathered such bits of intelligence, I recorded them for later retrieval by speaking into a small microphone tucked deep within my fist to shut out the noise of the speakers. The microphone was attached by a cord to a superb little tape recorder fastened to my belt and covered with a black leather case. When a gat-toothed young man inquired as to what I was doing when I put my mouth up to my obviously-wired fist, I told him it was electric dope, expecting no more than a smile or agreeable chuckle. Instead, his face exploded in delight and he asked if he could try it. I handed him the microphone, he took a couple of hits, shouted "Far f . . . . g out!" (an expression more freighted with enthusiasm than substantive content), declared to his friends that it was first-rate stuff, and demanded to know where he could get some for himself.

The Friday evening program was marred somewhat by the fact that it was being filmed by the Midnight Special television show. As members of the film crew walked in and out among performers and as the cameras swept around without concern for the fact that soft human bodies were in the vicinity, one got the impression the crowd was being regarded less as primary consumer than as studio audience. Even more offensive was the presence and behavior of Leon Russell, who would serve as Wolfman Jack's co-host for the Special when it aired in early August. Russell is a darling of the progressive country set, for reasons I cannot fathom. For three days he wandered around in what appeared to be a chemical daze, his pasty white pot-belly poking through an unbuttoned shirt and his wasted face peering out from under a straw hat perched on top of the grey hair that flowed down the sides of his face for at least two feet. Because he had obviously ordained himself to be the Big Star of the picnic, Leon felt free to walk onstage whenever an act was reaching its peak and share in the applause, just as if he had earned it. On one of his early appearances, he sprinkled beer on the crowd with his fingertips, in the manner of a Great High Priest. On another, when a groupie-aspirant handed him a box of strawberries, he took small bits from each and threw them into the crowd, to be shared in sacramental fashion. Most of the time, though, he just stood and gazed through eyes that betrayed a mind suffering from severe brown-out.

But not even Russell could ruin the evening. The Main Coonass, Doug Kershaw, gave a typically superlative performance. With his rubber face changing in an instant from Bayou Prince to Lunatic Frog, and his body contorting like a package of pipe cleaners on an acid trip, he bounded all over the stage, playing his gaudy fiddle at maniacal speed and working himself, his band, and the audience into a frenzied lather. Michael Murphey, splendid in his white cosmic cowboy suit, did a fine job with some exceptional songs, and Waylon Jennings got a good reception with his hard-driving music about men that represent poor marital risks. I think things closed down about one A.M. but I don't honestly know, because I finished before they did. As I was walking out, I heard Leon Russell take credit for getting the mass-gathering law suspended and then declare that "I never expected the Good Lord to bless me so much by having so many beautiful faces to look at me at one time on the Fourth of July." It was actually the sixth of July, but I doubt Russell knew it. In any case, his pronouncement strained my doctrine of special providence considerably, and I wished I knew where to find the young man who had hollered at Tim O'Conner late the night before. I think he might have had an appropriate word for Leon.

More from a sense of duty than desire, I went back again on Saturday. The main attraction of the afternoon was a middle-aged man who both looked and claimed to be a deputy sheriff, but who walked around giving freaks the soul-brother handshake and spending what time he could bridging the generation gap with a topless chick of generous endowment. Among the invited performers, Greezy Wheels, Doug Sahm, Spanky and Our Gang, and some others did a nice job, but Rick Nelson and David Carradine helped convince the faithful it was time to go home.

I suspect most of the people who stayed all three days managed to have a good time and would probably show up if Willie announced a similar event for next week. And I'm glad I went. I enjoyed myself, as well as a lot of other people, and I came to like redneck rock better than before. But late Saturday night, as I sat all showered and shampooed in my cool two-story house with the lawn and the shrubs and the bird-feeder and the basketball goal and the hopscotch grid, drinking iced tea and talking to my friends, admiring my teenaged boys and eight-year-old daughter, and thinking about my prize wife, whose eyes and smile reflect experience not just with love but with sex, I decided this year's picnic would probably last me a good long while.

ART

G. Phillips

Arrell Morgan Gibson

Arrell Morgan Gibson was born on December 1, 1921, in Pleasanton, Kansas. A noted historian of the Southwest, and Oklahoma in particular, he received his B.A. (1947), M.A. (1948), and Ph.D. (1954) degrees at the University of Oklahoma, where he has taught since 1957 and where he is currently George Lynn Cross Professor of History. In addition, Gibson has held visiting appointments at the Universities of Arizona, New Mexico, and Nebraska. His works include *The Kickapoos: Lords of the Middle Border* (1963); *Oklahoma: A History of Five Centuries* (1965); *The Chickasaws* (1971), for which he was nominated for the Pulitzer Prize in 1972; and *The West in the Life of the Nation* (1976). The following essay is from his *The Santa Fe and Taos Colonies: Age of the Muses (1900–1942)*.

Native American Muses

SHORTLY after 1900 northern New Mexico became a world-famous literary-artistic center. Writers, painters, musicians, playwrights, and poets founded colonies at Taos and Santa Fe and produced critically acclaimed paintings, sculpture, musical compositions, plays, poetry, and prose. Interestingly, while Anglo aesthetes dominated the colonies' creative and social life, Indians, most of them from neighboring pueblos, contributed substantially to the colonies' fine arts legacy.

From the earliest days of the Taos and Santa Fe colonies, painters had employed Pueblo Indians as studio models. These slender, supple-muscled natives became familiar figures in genre-type paintings that enjoyed sustained popularity. But besides being subjects of art, Indians of northern New Mexico also were creators of works of art. They too were caught up in the art spirit that dominated this region between 1900–1942, and they also contributed to the aesthetic legacy of the Taos and Santa Fe colonies.

Indians of the Southwest had a noble ancient tradition for aesthetic expression, confirmed by the abundant evidence archeologists and anthropologists had exposed in the prehistoric ruins of northern New Mexico. During three centuries of Spanish rule, they had endured periodic suppression of lifestyle, religion, and art, but, by cautious *sub rosa* application, they were able to preserve their muse techniques and tradition.

Soon after the United States absorbed this land in 1846, it began to attempt to transform the natives into hybrid Anglo-Americans.

Managers of the Americanization program believed that in order to accomplish this it was essential to erase all sign of Indianness. Aboriginal lifestyle, religion, and art were regarded as pagan and thus were forbidden. Indian children, coerced into attending government schools, were taught that tribal ways were inferior, that American ways were superior.

Artists and writers in the Taos and Santa Fe colonies challenged this federal policy of suppressing aboriginal culture. They had come to cherish their Pueblo neighbors; they found them charming, useful, and instructive; useful to painters as models, to writers as sources of inspiration for verse, and substance for fiction and nonfiction composition. And increasingly painters found Indians instructive in their art forms. For several years most artists in the Taos and Santa Fe colonies followed the conservative, traditional path of painting style, but after 1920 they increasingly searched for "fresh artistic forms and symbols." This led them away from the European and eastern art establishment for aesthetic guidance to more exotic sources. Several artists turned to "primitivism" on the assumption that there was feral strength in primitive art because it was believed "that 'savage' peoples created and responded to art more intensely than did their 'civilized' counterparts."

The symbolism and structured form found in survivals of Indian art greatly influenced Andrew Dasburg, Paul Burlin, Olive Rush, and other leaders of the Abstract, Cubist, and Expressionist movements in the Taos and Santa Fe colonies. They acknowledged the aboriginal influence on their art. Burlin disclosed that "his rugged, direct quality" in painting was "due in part" to his "study of the abstract elements in Indian art. . . [;] this source had a direct bearing on his early, semi-abstract style."

The artists and writers of the northern New Mexico colonies also adopted a protective stance toward their Indian neighbors. One of the purposes of the Society of Taos Artists, a professional and marketing organization formed at Taos in 1912, was "to preserve and promote the native art." Ernest Blumenschien and Bert Phillips, founders of the Taos colony, believed "the effort to standardize" the Indian "is resulting in a discouragement of racial customs which will eventually destroy their wonderful art. . . . There are many gifted artists among the Indians. Their conceptions are . . . individual and full of racial character." They pointed to paintings "done entirely without instruction, that were wonderful; the construction, the color, the whole feeling, splendid; and yet absolutely Indian in character. . . . [The Indian] has the instinctive skill of the generations that have preceded him."

Robert Henri, international art figure and Santa Fe colony pioneer, lamented that because of sustained and suppressive federal pressure on the Indians,

> materially they are a crushed out race, but even in the remnant there is a bright spark of spiritual life which we others with all our goods and material protections can envy. They have art as a part of each one's life. The whole pueblo manifests itself in a piece of pottery. With us, so far, the artist works alone. Our neighbor who does not paint does not feel himself an artist. We allot to some the gift of genius; to all the rest, practical business. Undoubtedly, in the ancient Indian race, genius was the possession of all; the reality of their lives. The superior ones made the greater manifestations, but each manifested, lived and expressed his life according to art. . . . Here in New Mexico the Indians still make beautiful pottery and rugs, works which are mysterious and at the same time revealing of some great life principle which the old race had. Their work represents the pueblo and stands for their communal greatness. It represents them, reveals a certain spirituality we would like to comprehend.

Until about 1920, Indian art functioned as a fugitive enterprise with some work being done primarily in ceramics and textiles. But Indian artists worked under considerable handicap as federal agents assigned to the Pueblos and tribes along the Rio Grande enforced the Americanization program by maintaining an unrelenting pressure on these hapless aboriginal wards. As late as 1919, George Vaux denounced the Taos art colony, accusing it of having a "deleterious and undesirable effect upon the Pueblo Indian in that it encourages him to retain his immemorial manner of dress and spoils him by offering him easy money to pose for paintings when he might be better employed at the handles of a plow. . . [,] painters are merely clogging the wheels of progress by making the Indian lazy and shiftless."

Kenneth Chapman, Frank Applegate, John Sloan, and Mary Austin, leaders of the Santa Fe colony, and Edgar Hewett, director of the New Mexico Museum in Santa Fe, were primarily responsible for mounting a defense for Native American creativity against the obscurantism of the federal Americanization program and for generating the renaissance in Indian art. In their analysis of the character and content of Indian art they found that natives used sand, bark, stone, clay, wood, bone, skin, quills, beads, metal, fibers, rushes, and wythes as media for aesthetic expression. They ground roots, bark, leaves, minerals, hulls, berries, and animal substances, such as gall, to produce red, yellow, blue, green, and brown pigments. Indians fashioned exquisite ceramic pieces without the benefit of the potter's wheel. And they created masks and costumes, regarded as characteristic of supernatural beings, to achieve "personation." They wore these masks and garments at dances, festivals, and rites to personate the supernatural beings. Also the natives carved deity figures, icons, called kachinas, from cottonwood, then painted them and fitted them with feathers. Hopis were the premier kachina makers. The southwestern Indians drew on a multitude of symbolic designs, some over 4,000 years old, to embellish their art, each an "abstraction of the cosmos of New Mexico—sun, and storm, lightning, thunder, rainbow, swelling rain cloud, rising fog, the stepped earth-altar outline of the hills, subtending the down-stepping arrangement of the storm cloud, the infiltrating rays of light and falling rain." The mythical thunderbird dominated the design galaxy. Natives painted in flat, stylized manner, "perspective and volume . . . suggested by the overlapping planes," on drum heads, pottery, their bodies, and walls of dwellings and kivas.

Austin and Sloan became the publicists for Indian art; they did much to introduce it to the eastern United States and to develop an interest there in it. Sloan was particularly concerned that the "primitivism" surge among artists had generated an appreciation for Inca, Aztec, Mayan, and African art, but the art of the southwestern Indians was assigned to natural museums as ancient curios. He urged that their dances, rituals, ceramics, textiles, icons, and other aesthetic compositions be recognized as art, concluding that theirs was "the only 100 percent American art produced in this country."

The renaissance of Indian art began in 1902. Chapman, on a field trip searching for variant pottery types, discovered Apie Begay, a Navajo, composing tribal scenes in crayon and pencil. About the same time he learned that Elizabeth Richards, a young Anglo teacher at the San Ildefonso Pueblo school, was encouraging her students to draw pueblo life scenes and paint them with water colors. Begay's drawings and the expressive renderings of the San Ildefonso Pueblo students caused Chapman to encourage Indians to paint, and by 1915 several had advanced to the stage that he believed they would benefit from studio experience. At his urging, Hewett brought several San Ildefonso painters to the School of American Research, Museum of New Mexico, and assigned them studios. In the group were Awa Tsireh and Crescencio Martinez.

Their successes attracted other young San Ildefonso artists to studios in the Museum of New Mexico at Santa Fe. The San Ildefonso painters "strongly influenced each other and developed a group tradition" that fused into the so-called San Ildefonso School of Water Colorists. "Their visual goals were initially illusionist, representational, and realistic." Sometime after 1920 Richard Martinez led "a major shift toward abstract decoration."

Aspiring painters from Tesuque, Taos, Hopi, and Zia pueblos joined the San Ildefonso artists at Santa Fe and were assigned studios in the School of American Research, Museum of New Mexico. Taos painters of note included John Concha, Alberto Martinez, and Raphael Pando. Fred Kabotie from Hopi and Ma-Pe-Wi from Zia emerged as the outstanding young artists. Kabotie, whose compositions emphasized Hopi ceremonials, came to be rated the "most versatile and accomplished of the early pueblo painters."

Indian painters from other parts also were attracted to Santa Fe and Taos. They included F. Overton Colbert, Chickasaw, Monroe Tsotoke, Kiowa, and Acee Blue Eagle, Creek-Pawnee, all from Oklahoma. Besides painting, Blue Eagle lectured on Indian art at Arsuna School in Santa Fe.

Native artists faced two supreme risks. One was the possibility of failure to produce compositions that met their aesthetic expectations or those of their painter peers and the art-buying public. The other was the possibility of provoking civic wrath ostensibly for revealing secrets of kiva ritual and ceremony in their paintings. Ones accused of pueblo blasphemy faced trial before the council of elders and a sentence of public whipping or even expulsion from the pueblo. Several Indian artists reportedly were so accused and banished, and the threat of peremptory punishment intimidated some artists, either conditioning their artistic response or causing them to abandon a career in painting.

Notwithstanding these risks, Indian art came to flourish in the simpatico aesthetic milieu fostered by the Santa Fe–Taos colonies. The range of recognized Indian art form expanded beyond painting to include work in clay, fiber, wood, metal, and sand. This development was in response to the pervading art spirit of the Santa Fe–Taos colonies, as well as an extension of the already established painting ventures by Indians, and it also was linked to the escalating tourist population. Each summer after 1920 more and more people visited northern New Mexico. An additional attraction for them was the growing Indian arts enterprise.

With Indian paintings, pottery was the most popular art form with the buying public. Several pueblos developed distinctive pottery styles. Picuris and Taos pottery had a micaceous gold clay cast; San Ildefonso and Santa Clara pottery was either "luminous black" or "earthy red." Santo Domingo and Cochití pottery characteristically was "creamy buff" with "bold . . . geometric designs." Zia potters decorated their ceramics with "deer, birds, flowers, and seeds." Zuñi pottery has been described as "cold red, with brown and white designs that unite complex triangular figures with rotund whorls"; Acoma pottery was identified by its "close-knit geometrics," and Laguna pottery by its "accurate cross-hatching of fine-line work."

Maria and Julian Martinez of San Ildefonso Pueblo were the potters ultimate in the Southwest. In 1921 Maria Martinez discovered a means of scribing dull black designs on a polished black background. Julian and Crescencio Martinez decorated unfired pottery, using yucca fiber brushes dipped in containers of vegetable or mineral color.

Weaving baskets, bowls, hampers, and mats from sedges, wythes, and fibers, each embellished with symbolic designs set in contrasting colors, a time-honored art, also became a profitable enterprise for southwestern Indians. In addition, they carved icons, and fashioned drums from cottonwood and aspen trunks, covering the heads with tightly stretched elk hide, and worked traditional figures and designs with beads and quills on soft, bleached buckskin.

The most popular weaving art form came from Navajo looms. Natives of this populous Indian nation had learned the technique of fiber selection, color and design application, and loom construction from their Pueblo neighbors. Spanish innovations included sheep for wool fibers and improved loom technology. Well before the aesthetic colonies were founded in northern New Mexico, Navajo serapes, blankets, and rugs were esteemed trade items at the Taos fair. Indians from Canada to northern Mexico knew of Navajo textiles and sought them. With

the renaissance of southwestern Indian art and the rise of the tourist market, both Pueblo and Navajo weavers concentrated on producing rugs for the visitor trade.

Indian metal art began with the Spanish advent. From Spaniards, natives learned silversmithing. Pueblo, Navajo, and Apache Indians melted Spanish silver coins and fashioned them into ornamental pieces—conchas (flat silver shells) strung on a leather strap and worn about the waist, buttons, bracelets, rings, harness pieces, and squash blossom necklaces. During their captivity at Bosque Redondo, 1865–1868, the Navajos were introduced to brass and copper wire, which they hammered into bracelets. After 1900 Indian metalsmiths began to fit turquoise, the precious stone of the Southwest, to silver pieces.

Sand painting was an ancient Navajo art form. Native artists produced intricate, exotic designs with colored sand and used their compositions for healing, contemplation, and aesthetic fulfillment. Traditionally, the paintings in sand were destroyed by sunset of the day during which they were made. Gradually sand painting became commercialized as Indian designers adapted religious symbolism to tourist demand. During the summer months Navajo artists presented sand painting demonstrations for visitors. One huge sand mosaic, fifteen feet square, was struck in the lobby of La Fonda Hotel in Santa Fe. For the tourist trade, native artists spread glue on the surface of small rectangular pieces of masonite or plywood and permanently cast vari-colored sand into attractive patterns and symbolic figures.

As interest in Indian art grew during the 1920s and the native painter population working in the New Mexico Museum studios increased, Hewett, Applegate, Chapman, Sloan, and Austin solicited support for them. Contributions of $5, $50, and occasionally $100 came from donors as far away as New York and California to further "Indian art in the Southwest."

A most important development in Indian art occurred around 1930 when federal officials began to relax the 150-year-old policy of eradicating Indian culture, including tribal art. A few daring teachers in the Indian schools of New Mexico had permitted native children to express themselves freely in art. During 1929, pupils of the second grade of Santo Domingo Pueblo school exhibited their drawings at the Museum of New Mexico in Santa Fe. However, the Indian artists surfacing during the 1920s were largely self-taught.

Mary Austin was largely responsible for the change in public policy concerning Indian art. She insisted that the humane and intelligent policy for the federal government was to lift the rule against expressing Indianness. Her position was that the most effective way to renew the Indian was to permit him self-determination rather than to require him to follow the white man's road. And the suppressed Indian arts, so vital to tribal as well as national culture, could be saved only through education. Austin became acquainted with officials in the Bureau of Indian Affairs and the Department of the Interior and pressed them for favorable action. Finally in 1930 she received from Secretary of the Interior Ray Lyman Wilbur a guarded promise to consider changing the federal policy of Americanizing Indians. At his direction, Dr. W. Carson Ryan, Jr., director of education for the Bureau of Indian Affairs, surveyed Indian schools for the purpose of implementing a plan to add native art to the curriculum. This changing federal posture led to the development of an Indian art center in the U.S. Indian School at Santa Fe.

There, during 1932, Superintendent Chester E. Faris asked Olive Rush, a leading artist in the Santa Fe colony, to decorate the walls of the school's new dining hall with murals. She countered with the proposal that Indian painters do the work under her supervision. Faris agreed. The call went out for Indian painters and twelve responded; they organized themselves into the Fresco Guild. Up to that time the native painters had only done small watercolors. Thus it was essential that they readjust their ideas to scale. But the "Indian instinct for placement, trained through generations of adjusting complicated designs to the surface of native pottery, came readily into play here, so that it was not more than a few days before the whole difficulty of scale and relative proportion was overcome." Indians and non-Indians came to watch the Fresco Guild at work. The project became for the Indians "a universal source of pride and the swelling of self-respect."

This success encouraged school officials to form an art department at the U.S. Indian School at Santa Fe called The Studio. It opened in September 1933 with Dorothy Dunn in charge. Dunn had been a student at the Chicago Art Institute. From research classes at nearby Field Museum and lectures in anthropology she became interested in Indian art. Dunn arrived in New Mexico in 1928 where she "found more Art than I had ever dreamed of in Chicago."

Dunn taught two years at the Santo Domingo Pueblo school and one year in the Navajo schools. After becoming acquainted with Chapman, she worked in the basement of the Art Museum in Santa Fe on an enlarging collection of Indian art, which would become the Indian Arts Fund Collection. Also she attended Indian ceremonials and worked with archeological crews on several prehistoric site excavations.

Rush, Gustave Baumann, and F. H. Doyles of the Denver Art Museum assisted Dunn in establishing The Studio. For several years during the 1930s The Studio enrollment averaged 130 pupils. They studied composition, drawing, design, and painting. Initially, Dunn had only one student helper, and she divided the students into eight classes of from fifteen to thirty-two. Elizabeth Willis DeHuff later taught art there. Students became teachers of art in the Indian schools of the Southwest, were employed as muralists, as illustrators and commercial artists, and some became freelance painters.

Most of The Studio students were from the southwestern Pueblos and the Navajo nation, although some came from Oklahoma, the old

Indian Territory. These included Allan Houser, Fort Sill Apache, George Keahbone, Kiowa, and Allan Bushyhead, Cheyenne-Arapaho, and some Indian students who had studied under Dr. Oscar Jacobson during the 1920s at the University of Oklahoma School of Art. The success of The Studio in Santa Fe led to an academic spread of Indian art; for example, in 1935, faculty of Bacone College in Muskogee, Oklahoma, an Indian institution of higher education, established an Indian art department.

One of the most successful Indian artists to study at The Studio was Oscar Howe, a Yanktonai Sioux from the Crow Creek Reservation in South Dakota. He arrived at Santa Fe in 1933 at the age of eighteen to study commercial art, but natural talent refined by The Studio training led to a full-time career as painter. Howe "explored time honored precedents of the Plains Indians together with a study of certain modern media and techniques." He presented several one-man shows in the Museum of New Mexico in Santa Fe that were rated as "exciting displays of regional themes from the Great Plains—rich and vivid in color—dynamic in composition." And he is credited with introducing "elements of European experimentation into Indian graphic arts."

Other Indian art instructional facilities in Santa Fe and Taos were Arsuna School—its curriculum included courses in native aesthetics— and Seton Village. Ernest Thompson Seton, the naturalist, established Seton Village near Santa Fe and formed within it what he called the "College of Indian Wisdom," a four-week summer term, based on the proposition that the Indian "possessed a transcendental view of the world. Rather than seeing themselves as superior to other creatures and attempting to dominate and change the world, Indians sought harmony with all things around them." The teaching schedule included lectures by Thompson Seton on environment and art, instruction by Ina Sizer Cassidy in Indian basketry, pottery design and symbolism by Chapman, and a pottery-making course taught by Indians from the Santa Clara and San Ildefonso pueblos. Enrollment in the College of Indian Wisdom for 1932 included Indians and non-Indians from New Mexico, California, Missouri, New Jersey, Iowa, Oklahoma, Michigan, and Illinois.

Initially, gallery display of Indian art posed a problem similar to that which confronted the Santa Fe and Taos colony pioneer painters. And the problem was resolved in a similar fashion. Each year Museum of New Mexico staff formed displays of Indian art and sent them on an exhibit circuit that began in Santa Fe and Taos and proceeded first to the East Coast, then westerly to the Pacific Coast. Sloan, Hewett, Rush, and Austin were chiefly responsible for maintaining contacts with gallery and museum officials and arranging for the showing of art produced by local native artists. Eventually they joined with Mrs. J. D. Rockefeller, Jr., Mrs. Dwight Morrow, Oliver La Farge, Witter Bynner, Alice Corbin Henderson, and Amelia and Martha White to form the Exposition of Indian Tribal Arts, an organization that promoted the production and exhibition of native art.

As early as 1920 the Museum of New Mexico established an "Indian Alcove" to display native drawings hailed as "new art indigenous to the soil." In 1922 the museum staff began to sponsor the Southwestern Indian Fair featuring native art in connection with the annual Santa Fe Fiesta. Through the years the Museum of New Mexico and the Harwood Foundation Gallery at Taos showed combined native art exhibits as well as one-person shows featuring the work of Allan Houser, Gerald Nailor, Eva Mirabal, George Keahbone, Vicente Mirabal, Pop Chalee, Awa Tsirch, Crescencio Martinez, Quincy Tajoma, Narenco Abeyta, Fred Kabotie, Ma-Pe-Wi, Tonita Pena, and Oqwa Pi.

In 1920 collections of Indian paintings, pottery, basketry, textiles, and metal work began to move from Santa Fe and Taos to the East Coast. In that year Sloan arranged for a showing of New Mexico native works at the Independent Art Show in New York, the occasion marked as "the first time that American Indian paintings had ever been exhibited as Art." Also in 1920, Austin was able to schedule an exhibit of Indian paintings at the Museum of Natural History.

During the 1920s Indian art gained a wider public acceptance. Galleries and museums in the East, the Midwest, and on the West Coast, particularly San Francisco, Los Angeles, and San Diego, increasingly accepted exhibits of native art from northern New Mexico. Thus in 1931, Sloan staged the largest collection of Indian art ever assembled, works by painters from thirty tribes that filled seven large rooms and included the "marvel of sand painting," in the Grand Central Palace Gallery in New York. The following year Rush exhibited work by Indian students from The Studio at Rockefeller Center in New York, Cochrane Galleries in Washington, D.C., and in Chicago at the World's Fair Galleries. Also, after 1930, Indian art from northern New

Mexico often proceeded from East Coast exhibitions to galleries in Geneva, Venice, Budapest, Prague, Paris, and London. By 1941, Indian art from New Mexico was accepted for display in the New York Museum of Modern Art.

Critics and writers on art were attracted to these exhibitions. The *New York Times* art critic was struck by Awa Tsireh's work: "His drawings are in their own field as precise and sophisticated as a Persian miniature. The technique that has produced pottery designs as perfect as those of an Etruscan vase has gone into his training."

Equally as vital to Indians as exhibition of their art was marketing. Resourceful natives sold paintings, metal work, pottery, and textiles to summer tourists at stands along major highways crossing their lands, in the pueblos, and in Santa Fe, Taos, and other northern New Mexico towns. Civic leaders made several attempts to establish a native market in Santa Fe until Hewett set up a sales place under the portico of the Governor's Palace on the Santa Fe Plaza in 1936.

Colony members also aided in native art sales. On lecture trips to Broadmoor Art Academy in Colorado Springs, Alice Corbin Henderson carried portfolios of Indian paintings. One season she sold fifty-seven pieces. Mary Austin, on trips to New York to meet with her publisher, also carried Indian paintings that she sold to acquaintances. Besides paintings, the most popular native art item was pottery. The nonpareil ceramics of Maria Martinez of San Ildefonso were featured in New York Fifth Avenue shops.

Sloan became concerned that tourist patronage might influence Indian art "for the worst." Most of the time Indians, near poverty and perennially in need of money, could be driven to produce at an unbecoming level. Also manufacturers in Massachusetts and other eastern states were producing and marketing jewelry and blankets with the claim that they were Indian-made. To guard against commercialism and corruption of native art, and alien competition, he, Austin, and other native art advocates in the Santa Fe and Taos colonies urged government officials to guard genuine Indian creativity. The Federal Trade Commission moved to ban the misrepresentation of native goods, and officials in the Department of the Interior issued an order that only authentic items made by individual Indians could be sold in the national parks. Also, Bureau of Indian Affairs agents established three schools for Indians to receive training in weaving and metal work—one at Santa Fe, one at Albuquerque, and one at Fort Wingate.

Another agency that sought to guard the integrity of native art was the Laboratory of Anthropology in Santa Fe. Its foundations were established during 1922 in the School of American Research, Museum of New Mexico, when Chapman, Austin, and other members of the Santa Fe colony formed the Indian Arts Association. Its purpose was to encourage the native artist to shun the growing tourist pressure for curios and to produce only the best, consonant with traditions of ancient Indian art. Mary Austin explained that collectors, museums, even tourists, were buying up the old pottery, and there was the fear that soon there would be nothing left by which the Indian Pueblo potters could refresh their inspiration and criticize their own output. . . . With nothing to feed the stream of living tradition [as things were bought up], it became quickly evident that the decorative quality of native design would grow thin, lose interest and value. So . . . the artist friends of the Indians, in the desire to preserve . . . the treasure of . . . living and authentic art, [helped establish] the Indian Arts Fund.

Pieces of pottery came from the abandoned Pecos pueblo, from Pojoaque, Isleta, and other settlements. "Local collectors turned in what they had" in the way of pottery; even curio dealers cooperated. The pieces were temporarily placed in the basement of the Museum of New Mexico."

The Indian Arts Fund received donations from friends of the cause, most ranging from $5 to $100, and gifts of Indian art. Then during 1928, John D. Rockefeller, Jr. presented $270,000 to the fund. Thereupon Indian Arts Fund trustees incorporated in 1929 to form the Laboratory of Anthropology; its collection was enlarged to embrace the best examples of native textiles, bone and wood carvings, metal art, and paintings. Architect John Gaw Meem designed a building compatible with the Santa Fe style and, when completed, provided a structure for storing, analyzing, and exhibiting the native art collection."

Through the years its holdings were increased by gifts and purchases. Trustees purchased a textile piece, rated the "finest Navajo blanket seen in the West," from a Denver woman for $2,500. The collection, which contained over one thousand pieces of fine pottery in 1929, was enlarged by the purchase of the Alice Corbin Henderson collection of native ceramics by Mary Austin, who gave it to the Indian Arts Fund. The Laboratory of Anthropology program included publishing and teaching; in cooperation with the University of New Mexico it presented a course each year in Indian art taught by Chapman, offered especially for teachers in the schools of the Southwest and for employees of the U.S. Indian Service.

During the Depression, native artists became involved in the federal Public Works of Art Project, the Treasury Relief Arts Project, and several PWA projects. Local Indians were employed to apply murals to new state and federal building interiors, including the New Mexico state capitol building and Indian Department building in Santa Fe and several post offices, courthouses, and schools across the Southwest.

Also they were assigned to PWA projects to produce baskets and bead, metal, and textile work.

The creative flair of the Santa Fe and Taos colonies to include southwestern Indians helped to liberate them from the suppressive federal Americanization program, precipitated a renaissance in native art, and provided Indians the means to achieve aesthetic fulfillment. And one writer contends that the interaction of Anglo and Indian artists also ameliorated the long standing Indian-white alienation and hostility; he explains "The red man and the white man for so long a time were on such bad terms and their relations at best were so strained." However, particularly in northern New Mexico, "the Indian has become a friend of the white man," this "due in no small measure to the artist, whose sympathetic understanding of human nature has helped to create an 'entente cordiale' in many Indian communities."

Trent Elwood Sanford

Trent Elwood Sanford was a practicing architect when he published *The Architecture of the Southwest* in 1950. The route between San Juan and Taos, New Mexico, which he describes here has changed little since Sanford toured and wrote about it more than thirty years ago. Today, however, the High Road to Taos is paved—a fact that may help to account for the snow-cone and taco stands that presently mar the entrance to the otherwise pristine Santuario de Chimayo.

The High Road to Taos

THE drive from San Juan to Taos on Highway 64, part of it along the Rio Grande Canyon, is a very pretty one. The road winds between the high walls of the narrowing canyon and then leaves the river to enter the wide valley of Taos, with that old Spanish town in the distance and the high mountains to the north as a backdrop for the scene. The drive is not at all difficult for the road is paved all the way.

But there is another road. It is longer and much poorer—unpaved, narrow, steep, winding, and slippery when there is snow—but infinitely more interesting scenically, historically, socially, and architecturally. This is the High Road (name unofficial—the maps and guidebooks call it 73, 75, and 3). It begins a few miles south of San Juan and leads almost immediately from New Mexico into Old. There are no cities; there are no towns of more than a few hundred people. There are no haciendas, no long, rambling houses of *ricos*, no peons—some of them are there, though they are no longer peons but independent property owners and Penitentes.

After winding through some ten miles of farming country the road leaves the valley of the Rio Grande and climbs up the mountain ridges, up and over them into high valleys a hundred years or more away from the world. In each of the valleys is a village, with a muddy plaza and an old church facing it, with horses roaming around at will and clusters of small adobe houses, some of them with exterior mural decorations. Each house has a beehive-shaped adobe oven outside the door and in the fall scarlet strings of drying chile adorn the walls.

Spreading out from the houses to fill the small valley are the fields where the *paisanos* harvest their crops by hand, goats or horses stamp-

ing out the grain as they did a hundred years ago. Streams, cold and clear, rush down from the mountains to water the valley and keep the village alive, and an aqueduct carved out of huge logs rests on timbered trestles to cross narrow gorges and bring water to a pool where the people come and get it. The villages have names as musical as the clear, cold streams which rush down into them: Córdova, Truchas, Trampas, Penasco.

Each valley—and its village—is a little world in itself, entirely surrounded by a wilderness unbroken except for the tortuous dirt road, dusty or muddy depending on whether or not it has snowed. If it has not, the surroundings are a mounting sea of deep-green waves; when it has, the wooded wilderness becomes, as far as the eye can see in any direction, a rising and falling tier upon tier of Christmas trees brilliantly decorated in the sparkling sunlight.

When the Spaniards settled New Mexico, the *ricos*, with extensive grants of land, brought with them a following of humbler folk. Some of them were Indians from Mexico, Tlaxcalans and Aztecs; some were mestizos, of mixed Indian and Spanish blood; and they included soldiers, artisans, and peasants. Many of them, after arrival, doubtless intermarried with Navahos and Apaches, to produce a varied mixture. Some of them took small homesteads in the less desirable locations which had not been gobbled up by the *ricos*; others came as servants and remained bound in peonage for generations. Some of the latter group, who could pay their debts and thus buy their freedom, took up land of their own, worked it, and achieved a degree of independence.

The rich lands of the valley near Albuquerque were largely in the hands of "the right people"; Santa Fe was the military and social center; and north of the capital and along the upper part of the river the Pueblo Indians had their grants of land. So these people of mixed blood, small homesteaders gradually joined by peons who had become free, took to the lands to the north farther away from the Rio Grande and in the high valleys among the foothills of the Sangre de Cristo Mountains. There they gained a foothold and still live—close to the soil. The mighty *ricos* have fallen but the meek have clung to the earth. In the high valleys they live on it, till it, water it, harvest the crops that grow on it, plant crosses in it, and eventually are buried in it. New Spain in New Mexico has all but vanished but Old Mexico remains—on the High Road to Taos.

Only about a mile from Highway 64 is the old Spanish town of Santa Cruz. For more than three hundred years it was on the main road between Santa Fe and Taos, but the new paved highway bypassed it and left it to sleep in the country. Spanish colonists who came with Oñate established a settlement there but it was not until 1695, after the Pueblo Revolt, when sixty families of colonists from Zacatecas were given grants and settled there, that it was made a *villa*, the second in New Mexico. Long outgrown by Santa Fe and Albuquerque, its official name was larger than the city ever became. It was La Villa Nueva de Santa Cruz de los Españoles Mexicanos del Rey Nuestro Señor Don Carlos Segundo.

A large cruciform church was begun in 1733 and it now dominates the plaza of the sleepy Spanish-Mexican town. The church formerly had a flat dirt roof, but because of damage done by heavy rains the present steep, gabled roof was superimposed about 1900. The simple front is flanked by square towers with buttressed bases and plain belfries with pyramidal roofs. The interior, with a flat ceiling of vigas and carved corbels, contains many old paintings, religious ornaments and vestments, and a particularly fine wood carving of Saint Francis. On either side of the altar there is a chapel, one dedicated to Our Lady of Carmel and the other to Saint Francis. Interestingly enough, a morada of the Penitentes is near by.

The road to the east (now paved for about ten miles) follows the Santa Cruz Valley and its rocky stream through cornfields and orchards, gardens of beans and melons, and villages of a dozen little adobe houses drowsing under rustling cottonwoods. Onions and corn lie drying on the flat roofs and strips of jerked meat hang from lines stretched across the *placitas*. Tiny chapels dot the roadside and here and there a cross rises out of a heap of stones to mark the place where a funeral procession has stopped to rest.

Eight miles from Santa Cruz is the town of Chimayo, built on the site of an Indian pueblo and long famous for its weaving. A bumpy, narrow road crosses ditches and winds among the scattered adobe houses, lined with hedges and shaded by cottonwoods, to the tiny Santuario de Chimayo, so well hidden behind two giant cottonwoods that it is almost sure to be passed by at first.

The sanctuary was built as a private chapel in 1816 by a pious *paisano*, Bernardo Abeyta, who had prospered, and who took that means of offering thanks for his good fortune. It remained in possession of his family until 1929, when it was purchased by the Roman Catholic Diocese of New Mexico. The sand on which it is built, some of it available through a hole in the pavement of a side room, is thought to have miraculous curative powers and pilgrims come from afar to worship at this New Mexican Lourdes.

Quite unprepossessing on the exterior, the little church has one of the loveliest settings in New Mexico and the interior has a great deal of primitive charm. Behind the towering cottonwoods an adobe-walled churchyard with a large cross in the center is entered through a wooden-grilled gate. The formerly flat-roofed façade and twin towers have now been protected by peaked roofs and between the towers is a shallow gallery with wooden posts supporting the roof. Dazzling with rich colors, the interior is a museum of primitive iconographic art. Beneath the round vigas of the ceiling, supported at the ends by carved corbels, beskirted, doll-like figures of saints in polychrome, wearing tin crowns and baby shoes—one of them holding an enormous flower—stand amidst curtained surroundings of similar richness of color and interest to form side altars. The reredos is richly decorated with painted conventional designs and religious symbols and in front of the altar is a rail with carved and painted balusters. Many flickering candles in pierced candelabra illuminate the interior.

On leaving Chimayo and the pavement the road begins to climb, and after about four miles a precipitous and narrow rocky trail leads past a large cross and morada of the Penitentes down to the right into Córdova. The one rough and twisting street is lined with adobe houses with doorways of pink and blue and yellow, some of them perched on the very edge of the steep hill which slopes down to the mountain stream. Several sharp turns lead to the Church of San Antonio de Padua, a small square structure with an arched doorway and a cubical belfry above. The bier is kept conveniently near the door, for there is no room in Córdova for a hearse.

The side road climbs as steeply back to 76, past wooden crosses planted among the rocks and bearing framed photographs of the departed ones. Once regained, the main road balances delicately on a hogback trying its unlevel best to keep from spilling over the sides. From the narrow ridge can be seen the whole panorama of the upper Rio Grande and, beyond, the Jemez Mountains and farther to the south the Sandías—almost lost on the sky line—all belonging to a world that is being left behind. Closer, on the right, the jagged Truchas peaks rise above a dense fringe of trees a full mile higher than our road only to drop into a bottomless sea of green or white. After many dips and climbs along the ridge the road reaches the village of Truchas, so sudden and startling as to be almost unbelievable.

Truchas is on the maps of New Mexico and on New Mexico Route 76, but it belongs in Norway, Finland, or perhaps Siberia. Its one street twists along the top of a narrow ridge which spills into a forested wilderness on either side. Steep-roofed log houses line the road, huge piles of wood banked up at their sides like bulwarks built to protect them.

In most Mexican villages the church faces the plaza in the center and the morada stands apart and apparently deserted, but in Truchas, with its sometimes arcticlike isolation, the morada is almost as large as the church and has a bell tower.

Across mountain ridges and high valleys the sky-line drive (described by the guidebook as being "safer as a pack trip") continues to Las Trampas, meaning "the traps" but known as the "Place of the Early Settlers." The village with its cluster of flat-roofed mud houses surrounding a plaza and an old church, completely hemmed in by high wooded mountains, seems quite out of this world. Yet there is a Spanish church there almost two hundred years old, in character much like the churches in the Keres pueblos of the Rio Grande.

Built of adobe, the Church of Santo Tomás Del Rio de las Trampas has walls four feet thick and thirty-four feet high. A gallery crosses the recessed front and from it, in days gone by, the choir sang while the procession moved outside around the plaza. At one time the church had bell towers, presumably much like those of the church at San Felipe. An old photograph shows a small wooden belfry on the remains of one while the stump of the other projects only a little above the roof; but today they have been cut down to approximately the level of the flat roof.

The church once had two bells, both said to have contained gold and silver. One, because of its soft tone, was called Gracia and was rung for Mass and for the deaths of infants; the other, Refugio, with a lower tone, was rung for the deaths of adults and for Masses for the Dead. Refugio was stolen a few years ago, so now Gracia is used for all occasions. Due to the deletion of the bell towers, Gracia hangs in front of the church from a beam supporting the gallery.

The interior has the typical flat ceiling supported by wooden vigas and corbels, old paintings adorn the reredos and side walls, and a wooden lattice railing serves as an altar rail. Of particular note are the fine wood carvings of the reredos and the pulpit.

For some unaccountable reason the tradition grew up that the church, first known as The Church of the Twelve Apostles and later as San José, is more than three hundred and fifty years old, thus antedating the settlement of New Mexico by Oñate, a tradition even copied on modern maps though some of them have toned it down to three hundred years. It was probably built about the middle of the eighteenth century; the Historic Building Survey gives its date as 1760.

Unlike the situation at Truchas, the Penitentes of Las Trampas have no morada competing with the church; they have simply absorbed the church. Their secret chambers are built onto the rear of the building itself and in the sacristy, just to the right of the entrance door, stands the death cart which is trundled in the Holy Week processions. In the crude two-wheeled cart, its three-foot wheels hewn from solid logs, sits a carved skeleton draped in black, a bow and arrow poised in her bony fingers. Doña Sebastiana, as the figure is called, is said to have once discharged the arrow and pierced the heart of an unrepentant sinner.

In a high valley of its own, reached by a branch road from Penasco, Picurís is the only remaining Indian pueblo in a mountainous land of little Mexicos. Once one of the most powerful and hostile of the Indian pueblos, it is now the smallest of all except Pojoaque. First visited by members of the Coronado expedition, it was assigned as a mission by Oñate in 1598 to Fray Francisco de Zamora. Some time after 1620 a church was begun there by Fray Martín de Arvide, who was later murdered on his way to Zuñi as a missionary. Father Benavides wrote in 1630 that there were about two thousand Indian converts at Picurís, the people of which pueblo he describes as being the most savage in the province.

At the time of the Pueblo Revolt, which had its beginning in the northern pueblos, Picurís was particularly active and its governor, Luís Tupatu, succeeded Popé as leader. But when in 1692 de Vargas reached northern New Mexico, Tupatu, mounted on a fine horse and in full Spanish costume, appeared at the governor's palace in Santa Fe and offered his allegiance to the conqueror.

Shortly afterward the Church of San Lorenzo de Picurís was begun. It has a walled forecourt with a stepped gateway surmounted by a cross. On the front of the church, at the center line, is a simple, square opening for a bell; but the former stepped gable, which was the pierced belfry, and the flat roof have given way to a pitched roof with a small wooden cupola above.

This forlorn and barren church and a few scattered, small square houses of puddled adobe, which the Indians occupy when they are not tending their goats, are all that remain of the once populous and powerful pueblo. In its setting, though not its architecture, the tiny hamlet is reminiscent of a Swiss mountain village.

Through Penasco, a string of several surviving eighteenth-century settlements with a church belfry crowned by a bulbous dome such as one might expect to see in Russia, the High Road continues, joining Route 3 to climb up through the woods onto Government Hill. After winding up and over it follows the heavily wooded curves of the Rito Grande del Rancho and then the Rio Chiquito for some twelve miles and finally comes down to earth at Ranchos de Taos.

Taos (it rhymes with house, not chaos) is divided into three parts, or rather one might better say that there are three Taoses: Ranchos de Taos, an old Indian farming center; Don Fernando de Taos, the Spanish town and modern art center, usually called simply Taos; and San Gerónimo de Taos, the Indian pueblo.

Ranchos de Taos is the first, approaching from the south. It is a peaceful, quiet village with a fine view of the broad valley and its background of rugged peaks. There is a large dirt plaza, with one-story adobe houses facing it, and a small Penitente chapel; but of greatest interest is the fat, buttressed Church of Saint Francis of Assisi. Facing the plaza, this church turns its rear to the highway, a view that is probably photographed more than the hindside of any church except L'Abside de Notre Dame de Paris. With a wide buttress against the apse and beehive-curved buttresses at the corners of the transepts, it is a fascinating study in planes and in lights and shadows.

The church was built at some time in the early eighteenth century but, falling into disuse, it was rebuilt about 1772. The white-stuccoed adobe building, one hundred and twenty feet long, has exceptionally massive walls and a front enclosed by a forecourt with almost equally thick adobe walls, rounded on top. Two wide buttresses on the front rise the full width of the twin bell towers and flank an arched entrance portal with surface tracery and double paneled doors. On the interior the vigas of the ceiling are unusually close together and rest on elaborate double corbels. The choir loft still has the original dirt floor but the main floor of the church, to make the upkeep easier for the venerable sexton-guide, has new flooring of wood. The large carved reredos, partitioned into panels, contains several old paintings.

In its rugged simplicity, its irregular yet soft contours, and its play of light and shadow the Ranchos de Taos church is one of the finest examples of the Spanish-Pueblo style.

Four miles to the north, over the sage-covered plain, lies the historic little city and popular artists' center of Don Fernando de Taos. The town's harassed postmaster in the 1880's requested that the prefix be omitted and it has been since, but the longer name—now little used—remains officially on the books.

Long a market center, Taos is still the meeting place of the three distinct cultures of the Southwest. During all of the Spanish regime its annual fair attracted Indians from the pueblos and from the plains, traders from Mexico, and *hacendados* and villagers from all the surrounding territory. The plaza is still the center of life in the little town. Now well filled with trees, it is lined on three sides with flat-roofed stores, a nondescript collection from various periods; yet the *portales*, though recent, give the square the appearance of New or Old Spain. Indians wrapped in cotton blankets, farmers in broad-brimmed black hats, bewhiskered artists carrying easels, and visitors from the East affecting the dress of the West, pass by under the *portales*, each thinking the other a little queer.

To the north rows of huge cottonwoods line the road as it leaves the town, headed for the Indian pueblo of Taos two and a half miles distant. Past gardens and fields where buffaloes graze the road leads directly to the gate, for Taos is still a walled town. Just inside the gate, to the left, are the ruins of the old mission built in 1704 and destroyed during the Mexican War in 1847, when it was used as a fortress by the Mexicans and their Indian allies. Remains of twin towers still stand and the low ruins of thick adobe walls, which once enclosed the nave, now contain a cemetery. A freshly painted little white cross with the date 1949 shows that it is still in use.

Not far away is the small adobe mission which was built about 1848, supposedly on the site of the original church built by Fray Pedro Miranda in 1617 and destroyed at the time of the Pueblo Revolt. Of whitewashed adobe, the church has a stepped gateway to the forecourt and a similarly stepped false gable on the façade above a square opening for a bell. A row of projecting vigas decorates the side walls. Visitors are not invited inside.

Scattered single houses now extend around part of the plaza on both sides of the entrance, *tapestes* (platforms) supported by poles alongside them for the storage of corn, alfalfa, and firewood. Beehive ovens are clustered about near the houses and the ends of tall ladders, projecting up from bound circles of poles, betray the presence of underground kivas.

But the most distinctive features of the pueblo are the two large, multistoried, terraced community houses facing each other across the creek which flows through the middle of the large central plaza, the finest examples in the Southwest of a survival of the ancient community-house builders. At either end of the plaza a bridge of hand-hewn pine logs connects the two parts of the village.

The people of Taos are quite conscious of their unique standing among the pueblos and jealously guard against innovations. It is only within the last comparatively few years that any single-family dwellings have been permitted. Their houses now have doors and windows but the old ladders are still used since the great community houses have no inside stairways. Though prosperous and in some ways progressive, the people cling to their old customs, to ancient ways and thoughts, to old ceremonies, and to old beliefs. Recently the chief men of the pueblo came to the conclusion that the road leading there should be paved and took the question up with the United States Government authorities. Agreed; but the road was too narrow; it would have to be widened first. Could not be done; that would interfere with the sacred plums.

From Isleta on the Rio Grande north to Taos is one hundred and fifty miles. There is probably no single stretch of country anywhere, of similar length or even much greater length, that is more thoroughly steeped in history, more diversified in its people, its thought, and its religion, more fascinating in its villages, more progressive in its commercial capital, or quainter in its political capital, the oldest in the United States.

The green valley made by that river, with its tributaries, is very abruptly bounded on either side by arid stretches; but within the limits of that valley three very different kinds of people have lived and built and are still doing so. The three kinds refer only to races or nationalities; blends and developments make the number much greater.

Penitentes rub elbows (when they cannot avoid it) with wealthy ranchers; artists paint Indians who live in the same kind of houses they lived in five hundred years ago; and atomic-age scientists discuss modern politics with businessmen in houses copied from those Indians, modified some by the Spaniards who in turn had been influenced by the Moors.

The Spaniards brought their art by way of Mexico and in a perfectly natural way it merged into the style of the Pueblo Indians, who carried out the feeling of their own art under Spanish direction and produced a blend that did credit to both. There is not a similar situation anywhere else in the country.

For more than three hundred years the Rain Dance and High Mass have been celebrated side by side with neither supplanting the other, and yet they are no nearer a blend than the practice of self-flagellation and the study of nuclear physics which go on in the same mountains.

But in artistic expression and especially in architecture the white people have had to lean on the Indians. Small wonder the Pueblos look upon the world with complacence. The Zuñis thought their villages the center of it. Those Pueblos Indians who lived between Isleta and Taos, especially those of the latter pueblo who dwell in five-story community houses beneath the high mountains, had an even better right to think the upper Rio Grande the center—until some of them, especially those of the former pueblo, driven out by their linguistic cousins of Taos, were forced to find another place along the same river, far to the south.

TALES

Leslie Marmon Silko

Leslie Marmon Silko, born in Albuquerque in 1948, is of Hopi, Mexican, and white heritage. Raised at Laguna Pueblo in west central New Mexico, she has said that while she is of mixed ancestry, what she *knows* is Laguna. Silko has published short stories, poems, and the highly acclaimed novel, *Ceremony*. Her book *Storyteller* is a collection of fiction, poems, folktales, and historical and autobiographical sketches that draw upon her early life at Laguna. Her work is clearly informed by the Indian tradition of storytelling—a tradition in which the *word* is central, the *language* is celebrated. The story that follows is one that first appeared in a collection of works by young Indians in 1974. The irony implicit in the title of this tale—that it is "a" Geronimo story—suggests that Silko is providing us with a fictional glimpse of a myth in the making. History tells us that in 1886 the Apache war leader Geronimo surrendered to Brigadier General Nelson A. Miles. With Geronimo at the time of his surrender were seventeen warriors, fourteen women, and six children. It had taken five thousand regular Army troops to capture Geronimo's band.

A Geronimo Story

ONE

MOST of the scouts were at the corral catching their horses and saddling up. I saw them there, busy, getting ready to go; and the feeling of excitement hit me in the stomach. I walked faster. The dust in the first corral was so thick I couldn't see clearly. The horses were running in crowded circles while the men tried to rope them. Whenever someone threw a rope, all the horses would bolt away from it, carrying their heads low. I didn't see our horses. Maybe Mariano thought that me and my uncle weren't going and he left our horses in the pasture.

For a while it had looked like my uncle couldn't go this time because of his foot: he tripped over a big rock one night when he was coming back from the toilet and broke some little bones in his foot. The "sparrow bones" he called them, and he wrapped up his foot in a wide piece of buckskin and wore his moccasins instead of cavalry boots. But when Captain Pratt came to the house the night after they got the message about Geronimo, Siteye shook his head.

"Shit," he said, "these Lagunas can't track Geronimo without me."

Captain said, "O.K."

Siteye sat there staring out the screen door into the early evening light; then he looked at me. "I think I'll bring my nephew along. To saddle my horse for me."

Captain nodded.

The other corral was full of horses; they were standing quietly because nobody was in there trying to catch them. They saw me coming and backed away from me, snorting and crowding each other into the corner of the corral. I saw Rainbow right away. My uncle's horse. A tall, strong horse that my uncle bought from a Mexican at Cubero; my uncle has to have a big horse to carry him. The horses that we raise at Laguna don't get as powerful as Rainbow; but they eat less. Rainbow always ate twice as much. Like my uncle, Siteye is a big man—tall and really big—not fat though, big like an elk who is fast and strong—big like that. I got the lariat rope ready and stepped inside the corral; the horses crowded themselves into the corners and watched me, probably trying to figure out which one of them I was going to catch. Rainbow was easy to catch; he can't duck his head down as low as the others. He was fat and looked good. I put the bridle on him and led him out the gate, watching, careful to see that one of the others didn't try to sneak out the gate behind us. It was hard to swing the saddle onto his back; Siteye's saddle is a heavy Mexican saddle—I still use it, and even now it seems heavy to me.

The cinch would hardly reach around his belly. "Goddamn it, horse," I told him, "don't swell up your belly for me." I led him around a little to fool him, so he would let the air out, then I tightened the cinch some more. He sighed like horses do when you cinch them up good and they know you've got them. Then, when I was finished, all I had to do was drop the bridle reins, because this horse was specially trained to stand like he was tied up whenever you drop the reins in front of him, and he would never wander away, even to eat. I petted him on the neck before I went to catch my horse. Rainbow was such a beautiful color too—dark brown with long streaks of white on each of his sides—streaks that ran from behind his ears to the edge of his fat flanks. He looked at me with gentle eyes. That's a funny thing about horses—wild and crazy when they are loose in a corral together, and so tame when they've got a saddle on them.

My horse was a little horse; he wasn't tall or stout—he was like the old-time Indian horses—that's what my father told me. The kind of horse that can run all day long and not get tired or have to eat much.

Best of all he was gold-colored—a dark red-gold color with a white mane and tail. The Navajos had asked twenty dollars for him when they were only asking twelve dollars for their other saddle horses. They wanted cash—gold or silver—no trade. But my mother had a sewing machine—one that some white lady had given her. My mother said it sewed too fast for her, almost ran over her fingers. So we offered them this new sewing machine with silver engraved trimming on it and a wooden case. They took it, and that's how I got my first horse. That day he was hard to catch. He could hide in between the bigger horses and escape my rope. By the time I managed to catch him I could hear Siteye yelling at me from the corral.

"Andy!" he called, "Andy, where's my horse? We're ready to go."

It was almost noon when we crossed the river below the pueblo and headed southwest. Captain Pratt was up ahead, and Siteye and Sousea were riding beside him. I stayed behind, because I didn't want to get in anyone's way or do anything wrong. We were moving at a steady fast walk. It was late April, and it wasn't too cold or too hot—a good time of year when you can travel all day without any trouble. Siteye stayed up ahead for a long time with Captain, but finally he dropped back to ride with me for a while; maybe he saw that I was riding all by myself. He didn't speak for a long time. We were riding past Crow Mesa when he finally said something.

"We'll stop to eat pretty soon."

"Good," I said, "because I'm hungry." I looked at Siteye. His long, thick hair was beginning to turn white; his thighs weren't as big as they once had been, but he's still strong. I said to myself, he's not old.

"Where are we going?" I asked him again, to make sure.

"Pie Town, north of Datil. Captain says someone there saw Apaches or something."

We rode for a while in silence.

"But I don't think Geronimo is there. He's still at White-Mountain."

"Did you tell Captain?"

"I told him, and he agrees with me. Geronimo isn't down there. So we're going down."

"But if you already know that Geronimo isn't there," I said, "why do you go down there to look for him?"

Siteye reached into his saddle pack and pulled out a sack full of gumdrops and licorice. He took two or three pieces of candy and handed me the bag. The paper sack rattled when I reached into it, and my horse shied away from the noise. I lost my balance and would have fallen off, but Siteye saw and he grabbed my left arm to steady me. I dismounted to pick up the bag of candy; only a few pieces had spilled when it fell. I put them in my mouth and held the quivering horse with one hand and rattled the paper bag with the other. After a while he got used to the sound and quit jumping.

"He better quit that," I said to Siteye after we started again. "He can't jump every time you give me a piece of candy."

Siteye shook his head. "Navajo horses. Always shy away from things." He paused. "It will be a beautiful journey for you. The mountains and the rivers. You've never seen them before."

"Maybe next time I come we'll find Geronimo," I said.

"Umm." That's all Siteye said. Just sort of grunted like he didn't agree with me but didn't want to talk about it either.

We stopped below Owl's Rock to eat; Captain had some of the scouts gather wood for a fire, and he pulled a little tin pot out of his big leather saddle bag. He always had tea, Siteye said. No matter where they were or what kind of weather. Siteye handed me a piece of dried deer meat; he motioned with his chin toward Captain.

"See that," he said to me, "I admire him for that. Not like a white man at all; he has plenty of time for some tea."

It was a few years later that I heard how some white people felt about Captain drinking Indian tea and being married to a Laguna woman. "Squaw man." But back then I wondered what Siteye was talking about.

"Only one time when he couldn't have tea for lunch. When Geronimo or some Apache hit that little white settlement near the Mexican border." Siteye paused and reached for the army-issue canteen by my feet. "That was as close as the Apaches ever got. But by the time we got there the people had been dead at least three days. The Apaches were long gone, as people sometimes say."

It was beautiful to hear Siteye talk; his words were careful and thoughtful, but they followed each other smoothly to tell a good story. He would pause to let you get a feeling for the words; and even silence was alive in his stories.

"Wiped out—all of them. Women and children. Left them laying all over the place like sheep when coyotes are finished with them." He paused for a long time and carefully rewrapped the jerky in the cheesecloth and replaced it in the saddle pouch. Then he rolled himself a cigarette and licked the wheat paper slowly, using his lips and tongue.

"It smelled bad. That was the worst of it—the smell."

"What was it like?" I asked him.

"Worse than a dead dog in August," he said, "an oily smell that stuck to you like skunk odor. They even left a dead man in the well so I had to ride back four miles to Salado Creek to take a bath and wash my clothes." He lit the cigarette he'd just rolled and took a little puff into his mouth. "The Ninth Cavalry was there. They wanted Captain to take us scouts and get going right away."

Siteye offered me the Bull Durham pouch and the wheat papers. I took them and started making a cigarette; he watched me closely.

"Too much tobacco," he said, "no wonder yours look like tamales."

I lit the cigarette and Siteye continued.

"The smell was terrible. I went over to Captain and I said, 'God-damn it, Captain, I have to take a bath. This smell is on me.' He was riding around with his handkerchief over his mouth and nose so he couldn't talk—he just nodded his head. Maybe he wanted to come with us, but he had to stay behind with the other officers who were watching their men dig graves. One of the officers saw us riding away and he yelled at us, but we just kept going because we don't have to listen to white men." There was a silence like Siteye had stopped to think about it again. "When we got back one of the officers came over to me; he was angry. 'Why did you go?' he yelled at me. I said to him, 'That dirty smell was all over us. It was so bad we knew the coyotes would come down from the hills tonight to carry us away—mistaking us for rotten meat.' The officer was very upset—maybe because I mentioned rotten meat, I don't know. Finally he rode away and joined the other officers. By then the dead were all buried and the smell was already fading away. We started on the trail after the Apaches, and it is a good thing that scouts ride up ahead because they all smelled pretty bad—especially the soldiers who touched the dead. 'Don't get down wind from the army.' That's what we said to each other the rest of the week while we hunted Geronimo."

TWO

We started to ride again. The sun had moved around past us, and in a few more hours it would be dark. Siteye rode up front to talk to the other scouts and smoke. I watched the country we were riding into: the rocky piñon foothills high above the Acoma mesas. The trail was steep now, and the trees and boulders were too close to the trail. If you didn't watch where you were going, the branches would slap your face. I had never been this far south before. This was Acoma land, and nobody from Laguna would come to hunt here unless he was invited.

The sun disappeared behind the great black mesa we were climbing, but below us, in the wide Acoma valley, the sunlight was bright and yellow on the sandrock mesas. We were riding into the shadows, and I could feel night approaching. We camped in the narrow pass that leads into the malpais country north of the Zuñi Mountains.

"Hobble the horses, Andy. We're still close enough that they will try to go home tonight," Siteye told me. "All four feet."

I hobbled them, with each foot tied close to the other so that they could walk slowly or hop but couldn't run. The clearing we camped in had plenty of grass but no water. In the morning there would be water when we reached the springs at Moss-Covered Rock. The horses could make it until then. We ate dried meat and flaky-dry sheets of thin corn-batter bread; we all had tea with Captain. Afterward everyone sat near the fire, because winter still lingered on this high mesa where no green leaves or new grass had appeared. Siteye told me to dig a trench for us, and before we lay down, I buried hot coals under the dirt in the bottom of the trench. I rolled up in my blanket and could feel the warmth beneath me. I lay there and watched the stars for a long time. Siteye was singing a spring song to the stars; it was an old song with words about rivers and oceans in the sky. As I was falling asleep I remember the Milky Way—it was an icy snow river across the sky.

THREE

The lava flow stretches for miles north to south; and the distance from east to west is difficult to see. Small pines and piñons live in places where soil has settled on the black rock; in these places there are grasses and shrubs; rabbits and a few deer live there. It is a dark stone ocean with waves and ripples and deep holes. The Navajos believe that the lava is a great pool of blood from a dangerous giant whom the Twin Brothers killed a long time ago. We rode down the edge of the lava on a trail below the sandrock cliffs which rise above the lava; in some places there is barely room for two horses to pass side by side. The black rock holds the warmth of the sun, and the grass and leaves were turning green faster than the plants and bushes of the surrounding country.

When we stopped for lunch we were still traveling along the edge of the lava. I had never walked on it, and there is something about seeing it that makes you want to walk on it—to see how it feels under your feet and to walk in this strange place. I was careful to stay close to the edge, because I know it is easy to lose sight of landmarks and trails. Pretty soon Siteye came. He was walking very slowly and limping with his broken foot. He sat down on a rock beside me.

"Our ancestors have places here," he commented as he looked out over the miles of black rock. "In little caves they left pottery jars full of food and water. These were places to come when somebody was after you." He stood up and started back slowly. "I suppose the water is all gone now," he said, "but the corn might still be good."

When we finally left the lava flow behind us and moved into the foothills of the Zuñi Mountains, Siteye looked behind us over the miles of shining black rock. "Yes," he said, "it's a pretty good place. I don't think Geronimo would even travel out there."

Siteye had to ride up front most of the time after we entered the Zuñi Mountains. Captain didn't know the trail, and Sousea wasn't too sure of it. Siteye told me later on he wasn't sure either, but he knew how to figure it out. That night we camped in the high mountains, where the pines are thick and tall. I lay down in my blanket and watched the sky fill with heavy clouds; and later in the night, rain came. It was a light, spring rain that came on the mountain wind. At dawn the rain was gone, and I still felt dry in my blanket. Before we left, Siteye and Captain squatted in the wet mountain dirt, and Siteye drew maps near their feet. He used his forefinger to draw mountains and canyons and trees.

Later on, Siteye told me, "I've only been this way once before. When I was a boy. Younger than you. But in my head, when I close my eyes, I can still see the trees and the boulders and the way the trail goes. Sometimes I don't remember the distance—things are closer or farther than I had remembered them, but the direction is right."

I understood him. Since I was a child my father had taught me, and Siteye had taught me, to remember the way: to remember how the trees look—dead branches or crooked limbs; to look for big rocks and to remember their shape and their color; and if there aren't big rocks, then little ones with pale-green lichens growing on them. To know the trees and rocks all together with the mountains and sky and wildflowers. I closed my eyes and tested my vision of the trail we had traveled so far. I could see the way in my head, and I had a feeling for it too—a feeling for how far the great fallen oak was from Mossy Rock springs.

"Once I couldn't find the trail off Big Bead Mesa. It was getting dark. I knew the place was somewhere nearby; then I saw an old gray snake crawling along a sandy wash. His rattles were yellowy brown and chipped off like an old man's toenails." Siteye rearranged his black felt hat and cleared his throat. "I remembered him. He lived in a hole under a twisted tree at the top of the trail. The night was getting chilly, because it was late September. So I figured that he was probably going back to his hole to sleep. I followed him. I was careful not to get too close—that would have offended him, and he might have gotten angry and gone somewhere else just to keep me away from his hole. He took me to the trail." Sitcye laughed. "I was just a little kid then, and I was afraid of the dark. I ran all the way down the trail, and I didn't stop until I got to my house."

FOUR

By sundown we reached Pic Town. It didn't look like Geronimo had been there. The corrals were full of cows and sheep; no buildings had been burned. The windmill was turning slowly, catching golden reflections of the sun on the spinning wheel. Siteye rode up front with Sousea and Captain. They were looking for the army that was supposed to meet us here. I didn't see any army horses, but then I didn't see any horses at all. Then a soldier came out of the two-story house; he greeted Captain and they talked. The soldier pointed toward the big arroyo behind the town.

Captain told us that they were keeping all the horses in a big corral in the arroyo because they expected Geronimo any time. We laughed while we rode down the sloping path into the wide arroyo. Siteye handed me Captain's sorrel mare and Rainbow for me to unsaddle and feed. I filled three gunny-sack feed bags with crushed corn that I found in the barn. I watched them eat—tossing their heads up in the air and shaking the bags to reach the corn. They stood still when it was all gone, and I pulled the feed bags off over their ears. I took the feed bags off the other Laguna horses, then I tossed them all a big pile of hay. In the other half of the big corral the Pie Town horses and army mounts had gathered to watch the Laguna horses eat. They watched quietly. It was dark by the time I finished with the horses, and everyone else had already gone up to the big house to eat. The shadows in the arroyo were black and deep. I walked slowly, and I heard a mourning dove calling from the tamarack trees.

They would have good food, I knew that. This place was named for the good pies that one of the women could make. I knocked on the screen door, and inside I could see an old white woman in a red checkered dress; she walked with a limp. She opened the door and pointed toward the kitchen. The scouts were eating in there, except for Captain who was invited to eat with the white people in the dining room. I took a big plate from the end of the table and filled it up with roast meat and beans; on the table there were two plates of hot, fresh bread. There was plenty of coffee, but I didn't see any pies. Siteye finished and pushed his plate aside; he poured himself another cup of coffee.

"Looks like all the white people in this area moved up here from Quemado and Datil. In case Geronimo comes. All crowded together to make their last stand." Siteye laughed at his own joke. "It was some Major Littlecock who sent out the Apache alert. He says he found an Apache campsite near here. He wants us to lead him to Geronimo." Siteye shook his head. "We aren't hunting deer," he said, "we're hunting people. With deer I can say, 'Well, I guess I'll go to Pie Town and hunt deer,' and I can probably find some around here. But with people you must say, 'I want to find these people—I wonder where they might be.'"

Captain came in. He smiled. "We tried to tell him. Both of us."

Siteye nodded his head. "Captain even had me talk to him, and I told him in good English, I said, 'Major, it is so simple. Geronimo isn't even here. He's at White Mountain. They are still hunting meat,' I told him. 'Meat to dry and carry with them this spring.'"

Captain was sitting in the chair beside me. He brought out his tobacco and passed it around the table. We all rolled ourselves a cigarette. For a while nobody said anything; we all sat there smoking and resting our dinner.

Finally Mariano said, "Hey, where are we going to sleep tonight? How about this kitchen?"

"You might eat everything," Siteye answered.

"I think it will be O.K. to sleep in the kitchen," Captain said.

Then Major Littlecock came in. We all stared, and none of us stood up for him; Laguna scouts never did that for anyone. Captain didn't stand up, because he wasn't really in the army either—only some kind of civilian volunteer that they hired because once he had been in their army. Littlecock wasn't young; he was past thirty and his hair was falling out. He was short and pale, and he kept rubbing his fingertips together.

He spoke rapidly. "I will show you the Apache camp in the morning. Then I want you to track them down and send a scout back to lead me to the place. We'll be waiting here on alert." He paused and kept his eyes on the wall above our heads. "I can understand your er-

ror concerning Geronimo's location. But we have sophisticated communications—so I couldn't expect you to be aware of Geronimo's
movements."

He smiled nervously, then with great effort he examined us. We
were wearing our Indian clothes—white cotton pants, calico shirts,
and woven Hopi belts. Siteye had his black wide-brim hat, and most of
us were wearing moccasins.

"Weren't you boys issued uniforms?" the Major asked.

Siteye answered him. "We wear them in the winter. It's too hot for
wool now."

Littlecock looked at Captain. "Our Crow Indian boys preferred
their uniforms," he said.

There was silence. It wasn't hostile, but nobody felt like saying
anything—I mean, what was there to say? Crow Indian scouts like
army uniforms, and Laguna scouts wear them only if it gets cold. Finally Littlecock moved toward the door to leave.

Captain stood up. "I was thinking the men could sleep here in the
kitchen, Major. It would be more comfortable for them."

Littlecock's face was pale; he moved stiffly. "I regret, Captain, that
isn't possible. Army regulations on using civilian quarters—the
women," he said, "you know what I mean. Of course, Captain, you're
welcome to sleep here." Littlecock smiled, he was looking at all of us:
"You boys won't mind sleeping with the horses, will you?"

Siteye looked intently at the Major's face and spoke to him in
Laguna. "You are the one who has a desire for horses at night, Major,
you sleep with them."

We all started laughing.

Littlecock looked confused. "What did he say, Captain Pratt?
Could you translate that for me, please?" His face was red and he
looked angry.

Captain was calm. "I'm sorry, Major, but I don't speak the Laguna
language very well. I didn't catch the meaning of what Siteye said."

Littlecock knew he was lying. He faced Captain squarely and
spoke in a cold voice. "It is very useful to speak the Indian languages
fluently, Mr. Pratt. I have mastered Crow and Arapaho, and I was
fluent in Sioux dialects before I was transferred here." He looked at
Siteye, then he left the room.

We got up from the table. Siteye belched loudly and rearranged his hat. Mariano and George reached into the woodbox by the stove and made little toothpicks for themselves out of the kindling chips.

We walked down the arroyo, joking and laughing about sleeping out with the horses instead of inside where the white soldiers were sleeping.

"Remind me not to come back to this place," Mariano said.

"I only came because they pay me," George said, "and next time they won't even be able to pay me to come here."

Siteye cleared his throat. "I am only sorry that the Apaches aren't around here," he said. "I can't think of a better place to wipe out. If we see them tomorrow we'll tell them to come here first."

We were all laughing, and we felt good saying things like this. "Anybody can act violently—there is nothing to it; but not every person is able to destroy his enemy with words." That's what Siteye always told me, and I respect him.

We built a big fire to sit around. Captain came down later and put his little teapot in the hot coals; for a white man he could talk the Laguna language pretty good, and he liked to listen to the jokes and stories, though he never talked much himself. And Siteye told me once that Captain didn't like to brew his Indian tea around white people. "They don't approve of him being married to an Indian woman and they don't approve of Indian tea, either." Captain drank his tea slowly and kept his eyes on the flames of the fire. A long time after he had finished the tea he stood up slowly. "Sleep good," he said to us, and he rolled up his big gray Navajo blanket. Siteye rolled himself another cigarette, while I covered the hot coals with sand and laid our blankets on top.

Before I went to sleep I said to Siteye, "You've been hunting Geronimo for a long time, haven't you? And he always gets away."

"Yes," Siteye said, staring up at the stars, "but I always like to think that it's us who get away."

At dawn the next day Major Littlecock took us to his Apache campsite. It was about four miles due west of Pie Town, in the pine forest. The cavalry approached the area with their rifles cocked, and the Major was holding his revolver. We followed them closely.

"Here it is." Littlecock pointed to a corral woven with cedar branches. There was a small hearth with stones around it; that was all.

Siteye and Sousea dismounted and walked around the place without stopping to examine the hearth and without once stopping to kneel
down to look at the ground more closely. Siteye finally stopped outside
the corral and rolled himself a cigarette; he made it slowly, tapping the
wheat paper gently to get just the right distribution of tobacco. I don't
think I ever saw him take so long to roll a cigarette. Littlecock had
dismounted and was walking back and forth in front of his horse, waiting. Siteye lit the cigarette and took two puffs of it before he walked
over to Captain. He shook his head.

"Some Mexican built himself a sheep camp here, Captain, that's
all." Siteye looked at the Major to make certain he would hear. "No
Geronimo here, like we said."

Pratt nodded his head.

Littlecock mounted; he had lost, and he knew it. "Accept my apol-
ogy for this inconvenience, Captain Pratt. I simply did not want to take
any chances."

He looked at all of us; his face had a troubled, dissatisfied look;
maybe he was wishing for the Sioux country up north where the land
and the people were familiar to him.

Siteye felt the same. "If he hadn't of killed them all off, he could
still be up there chasing Sioux; he might have been pretty good at it."

It was still early in the day; the forest smelled green and wet. I got
off my horse to let him drink in the little stream. The water was splashing and shining in sunlight that fell through the treetops. I knelt on a
mossy rock and felt the water. Cold water—a snow stream. I closed my
eyes and I drank it.

"Precious and rare," I said to myself, "water that I have not tasted,
water that I may never taste again."

The rest of the scouts were standing in the shade discussing something. Siteye walked over to me.

"We'll hunt," he said. "Good deer country down here."

By noontime there were six bucks and a fat doe hanging in the
trees near the stream. We ate fresh liver for lunch and afterward I
helped them bone out the meat into thin strips, and Sousea salted it
and strung it on a cotton line; he hung it in the sun and started to dry
it. We stayed all afternoon, sleeping and talking. Before the sun went
down I helped Sousea put the pounds of salted meat strips into gunny

sacks and tie them on the kitchen burros, who hardly had anything left to carry. When we got back to Pie Town it had been dark for a long time.

In the morning the white ladies made us a big meal; we took a long time to eat, and it was almost noon before we started northeast again. We went slowly and stopped early so Sousea could hang the meat out to dry for a few hours each day. When we got back to Flower Mountain I could see Laguna on the hill in the distance.

"Here we are again," I said to Siteye.

We stopped. Siteye turned around slowly and looked behind us at the way we had come: the canyons, the mountains, the rivers we had passed. We sat there for a long time remembering the way, the beauty of our journey. Then Siteye shook his head gently. "You know," he said, "that was a long way to go for deer hunting."

Frank Waters

Frank Waters was born and spent his early life in the shadow of Pike's Peak, around Colorado Springs. He has spent most of his adult years in northern New Mexico and presently divides his time between his summer home in Taos and his winter residence in Tucson, Arizona. Waters's novels include *People of the Valley*, set in the Mora Valley of northern New Mexico; *The Woman at Otowi Crossing*; and *Pike's Peak: A Family Saga*. In addition, his *Masked Gods: Navaho and Pueblo Ceremonialism* and *Book of the Hopi* are standard works on Indian culture.

Waters's best novel is *The Man Who Killed the Deer*. A novel of Pueblo Indian life, it is the story of Martiniano, a young Taos Indian who, returning from his stay at the white-run boarding school for Indians, finds himself caught between the ritual ways of his tribe and the white world that educated him. He refuses to see the logic in a white law that says he may kill a deer on one day but not on the next, and in a tribal custom that chastises him for not having performed the ritual proper to that killing. Tormented by the spirit of the deer, Martiniano struggles to discover his place in the scheme of things.

The problem of translating the mysticism that is so much a part of the Indian way of life into the printed word has been a difficult one for writers, be they Indian or otherwise. Waters has said that Indians "believe in the intangible as strongly as [the white culture] believes in the tangible," and that this belief is "a fact of existence one can't ignore." The following passage from the novel illustrates this mystical aspect of the Indian. The beating of a man's heart in concert with the pulse of nature, while perhaps difficult for the Anglo consciousness to comprehend, simply cannot be ignored.

From *The Man Who Killed the Deer*

THE last piñon knot crumpled in the small conical fireplace. Its coals blazed redly alive, then slowly clouded over with a gray film like the eyes of a dead hawk. The whitewashed adobe walls began to lose their pinkish pallor and dim outlines. A rat scampered across the dark earthen floor into silence. There sounded in the room only the rhythmic breathing of sleep.

It came loudly from a woman and a young girl lying on a wooden bedstead; more softly from the man-child wrapped in a serape on the adobe seating ledge extending along the wall. But the man stretched out on floor mat and blankets between them could not sleep. It was as

if an invisible hand was pulling at his spirit . . . pulling it out of his chest . . . pulling it outside the great sleeping pyramid of adobe in which he lay.

There were no windows in the room; only a small, square breathing shaft opening in the ceiling above. Yet he heard the October wind prowling along the walls, moaning in the outdoor ovens dotting the plaza like ant-hills. From the willow thickets along the stream rose clear, deep voices. "Hi-yah! Ai! Hi-yah!" They came from young men wrapped palely as ghosts in sheets and blankets who had been singing, hour after hour, at the rising moon. Across the pastures came the sound of a little water drum. But beyond, the dark pine mountain throbbed deeper. It was the shape of a recumbent woman's great soft breast flattened at the point, really incurved like an old buffalo bow. And the beat, from deep within, from the heart of the world, pulsed steadily, inaudibly, like the beat of the man's blood. Each was the echo of the other, indivisible. But they were not quite in tune.

So the man could not sleep. He rose quietly, pulled on his pants.

Squatting before the fireplace, he gently turned over the coals with a stick. In the faint glow his ruddy brown chest and shoulders emerged soft, hairless and fleshy, like a woman's, but powerful. His black eyes, big nose, full lips and massive cheek bones were the features of a mahogany mask. The face was somber and relaxed, yet intent—the rapt face of a man who would see without what he felt within.

As he waited, it came again—a long, wavering but insistent cry from the lower pine slopes. It was the frosty, eerie voice of a coyote. He had heard it thrice before; but now, with the pull upon his spirit, the cry held a summons he could not ignore.

His dark immobile face changed. It was still trance-like, but decisive. He dressed slowly and unhurried; in wool shirt, store boots with the heels removed, a dirty leather jacket and blanket. A waterfall of long black hair poured down his back. He did not wait to braid it with colored hair-strings into two long pig-tails falling to his waist. He bound it simply, the old way, into a chignon tied at the back with a strip of dirty cloth. Softly, so as not to awaken wife and children, he glided across the dark room. His strong, sensitive hands took down a rifle from a pair of mounted deer horns. He opened the door and stepped quietly outside.

The moon was high. A light frost covered the smooth beaten earth of the plaza. The halves of the pueblo on each side loomed up like great lumpy cliffs. There were no lights. Even the dogs were asleep. The young men had gone, and the stream sang alone over the frosty stones.

He reached the corrals outside the town wall. Already fresh evergreen branches were stacked along the logs to keep out wind and snow. The sorrel mare smelled him and hushed her whinny. He bridled, blanketed and saddled, led her outside to mount. She stepped daintily, distastefully, through the cold stream.

At one of the two great ash piles which still slowly rise upon hundreds of years' refuse, broken pottery and old bones, the mare hesitated. But not the rider. He pressed with his right knee, and shook loose the reins. It was as if an invisible cord, the invisible hand upon his spirit, was pulling him to the rocky upper trail.

Beautifully it all spread out below: the narrow valley ascending with the stream, great clumps of paling cottonwoods, thickets of wild plum and chokecherry, corn milpas and patches of open fields. But in the green-gray moonlight trance-like and empty as a dream. The dry pale cornstalks rattled in the wind. An overturned wicker basket left that afternoon by a group of women frightened away by a bear spilled chokecherries across the path.

The man looked up into the clear dark sky. The Deer were up. Some crows were calling. He listened attentively and rode on.

The trail led upward over the sloping thigh of the mountain. It was rough and sharp with black volcanic tufa. The mare shied round a boulder: the one marked with the strange signs of the Old Ones—a circle enclosing a dot, the imprint of a hand, a strange long-legged animal with a longer neck. The rider felt, as the mare, the lingering vibrations of the life that had never died but only lost its nonessential bodily form.

On the shoulder of the mountain they stopped. The mare to stand heaving, with sweat trickling down withers and flanks. The rider to stare dreamily down at the low town wall enclosing the two communal mud pyramids like the halves of a nutmeat within a broken shell; at the stream between them, with its two bridges of square-hewn timbers, flowing through the plaza; the conical outdoor ovens repeating in miniature the pattern of the mountain above; and at the ceremonial round kivas with ladders coming out of the top. But here, from high above and in the moonlight, it was all compressed and blended into a self-inclosed, impenetrable unity. The two opposite halves of the pueblo appeared like the fragments of a great headless drum, like the walls of an ancient kiva unearthed after a thousand years. There was the same dead weight of earth once raised and slowly sinking back. The same indifferent non-resistance. A curious non-aliveness. Not deadness, for nothing dies, but as something living with a slow serpent-pulse in a perpetual dream of time.

When the pull upon the man's spirit tightened he rode on. Through a thick, dark forest of pine and spruce. To the mouth of a steep and narrow cañon. The trail was narrow. Brush scraped his legs and the hanging rifle. He lowered his bare head under outflung branches.

It was high country now. Perhaps nine thousand feet. The shadowy forest dropped behind. Between the tips of tall firs he saw the pale sage desert stretching away beyond the river. And beyond it, the hazy western range wherein lay the Sun's house. But the gentle, insistent pull led him still higher.

The cañon walls drew back. The stream poured whitely down the falls, rushed through small glades, spread into great still trout pools. Here the beavers worked. Felled trees crossed stream and trail. Others on each side stood smooth and straight, but with an X-shaped notch where they were being gnawed in two, and with a talus of fresh chips below.

After a time the man reined up his mare. He stared upward and ahead at the bare granite face of the mountain above timberline. It was calm, expressionless, stoical as his own. There over the lower crest, the in-curved bow, lay the sacred tribal lake. The little blue eye of faith. The deep turquoise lake of life. But now there was no pull upon him. He listened to the deep pulse of the mountain, and he felt it as one feels a drum which has been beating so long that he is no longer conscious of the mere sound. He listened to the pulse of his own blood. They beat together now, in time. And he knew he was to go no farther.

So he waited, sitting patiently on his mare. At the edge of a small clearing. Hidden in the grove of tall pale aspens. The clouds drifted on. The Night People twinkled clearly again. Wind Old Woman blew cold off the first ice above, rattling the pale brittle leaves which fell like flakes of snow. Still he did not stir.

A shadow flitted from tree to tree-top. A deer bounded into the glade. It stood an instant nose forward, the petals of its ears up; then with a flick of its white tail-piece vanished into the brush. The man did not reach for his rifle. His hand lay heavily and calmly upon the neck of his mare. Still there was no sign.

After a while he rode out into the clearing, looked around him, then dismounted and led his mare to the stream. Six paces from the edge she suddenly whinnied and reared up on her hind legs. The man jerked her down with a powerful but steady hand. Before her front feet touched earth, the rifle was in his other hand. He stood bent forward in a crouch, no longer trance-like, but intensely aware.

He heard a muffled moan. It came from a man lying in the shadow of a boulder. He was lying on one side, legs doubled up, arms outspread, his face to the ground. But even as the rider bent down, scratching a match with his thumb-nail, the head rolled sideways, and there stared up at him a face whose features were familiar but drained of color to a sallow yellow.

"Martiniano!" the rider called softly and clearly. "I have heard your call. I am come."

William Eastlake

William Eastlake was born in 1917 in New York and grew up in New Jersey. While serving with the Army in World War II, he was wounded in the Battle of the Bulge—an experience recounted in his novel, *Castle Keep* (1965). After the war he settled on a ranch in northern New Mexico in a "high, dry, beautiful mesa country between the Apache and Navajo Reservations. This is a handy location," he has written, "because I am able to arbitrate differences between the Apaches and the Navajos. There has been no serious war between the tribes since I settled here; both seem content to steal what they can from me." He now makes his home in Bisbee, Arizona.

Eastlake's early novels are set in the "Checkerboard" region of the Navajo Reservation and northern New Mexico. *Go in Beauty* (1956), *The Bronc People* (1958), and *Portrait of an Artist with Twenty-six Horses* (1963) comprise what has been called Eastlake's trilogy. *Go in Beauty* begins and ends on the New Mexico ranch of George Bowman, a white Indian trader. *The Bronc People* is concerned with the relationship between Little Sant Bowman and his black foster brother, Alastair Benjamin. In *Portrait* we meet Ring Bowman and his Navajo friend, Twenty-six Horses. The story takes place during a single day—the summer solstice, the longest day of the year. Ring, riding the mysterious horse Luto alone on the reservation, falls into quicksand and is sinking slowly to his death. The narrative proceeds with a series of flashbacks—in fact, a series of short stories, some previously published—which Eastlake weaves into the structure of the novel.

The following selection, chapter 3 of the novel, is Eastlake's adaptation of the short story "A Bird on the Mesa," which first appeared in *Harper's* in 1961.

From *Portrait of an Artist with Twenty-six Horses*

THE sleeping Child Mesa rose through the clouds like an atoll. From above there was nothing more to see, nothing, no land or life, not even water or sand anywhere, nothing, only this mesa in all the universe—nothing more.

"Jesus Christ," Ring said. "Jesus Christ, what's anyone doing out here?"

The two on horseback below the mesa could hear the airplane in those clouds shrouding the mesa, the roar going round and round like a distant high whining toy held on a long twirling string by a child.

Now they wondered when the airplane would run out of gasoline and sink to earth.

"It's been about an hour now."

"Yes. He must have been short of gas when he began to circle. I bet he can see the top of the mesa; why doesn't he land there?"

"Because he'd never get down from the mesa."

"That's true. Not without us."

The two young men on horses could have been sitting here on horses a hundred years before. That's the way they were dressed, in blue hard pants, rough shirts; and this land of northern New Mexico looked still raw and unshocked too, still virgin and bright, with gray-green sage and mesas that rose like undiscovered islands in the clouds.

"He must have all the gasoline in the world."

"He'll come down."

"We've got to be patient."

"It really doesn't make any difference to me. I've got all the time in the world."

"The heifer can wait."

"Boy, can she wait!"

They both watched up from atop their nervous cow ponies to the thick, ugly, dark, swirling-in-gray, slow-moving clouds above, where the heavy hornet buzzing of the plane was inconstant as it whirled, unremitting and mad.

"What would an airplane be doing out here in nowhere?"

"Oh, this is somewhere, Twenty-six Horses. The most important place can be nowhere."

"Like the heifer we're following who's going to calve. She's going nowhere to do it."

"Yes, or that plane up there above the mesa."

"I wonder what they're up to that they came here to nowhere."

"Well, we're close to the Mexican border; they could be trying to smuggle something across."

"Like what?"

"People."

"You mean Mexicans? They can cross the river at night."

"They've got a high fence on this side now. This way they are flying them over that fence."

"To this mesa? It's a long way over."

"Yes, it is, Twenty-six Horses."

"You know, Ringo—" Twenty-six Horses let the rein fall on the fabulous horse. "You know—how do you know there are people up there?"

"Well, it's not a bird above the mesa."

"That's true," Twenty-six Horses said.

Yes, there were people above the Sleeping Child Mesa, but right now there seemed only one, the man at the controls of the old, gaudily painted DC-3. The soft light from the fantastic and myriad panel of instruments lit only the bony jaw outlines, throwing the face and brow in hard relief. It was the face of a murderer. There seemed no one else in the ship.

"You can come out now," the pilot said, almost to himself, and then again, "I said you could come out. Venga!"

"Okay, okay, okay," a man said, getting off the floor, and then nine others rose. The Mexican up first leaned over the pilot and said, "We there?"

"No," the pilot said. "The weather's been bad all the way. We're going to have to land down there." He pointed. "It looks like a flat-top wallowing in the ocean, doesn't it?"

"A what?"

"An aircraft carrier."

"You were supposed to land us near Albuquerque," the Mexican said, annoyed. He was the only one of the ten Mexicans who spoke English and he did all the negotiating with the gringo who had agreed to fly them into the States of the United States for three hundred dollars apiece.

"Are we in the States of the United States?" a wide peasant-faced Mexican asked in Spanish.

"No," the tall, thin-faced spokesman who leaned over the pilot said. "We're over an aircraft carrier."

"Actually a mesa," the pilot said.

"*Una mesa*," the spokesman explained to the others.

"Can we get down off it?"

"I never hard of one you couldn't," the pilot said, adjusting a large red mixture knob. The interpreter translated this and all the Mexicans seemed satisfied except the wide-faced peasant who thought about it a while and then touched himself and said, "*Yo, sí*."

"What's that?"

"He says he has," the interpreter told the pilot.

"Well, we're going to land on the top of that mesa anyway," the pilot said, and he touched back the throttle and he thought: I can land there all right. It's long enough to land. I don't know about taking off again with this load. I don't think so. The thing to do is land and conserve gasoline and when the weather clears I will take off again without the Mexicans. I'm very sorry, but I have fulfilled my contract. I told them I would land them someplace near Albuquerque. I'll be sorry if they can't get down off the mesa. If they can't get down off the mesa then no one will ever find out I brought them in. After a reasonable time, when this bunch is dead, I could bring in another bunch. It could work forever. I guess half the people in Mexico would like to come to the United States. The top of that mesa is the United States. Well, anyway you could get away with a few more loads. This is quite a discovery, a new island entirely surrounded by clouds.

The pilot felt like Magellan or Balboa, but lighted by the yellow deep shadows of the instruments he looked more like a pirate, a well-dressed, successful and even bow-tied Captain Kidd. But no one walked the plank, just that mesa, he thought. The pilot kicked the plane into a long glide towards the high flight strip, the steep sides of the mesa, raked by long combers of clouds breaking in on the scrub oak and piñon and then sweeping back into the turbulent big sky. Now the port engine sputtered. The pilot listened and then the pilot heard, really heard, the engine sing perfectly again and he began to let her down. The Mexicans got down on the floor and held onto each other. She hit, then hit again and again, and then a hard, awful once more, before she held the ground and rolled to a perilous halt on one leg.

Ring leaned back and touched the crupper of the horse. "Whatever it was, it lit."

"The bird's on the mesa," the Indian said.

"And they can't get down."

"Maybe they'll take off again."

"If it could fly it would not have landed."

Twenty-six Horses tried to think of something wrong with this proposition but he couldn't so he confounded Ring. "Do you know what, Ringo? We've never been on that mesa. Why do they call it the Sleeping Child Mesa? I think it's because at a certain angle the mesa is shaped like a sleeping child."

"You sure?"

"Sure I'm sure. But maybe my forefathers—"

"Do you know what forefathers means?"

"Indians?"

"No, it means you had four fathers. Now which one of them was looking at the Sleeping Child Mesa?"

"Does it make any difference?"

"I don't suppose it does. Did you hear that? It sounded as though the engine, the bird, started again and then quit."

"I like another idea now."

"What's that?"

"That they're smuggling dope in that airplane, or running arms."

"What's running arms?"

"It's an expression."

"I like our first idea best."

"Running people?"

"Yes. Running people is better than running arms. Running legs would be more apt."

"Apt? Apt? Listen, do you hear the bird again?" There was a faint mechanical coughing on the mesa and then silence. "The idea of running people is ridiculous when you think about it." The Indian sat his horse straight and felt secure in his judgment.

Ring swung around backwards on his saddle and looked over the long country, then up at the dark ceiling where the bird had lit. "Ridiculous when you think about it, yes," Ring said. "But so is Twenty-six Horses."

"What?"

"Don't think, Twenty-six Horses," Ring said.

The man on the mesa, the pilot, was thinking into the overcast. The Mexican illegal entries tumbled out when the plane came to an awkward stop. The front right wheel was off the ground, the left leg of the plane was in a hole. The Mexicans were under the shadow of the wing and waiting for the pilot to come out and tell them where to walk to get to Albuquerque.

"First we better get this plane out of the hole, then I'll show you how to walk to Albuquerque," the pilot called from the open hatch of the cockpit.

The interpreter got the Mexicans pulling and lifting on the plane and soon they had the purple-with-blue-wings and red-tailed bird that had brought them so far sitting alertly on a yellow apron of sandstone surrounded by low junipers.

The pilot turned on the radio to try to get a weather report while the Mexicans began to scout the mesa for a way down and out to Albuquerque, excepting the Mexican with the thin mustache. He stayed put beneath the wing.

The pilot could not call in for weather information because he had, of course, filed no flight plan. He had left a small field with his live cargo outside Guaymas, Mexico, five hours ago and he had hoped to land at the foot of the Sandia between Bernalillo and Albuquerque and get rid of the illegal Mexicans, then fly back to Guaymas for more if all went well. The radio told him nothing but loud squawking so he turned it off and watched the sky boiling around him to figure when he could take off. It was too bad he would not be able to take the Mexicans but he had gotten them to their States of the United States and that was all he was hired to do. There was a hole in the weather now towards the east so he started up the engines and let her idle to be able to get off quickly if there was an opening. It would be best to get off while the Mexicans were looking for a way down. There was no way down.

"Shut her off!"

"What?" the pilot called down to the Mexican interpreter.

"Shut off the engine. You're not going anyplace without me."

The pilot killed the motors and the propellers finally coughed to a jerky standstill.

"You're not going to leave me here to die. I could see from up there that there wasn't any way down off this mesa."

"Let's not be melodramatic."

"What?"

"Let's make a deal."

"All right." The interpreter seemed relieved. This was the kind of language he was used to interpreting. He had made a deal to be flown along for half fare if he would do the interpreting. But he did not want to die for half price on this mesa. "What's the deal?"

"Keep the others in ignorance and I'll fly you off with me."

"What you want me to keep them inside of, did you say? Speak more clear."

"Keep them occupied when they get back."

"*Ocupado.* Keep them busy when they get back. It's a deal."

"It's a deal."

"Remember, the deal is we go off together."

"That's the deal," and the pilot wondered how he was going to get rid of this Mexican who seemed more than willing to interpret his comrades out of their lives. The sandstone landing strip was about twelve hundred feet long and he doubted very much whether the ship could make it off the mesa with both of them—it would certainly be critical. Why take chances? There was not only the risk of not getting off, there was the risk of another living witness if you got him off. Why risk double jeopardy? Wait. I think there was a real break in the clouds. I think I saw some blue.

"The *muchachos* are coming back," the interpreter called up. "Can we take off fast now?"

"Not quite now," the pilot said down quietly. "You'll have to placate them."

"Are you sure you're speaking English?"

"Con them."

"Okay." The Mexicans came up and circled the plane with folded arms, their legs wide apart. They stared at the plane with small dark eyes, with somber and certain knowledge. They all wore loose-fitting, once-white clothes, but not the enormous wide hats you see in the cartoons and the movies. They didn't have any hats at all and their hair was very black, cut short and stood up like coarse dark wire in continuous amazement, and now imminent attack, like the hackles of a bear.

"What did you find?" the pilot asked down calmly from his perch above the blue wings.

"*Es una isla.*"

"It's an island," the interpreter repeated.

"Yes," the pilot said surely. "But it's in the United States and it's near Albuquerque. What more—?"

"*Qué mas?*"

One of the Mexicans reached out a great arm and broke off a thick branch from a juniper tree and tapped it on the ground. "*Este.*"

The translator did not have to translate the word "this" for the pilot. The pilot understood the weapon and he thought Well, I didn't want to produce my Smith and Wesson, but a thirty-eight is very small and there are ten of them, but here goes because it is the only language that any of us seems to understand, the only communication we've got left, and he reached under the seat and felt first with his fingers to feel if the clip was home and then he brought the blue gun over the wheel and pointed it down over the big blue wing straight at the faces of the marooned Mexicans. "*Mira,*" he said, using one perfect

Spanish word and shaking the automatic. "*Mira!*" Then he said more quietly to the interpreter, "Ask them in Mexican, how they want to go." There was a great silence. The clouds, the ocean of solid clouds around the mesa began to shift and, if not yet to break up, then to allow the first white light to beat down on the quiet tableau around the big blue bird on the high island mesa.

Now the pilot fired one loud echoless shot to cow the Mexicans and lend himself courage.

"I think we been up on this Sleeping Child Mesa," Ring said.
"When?"
"When we chased the polled bull."
"No."
"When we lost the bronc."
"No."
"When we saw into Old Mexico."
"Not then either."
"When was it then?"
"We were never on this mesa, Ringo."
"Then this will be the first time."
"No, someone else just made it."
"The first time for us then."
"If there is a way up."
"Well, there was a way down."
"If there is a way up," Twenty-six Horses repeated.
They stared at each other from their glaring horses. The horses wore identical yellow látigo hackamores; they had twin crazed ceramic eyes and now both pawed the red earth in furious frozen attitudes of Greek bronze and cow horse impatience.

"We should ought to find that heifer first."
"One heifer in three will need help having her first calf."
"So we should ought to find that heifer first, but—"
"Take this heifer though, I bet it's the two in three that don't need help. It's like you said, I think, about my forefathers."
"No, it's nothing to do with that, Twenty-six Horses. It's that you're right about it being the two in three. Why didn't I think of that?"
"You were distracted by the bird on the mesa."
"Yes. How are we going to get it down?"

"How are we going to get up to get it down?" Twenty-six Horses looked around wisely and then up at the heavens. "She's beginning to break up."

"Yes, the bird will escape. Let's see if we can find a trail up."

They couldn't. They walked, then trotted, cantered, finally ran their horses around the tall mesa, examining carefully the steep crenelated sides that rose like a Roman temple in the west, but forever and up into the once blue, now pressing sky, the mesa punching through and hidden up there, hiding and hidden and itself concealing—what was it? That noise, the big toy whir of a new bird on the mesa.

"I thought I saw—"

"What?"

"I thought I saw a way up."

"Where, Twenty-six Horses?"

"There. That cave."

"It's dark."

"And it goes in, not up."

"And it's dark, very dark. You're right, Twenty-six Horses, it goes in, not up."

"I guess that's it." Twenty-six Horses placed his hands on his hips and looked around solemnly. "If we can't get up we better locate that cow."

"That heifer before it becomes a cow."

"If we don't it may never live to be one."

"I said it much better," Ring said. "Don't always try to improve on what I say."

"After all I'm only an Indian."

"It's okay to be an Indian, Twenty-six Horses, it's okay, but remember the war's over. Don't still try to count coup."

"What's that?"

"Take scalps."

"Keep me filled in on all the Indian lore, Ringo."

"I'll fill you in with a rock in your head," Ring said. "Now what are we going to do?"

"Chase the heifer."

"All right, we'll chase the heifer, but I hate—"

"Me too."

"It's only a plane that got lost. Soon it will take off and go home."

"Me too."

"No, no, Twenty-six Horses, see if you can pick up a track of the heifer. That's what Indians are supposed to be good at, but in my experience they tend to confuse things."

"You only know a few Indians, Ringo."

"Oh, that's plenty," Ring said. "Now please see if you can pick up the heifer's track, won't you, Twenty-six Horses, like a good Indian?"

"The bird will escape, Ringo."

"That's too bad."

"You had them smuggling dope, arms, people, legs, everything."

"It was a weak moment."

"No, no, no," Twenty-six Horses said and he swung his horse in repeated half circles to pick up the track. "No, that's good, Ringo. It shows imagination. Why, in a little while, if you keep your nose to the—grindstone, is it?—why, soon you'll know as much about crime lore as Indian lore, if you rub two criminals together—"

Ring hurled his black horse into Twenty-six Horses' paint and they bumped and swayed, pitching and tossing across the sage; then a shot rang out. They pulled up their horses and stared around, then up at the mesa.

"If we can't get up, there is nothing we can do," Ring said.

"Look," Twenty-six Horses remarked, pointing. "There's the heifer."

It was the track of the heifer and they followed it. It took a circuitous, wandering, faltering route, stopping and searching for something, the way a heifer will, to find a perfect spot for her first calf. The animal is afraid, confused, worried and alarmed, but proud and secretive too and wanting a high dry sanctuary.

"Look, it's making for the mesa."

"The cave in the mesa."

"It might go up after all."

"It's very dark in there."

"You shouldn't be afraid of that, Ringo. Follow me. Follow the Indian."

They tethered each horse to its left stirrup with its own rein. The horse thinks it's tied. These did. Ring followed Twenty-six Horses and Twenty-six Horses followed the heifer tracks until the light got dim, but the cave was narrow now and slanting upward so that the animal could not be avoided.

"We're going up, Ringo. Follow the Indian."

"Did you hear that?"

"Another shot. Don't be afraid, Ringo. Follow the Indian."

I'd rather beat him in the head, Ring thought, but he followed the Indian, followed the faint dry noise, smelling old dust and cheap hair oil you bought at the trading post, smelling of secret places and Twenty-six Horses.

"Can you see anything?"

"Not yet, Ringo, but we're going up fast."

"If you can't see anything—"

"Don't worry, Ringo, follow the Indian."

Above on the mesa, leaning out of the great airplane, the pilot with the long piratical face repeated down to his illegal cargo of Mexicans, but particularly to the interpreter, "Ask them how they want to go." While the interpreter translated, the pilot waved the blue gun for attention.

The pilot waving the small blue gun, who was very shortly to be killed, had now lived almost exactly thirty-four years. Three weeks short. His name was Peter Winger and his friends, when he had friends, called him Wingy. Peter Winger had been born and lived his early life in New Haven, Connecticut, until he was turned down by the Air Corps because of chronic conjunctivitis, whatever that means. Peter Winger found out what it meant, but he didn't tell anyone else what it meant. Peter Winger learned to fly but couldn't get a commercial license in the United States so went to Old Mexico where he could not get a legitimate job either and was now hauling illegal immigrants. But he never thought he would have to use this gun. There seemed no other way out.

"Do they understand? Tell them to get out of the way. Tell them I am going to turn the ship around."

"Yes, but don't forget me," the translator called up.

The pilot, Peter Winger, started the engines and the great bird made a terrible roar as she began to pivot in a circle. "I won't forget you," Peter Winger called down to the translator from the still open cockpit. Now he slammed the window and began to taxi the huge, awkward, slow-moving bird towards the other end of the mesa for take-off. The translator screamed something at the other Mexicans and they all ran after the slow waddling DC-3 and one after another threw themselves on the tail of the plane, flat, and held on so they were all lying and holding on to the horizontal stabilizers as the plane trundled slowly down to the take-off point.

They are like flies on my tail, Peter Winger thought. How could they be so stupid? I've not met people so stupid since those doctors who turned me down for the Air Corps for poor vision. My vision is not so poor that I cannot see them trying to get off this mesa on my plane, and my eyes will not be so bad that I will not see them brush off like flies when I get up some speed.

The pilot, Peter Winger, now had the DC-3 all the way down at the far edge of the mesa where he had so perfectly hit while landing. The sky was clearing nicely now and in a few hours he would be back in Guaymas. Peter Winger applied full brakes and gunned the engines. He could see the Mexicans on the tail begin to flutter and stream like old rags, their eyes and tongues pop out when the giant raging wind from the backwash of the roaring eighteen-cylinder engines hit them. But there's more to come, Peter Winger thought. Wait till I get this thing up to two hundred miles an hour. There will be no more Mexican flies on the tail. As a matter of fact they will be off before I get fifteen feet. As a matter of fact, there they go now.

The Mexicans could take no more punishment and they were fleeing the plane. Now they were all off. A few of them picked up sticks and rocks and hit the side of the tinny bird, making a hard tinny noise, but even they now had fled from the great wind as Peter Winger made the engines roar still more. Peter Winger tried the ailerons and the rudder and checked out all the instruments. He could see the instruments fine and everything was okay. He was heading into the wind. He released the brakes and the great bird leaped forward for a perfect take-off, except that the heifer now moved into the middle of the runway. The heifer moved into the middle of the runway. The heifer moved into the middle of the runway: everyone said that a thousand times afterwards. Peter Winger would never live to say it to anyone. Now he was saying everything is perfect, I'm going to get off, I'm going to get off. But he wasn't. He could see to a point of piñon and he knew when he passed this point as he thundered down the strip that he could no longer abort the take-off, the plane then was committed to fly, and if something went wrong and she could not become airborne, then neither could she be stopped and the great DC-3 with Peter Winger, who could not quite see the heifer, would go skidding off the edge of the mesa and smash on the rocks nine hundred feet below on the desert floor. Now he gave the twin engines full throttle and the plane leaped down, down the runway, speeding past the rock and cactus like a hurtling horizontal rocket. Now it reached the point of no return, the point of piñon, and at this exact second Peter Winger saw the heifer where it had emerged from a motte of scrub oak, where it stood and gazed around at the high big blue world. Peter Winger killed the engines and touched the brakes and the hurtling bird lost all its grace and purpose and began to career drunkenly at a wild speed as though it were being torn apart.

"Oh!" Peter Winger saw the edge of the world coming up. "Oh, the damn cow. Oh God, the damn cow. How did a cow get up in the sky? Oh, the damn cow."

The plane bucked now on one wing, then began to skid at a ridiculous cruel angle and make a terrible cracking noise as it fled to the wrong side of the mesa and then flared out over the edge and dropped, wingless, flightless, like a house in a hurricane, to the great rocks below.

"The cow. I never saw. I never saw. I never saw that cow in the sky," were Peter Winger's last words on the mesa and on earth. Peter Winger repeated them over the broken wheel as the plane fell; he mumbled with stubborn, pathetic repetition as though he had seen a ghost. And yes, was Peter Winger's final thought, no one will believe, even with perfect eyesight, that there are cattle in the air after storms on the island mesas of northern New Mexico.

Ring and Twenty-six Horses peered out of the scrub oak after the cow just as the plane went over the edge.

"We missed it."

"No, there it is. The heifer."

"I mean the bird. It just flew."

"No, fell."

They both silently agreed about this, then looked around the high island mesa in wonder.

"Look, Ringo, your heifer is going to become a cow."

And it was too, and all the Mexicans appeared from nowhere with advice and wisdom. This was something they understood and knew a great deal about, something that was not shocking, mechanical, different and indifferent, but was the same in Mexico as it was, as it obviously is, in the States of the United States.

The calf flew out now from the heifer, suddenly and quickly, like a dolphin, a copy, a miniature replica of the cow, and the flat-faced Mexican dropped his weapon stick and reached in quickly with his hand and broke the caul and the calf careened its head and breathed air, was alive for the first time on earth.

"*Es un buen torito.*"

"What?"

"He said it's a fine little bull," the translator said.

"Yes," Ring said. "And Twenty-six Horses here is an Indian. He doesn't look too Indian but he's an Indian, and you gentlemen I presume are all Mexicans," Ring said portentously, "trying the hard way over the border fence. Well, no matter. We came up here looking for an airplane, a big bird we heard—"

"That rhymes."

"Twenty-six Horses is conscious of poetry, being a painter," Ring continued to the Mexicans. "He— Never mind. Follow me down. We—after all the noise, the shooting, we expected something terrible and we found life on the mesa. Life as we know it on earth. How am I doing, Twenty-six Horses?"

"Terrible. You should have quit while you were ahead."

"Twenty-six Horses doesn't understand," Ring called back to the others as they emerged from the tunnel.

"I'm only an Indian."

They marched down to the wreckage of the blue plane where Luto was grazing near the cockpit. Ring laid his hand on the withers of the big black horse and looked up at the huge, lonely Sleeping Child Mesa that was all visible now.

"God never," Ring said, "nature never, I mean people were never meant to fly. If we were I guess we would have been born with wings. Ask Luto. Luto knows."

The Indian didn't seem to be appreciating this. Then Ring quickly mounted the high horse and said proudly, "Certainly people shouldn't fly without passports, not on Monday."

The interpreter translated this and the Mexicans scratched their black stiff heads and shrugged their shoulders and watched the boy on the black horse. "*Quién sabe?*"

Now the procession led by the great black horse wound through the bright cliffs that Twenty-six Horses had painted, the Indian-painted section of Indian Country, followed by the heifer, now a cow. The lead Mexican right behind the horses bore the calf beneath the gaudy cliffs. He carried the calf as if the new life were a thing of great portent, a redeeming and saving angel that by some mysterious mission had arrived in the sky at a zero hour to return them safely to these bright rocks and these beautiful, odd inhabitants of these States of the United States.

"Look," Ring said to Twenty-six Horses, pointing upwards. "Look, from this angle down here your painting looks like a threat."

"What?"

"All red and angry."

"No. It's a monument."

"To that flyer?"

"Anyone."

"Not me."

"Anyone, Ringo," Twenty-six Horses said. "Anyone at all. Anyone who dies here."

"Not me."

"Okay, not you," Twenty-six Horses said.

"Because you would save me."

"Would I?" Twenty-six Horses asked.

Clancy Carlile

Clancy Carlile is a native of Oklahoma who has lived most of his adult life in California. He is the author of *When I Was Young and Easy* and *Spore Seven*. In addition to being a novelist, Carlile is a songwriter and a musician with a country-and-western band. The following excerpt is from his novel *Honkytonk Man*, from which Carlile adapted the screenplay for the 1982 Clint Eastwood movie of the same name. *Honkytonk Man* begins in Dust Bowl Oklahoma in 1938. It is a coming-of-age story about fourteen-year-old Whit Wagoner and his Uncle Red Stovall, a country singer–songwriter whom "Hoss"—as his Uncle Red calls him—idolizes.

From *Honkytonk Man*

"TURN off the lights," he said.

We were approaching old man Vogel's chicken farm. The caliche road shone in the dim moonlight, so I didn't need the headlight to see where I was going. When we got to the high chicken-wire fence that enclosed Vogel's place, Uncle Red told me to pull over and stop. Beyond the fence were the oak and blackjack trees, in which roosted the chickens we were going to steal—that we hoped we were going to steal, that is, because I had no confidence at all that we were going to succeed.

"Bring the board," Uncle Red said in a whisper. He got the wire cutters from the glove compartment, replacing them with his bottle of whiskey, and then we got out and sneaked up to the fence. We were hidden from view of the Vogel house by the trees, and it must have been about three o'clock in the morning, so there were no cars on the road, which meant that we were in no danger of being seen for the moment. I knew, however, that as soon as those chickens started squawking, all hell was going to break loose.

Uncle Red, still humming a little tune, as nonchalant as you please, snipped away at the strands in the chicken wire until he had opened a hole in the fence big enough for us to duck through. Then he took the board from me and whispered, "What's the matter with you? You shaking like a dog shitting peach pits."

"If Mama knew what we was doing . . ." But the thought was too fearful to complete.

"Well, she won't know 'less you tell her, and what she don't know won't hurt her—or you, either," he said. "Come on."

I followed him as he staggered through the hole in the fence. When we got under the first tree, we could see the roosting chickens on the limbs as thick as fleas on a dog's ear.

"Now when I lower 'em down," Uncle Red said, whispering still, "you grab 'em by the beak and the legs at the same time, and run 'em back to the car. Put 'em in them gunny sacks, then hightail it back here, quick as you can, y'hear? And 'member, now, grab 'em by the beak so they can't squawk."

"Okay," I said, but I was wondering how he was going to keep them from squawking as he got them out of the trees.

I found out soon enough. And it was the darnedest thing I had ever seen. He just pushed one end of the board up under a sleeping chicken's breast, put a little pressure on it, and that chicken made a sleepy little *pauuuuuk-puck-puck* sound and stepped right up on the end of that board. Uncle Red then lowered the board, with the chicken on the end of it still sleeping, and I grabbed it by the beak and legs at the same time, and ran for the car. The chicken came awake, of course, as soon as I grabbed it, but all it could do then was flap its wings a little, and that didn't disturb any of the other chickens.

I shoved it into one of the gunny sacks and tied the mouth of the sack, and even though the chicken then started squawking its fool head off, none of the other chickens could hear it. I ran back to Uncle Red. Up went the board, down came another sleeping chicken, and back to the car I ran.

It was fun. I had to admit, as soon as I saw how slick it all was, that this kind of chicken stealing was more fun than Christmas morning. I worked up a sweat running back and forth between the trees and the car, and by that time I was so excited I could hardly suppress a giggle.

It probably took no more than thirty minutes for all the gunny sacks to be filled with plump chickens. And once there were two or more chickens in a sack, they sort of settled down and stopped squawking, except for a protesting cry of discomfort now and then from one of the chickens on the bottom.

"The sacks're full," I said to Uncle Red in a panting whisper.

"How many we got?"

"Don't know. Maybe forty or fifty. Enough. Let's get outa here."

"One more," he said.

But all the chickens were gone from the lower limbs now, so Uncle

Red had to reach up as high as he could, even going up on the tips of his toes, to get another chicken off the higher limbs. And that's when it happened. He staggered, almost fell, and the board, on top of which perched a big red rooster, slid down along the limb, knocking into the other chickens, and suddenly chickens started toppling out of that tree all around us. Each one hit the ground shrieking and flapping its wings, and the alarm immediately spread to the chickens in the other trees, who must have thought a big coon or fox was after them. They panicked. I had never heard such a godawful racket in my life. They dropped like ripe fruit from a shaken tree, *plop plop plop*, and hit the ground running. But they didn't know where to run to, so they just ran in circles, all the while shrieking with a crack-brain hysteria.

"Holy shit!" Uncle Red said.

"Come on!" I cried. "Let's get out a here!"

And by then I could hear dogs barking. As I started to run, I glanced in the direction of old man Vogel's house and saw a light flick on.

"Run for it!" Uncle Red said.

And now I could hear the dogs coming. They had been released, and were coming through the trees toward us like demons from hell.

"Hurry!" I cried, and shot ahead of Uncle Red so fast that I was maybe twenty feet ahead when I ducked through the hole in the fence. By then I could hear the distant voice of old man Vogel yelling, "Hey! What the hell's going on out there?"

Scared half to death, I reached the car just in time to turn and see Uncle Red hit the fence. He had been running with his body bent forward so he would go through the hole, but he must have forgot where the hole was. He hit the chicken wire head first. The fence bulged outward under the force of his charge, then snapped back, tossing Uncle Red on his butt, his cowboy hat jammed down on his head.

The dogs—two vicious black dogs, growling and barking as if they were prepared to tangle with a bear—were closing in on him, and in the distance, coming through the trees in a white nightgown, was old man Vogel, yelling, "Stop, thief! Stop, or I'll blow your ass off!"

Uncle Red scrambled through the hole in the fence just as the dogs were coming up behind him. I ran around and jumped into the car and started the engine and reached across to open the door for Uncle Red, who was kicking at the snapping and snarling dogs.

"Holy shit!" he yelled. "Get away! Get away! Holy shit!"

When he finally jumped into the car, the rear wheels were already spinning in the dirt, and I had hit second gear before Uncle Red got the door closed, and was already in high gear when I heard the shotgun fire. The rock salt spattered pinging against the back of the car, but we were too far away for it to do any damage.

"Whooo-eee!" Uncle Red shouted. He was panting like a man who had just run two or three miles. "Goddamn, we made it, Hoss! We made it!" He laughed as he tugged the hat off his head and fixed the crease in its crown.

My heart was pounding so hard I could hardly breathe, but when Uncle Red laughed, I felt myself smiling a little, and when he said, "Whooo-eee! Boy, I thought them dogs was gonna make hamburger of my ass," I heard myself sort of chuckle—a nervous chuckle of relief, to be sure, but a chuckle nevertheless.

The chickens in the sacks in the back seat had burst into a flurry of squawks and cackles when we first roared away from the farm, but by the time we had gone a few miles, they had begun to settle down again. Uncle Red, once he had caught his breath, took the whiskey bottle from the glove compartment and had a swig; then, with only a slight hesitation, offered the bottle to me. I smiled and shook my head, and he said, "Just as well. You got some driving to do. Let's head on out for Tallapoosa."

By the time we got through Roscoe, Uncle Red had begun to sing—softly at first, and then louder and louder as the whiskey got lower. Without even trying to sound good, he bellowed,

> When I die, take my saddle from the wall,
> Put it on my pony, lead him from the stall

"Come on, Hoss," he said—almost shouted. "Help me out."

I joined in, timidly at first, but when I saw that he wasn't going to be bothered by my alternating soprano and baritone, I began to bellow the song almost as loudly as he.

> Tie my bones to his back, head him toward the west,
> And we'll ride the prairies that we love the best.
> Ride around. . . .

At some point along the way, I realized that I had never felt so good, so elated, so alive in all my life. With wild abandon, we raced

down the empty highway in the limousine, both of us singing at the top
of our lungs, while Uncle Red, using the whiskey bottle for a baton,
conducted.

> *Ride around, little dogies,*
> *Ride around slow,*
> *For old Fiery and Snuffy*
> *Are raring to go. . . .*

In a way, though, it was too bad that we got so wrapped up in our
singing. We might have been able to prevent the sudden explosion of
squawks and flapping wings that occurred in the back seat when we
were about halfway to Tallapoosa. Evidently I had been careless when
I tied up one of the gunny sacks, for all of a sudden about ten chickens
burst loose. They erupted in a horrible pandemonium of squawky cries
and earpiercing cackles, and were suddenly everywhere—on our
heads, on the back of the seats, banging against the windows and windshield. Uncle Red ducked and batted them away, yelling, "Shoo! Shoo!
Goddamn!"

I tried to steer the car with one hand while slapping the hysterical
chickens away from me, ducking their flapping wings, and for a brief
moment one old hen perched precariously on the steering wheel, her
tailfeathers in my face.

So there we were, careening down the highway from one side to
the other, with Uncle Red yelling, "Stop the car! Shoo! Holy shit! Stop
the car!"

I was trying to bring the car to a stop, but I could only get brief
glimpses of the road between the flopping and flapping chickens, and
then suddenly the car stopped without any help from me. There was
a sickening *whunk* when it hit and flattened a metal signpost, then
both wheels on the right side skidded into the ditch, and the car drag-
ged along on high center for a few feet before it came to a metal-
grinding stop.

The door on Uncle Red's side flew open and he fell out into the
ditch, followed by about a half-dozen chickens. The interior overhead
light came on, so I could see Uncle Red lying there on his back, head
down in the ditch, with his feet still on the running board. And for a
moment a rooster stood on his chest. The rooster, in his confusion and
hysteria, must have mistaken the car's overhead light for a sudden sun-

rise, for he suddenly flapped his wings and crowed. It was a very strident and uncertain *cockle-doodle-doo*, which was sharply cut off somewhere between the *doodle* and the *doo* when Uncle Red violently knocked him off his chest.

"You all right?" I asked.

"Don't know," he said. He didn't sound as if he were injured, but he didn't make any move to get up right away. Panting heavily, he stayed there for a few moments in the weeds, as if he were contemplating the stars.

There were still four or five chickens left in the back seat. They made weak, exhausted efforts to plunge through the closed windows now and then, but mainly they just perched on the back seat, or on the chicken-filled gunny sacks on the floor. The car was littered with feathers and big blobs of chickenshit here and there.

I slid over and looked down at Uncle Red. "Need a hand?"

"Sure," he said. "I could do with a little applause right now."

After floundering around a little in the dusty weeds, he finally caught hold of the door and pulled himself up. He dusted the seat of his pants and then walked around to the front of the car, assessing our predicament.

"We gonna be able to get this thing outa here?"

"I don't know," I said. "I think it's on high center."

"Start 'er up, see what you can do."

The engine started up again readily enough, but when I put it in gear and tried to drive back onto the pavement, the rear wheels spun and squeaked in the dirt and on the blacktop. The car didn't budge.

"Turn it off," he said after he got down on his knees and looked under the car. "It's stuck tighter'n a big-dicked dog."

I killed the engine and turned off the headlight, then got out to inspect the damage by moonlight. There was a dent in the middle of the front bumper, and the right section of the steer horns had been broken off. But the real worry was what damage might have been done to the underside of the car.

"Well, there ain't doodley shit we can do about it tonight," Uncle Red said. He looked both ways up and down the dark highway. "Have to wait till morning, see if somebody comes along that can pull us out. Meanwhile, might as well get some sleep."

He crawled into the back seat, using the uphill door so the gunny sacks full of chickens wouldn't fall out. He rolled the window down and shooed the remaining chickens out of the car. Cursing softly, he used the newly emptied gunny sack to wipe the blobs of chickenshit off the seat.

"Didn't tie that one sack too good, did you, Hoss?" He checked the other sacks to make certain they were tied securely; then he stretched out on the seat, his feet propped up on the windowsill, and went to sleep.

Lawrence Wharton

Lawrence Wharton was born in Wichita Falls, Texas. Raised in Oklahoma, he received his B.A. and M.A. degrees from Oklahoma State University and his Ph.D. from the University of Utah. He now lives in Birmingham, where he teaches contemporary fiction and writing at the University of Alabama. He has contributed short fiction to a number of magazines and is currently at work on a historical novel set in Oklahoma.

There Could Be No More To It

BILLY SIMPSON and Jim Byers worked as mechanics in the double garage of what had been once a Phillips service station. The place was a fiftyish-looking design surrounded by concrete on a fat corner lot, and in the drive beneath the leaking canopy, winged and peaked so that it looked as if it might become airborne, the pumps remained, glass broken out and the hoses disconnected.

They both worked silently on the cars and trucks brought to the garage. They did not own the place, but they controlled it. The owner, Bill Felton, lived in Florida and ran three Exxon stations near Disney World. He paid them well, and in return they did careful and fine work. Billy Simpson and Jim Byers were honest; you could take your car or truck to them and know that when either one of them got to it, only what was necessary would be fixed or replaced.

Both Billy and Jim were over six feet tall, lanky, and slump-shouldered, and to strangers they appeared nearly carefree. But each, in his own way, was rather distracted and prone to dream.

Billy Simpson, whom the customers called Sims for no particular reason other than his easy and friendly manner, had begun to look westward, away from his present, which was no more to him than the routine of his past. Billy was married to his high school sweetheart, Linda. She was not as distracted as Billy, or Jim, but she, too, just recently had begun to dream.

When Billy and Linda married, she was thin and plain, looking perfectly suited for life in a small wheat-country town in which she was born and, had she no luck at all, might have spent the rest of her life. As some of the plainer young girls who marry early dream of, Linda aged into a quite attractive young woman. Each year found her changed: her blue eyes deepened; her girlish and round face molded into a tight

structure of high cheek bones that curved downward softly into a narrow jaw. The pale and pimply flesh she had so despised as an adolescent became smooth and elegant against bone, alive with color. Her muscles were hard and precise, with no trace of having already borne one child. She was just too striking for strangers to think of as carefree. When Linda and Billy and Billy Jr. were together, people usually noticed them because they made being together as a family look so easy and natural. And those people who noticed them thought things could not have turned out much better for the three of them.

Jim Byers was single and twenty-seven, a year older than Billy, three years older than Linda. He was from northeastern Oklahoma, where the hills were rugged and harsh, where ugliness was hidden by scrub growth. He never became accustomed to flat, windswept Oklahoma City, and the gritty, exposed life there became his one practiced topic of conversation with the prettier barmaids in those joints where he spent most of his nights drinking beer. They always agreed with him, and Jim knew they would, whatever he said. Once in a while one of these women would return with him to his apartment to make all-night love that was too furious and too exhausting to be much fun. After such nights he worked in a daze, his stomach muscles sore and his eyes red and dry with dull pains lingering behind them.

Every Saturday, Jim went to Billy and Linda's, where Billy cooked hamburgers on the grill outside and the three of them drank too much beer. These evenings were pleasant enough, but Jim drank more beer than normally, to return to his apartment afterward drunk and miserable. The beer bloated him and made his head thick, but he was miserable because he was in love with Linda. And Linda, he could never forget, was Billy's wife: there could be no more to it. It was the same loyalty, if he were married, he would expect of friends. So Saturdays, all day, were painful. At work he covered it well by joking and talking easily about what they all would do and how much they might drink that night. As he talked, though, he skinned his knuckles against remote, sharp edges, he stabbed his palms with screwdrivers, he burned his fingers against hot manifolds. Every Saturday he arrived at Billy and Linda's with cuts and scrapes that took until the following Saturday to heal. The red orange dots of merthiolate on his hands embarrassed him, and for the whole evening he tried to keep his hands hidden. He tilted beers hurriedly, drinking in huge gulps that made belches he suppressed around Linda to bellow out freely when outside with Billy. He ate too fast, and Linda always cautioned him: You'll get an ulcer for sure. Jim would then fold his hands in his lap under the table. That's what you keep telling me, he answered her.

Billy was replacing the plugs in an old pickup that had a weathered broom stuck upside down just behind the cab on the driver's side. I've always wanted to be a cowboy, he said, as he turned the ratchet slowly to tighten a plug.

A cowboy? Jim asked. In the three years they had worked together, Billy had never mentioned this. Weren't you born on a ranch west of here?

Oh yeah. A goddamn thirty-acre wheat farm near Perry. I mean a real cowboy, on a working cattle ranch in Wyoming or Montana, where the late summers are spent driving herds down from the foothills. And here, Billy's voice trailed off. Before him were high mountains, scattered clumps of lodgepole pines and aspens, a hard, dark blue sky.

When Billy looked out from beneath the hood through the door of the garage, the traffic was thick and steady and the heat waves made even the sharpest of edges wavy and obscure. Across the street, the Taco Bell filled with dancing teen-agers hurrying to eat lunch.

I want to be a fishing guide, Jim said, sensing his turn. I don't want much. He, too, stopped working. Instead of a clear lake and the sheen of new fishing gear that should go with his dream, Jim saw Linda waiting beside the door of a small frame cabin. The wind blew her thick, black hair across her eyes, and after brushing it back several times, she kept her hand against the hair at the side of her head. Even in the shadow of her head, he saw her black eyebrows, her sky deep eyes.

A small boat, he said to Billy, a johnboat, some good gear, a small frame house down a dirt road, a garden; but he couldn't bring himself to finish the rest of the dream. He was surprised and embarrassed that he revealed what he had.

I don't want much, he said again to Billy.

Jim couldn't bear to look out from under the hood of the car he worked on. The pain in his heart increased, edged its way down to his fingertips, up to his eyes. He tasted the pain as the slightly salty taste to Linda's cheek as he kissed her. He felt the warmth of her hands on his back, the warmth of her back through her blouse in his hands.

Billy returned to the truck, wrenching the other plugs unnecessarily tight. If I was single, he said, I wouldn't even hesitate. I'd have been gone by now, heading west.

You'd leave Linda? Jim asked hurriedly. The question came automatically and without shame before he thought about it.

A wife's okay when you don't have one, Billy answered, and he was struck with the words of his own wisdom. Last night they had gone to a drive-in to see a western, and Linda complained the whole time about how bad the movie was. He had argued, but the truth was, he knew, even as he had argued, she was right. He had liked only the long shots of the landscape and the fine horses the actors rode badly. They went home sullen and bored. They both had felt cheated.

I don't know, Jim said. But he did.

Let's go to lunch, Billy said.

Jim followed Billy across the street to eat greasy burritos and to stare at the teen-aged girls.

They're still as pretty as they were when I was in school, Billy said. He remembered how plain Linda was then and how he had always stared at the more popular and more beautiful ones, those who dated his friends in the backfield. He had been an end, a position that allowed only his pick of the plain girls. As far as he was concerned, Linda was the same as she always had been, and he wondered if he could have done better for himself.

Jim stared with the same care trying to reckon what Linda must have looked like before she and Billy were married. He had spent most of high school in small, out-of-the-way bars where the women were always between twenty and forty, and always tried to look younger or older. For him, Linda had to be as beautiful then as now. There wasn't much else to figure out.

That was Monday.

Tuesday, Billy talked about becoming a cowboy, riding the high mountain pastures, sharing more and more of his dream with Jim. It made Jim nervous, as he could share no more of his dream than he had. So each time Billy talked of the mountains and the west, Jim said only: I don't want much. Billy saw that this was so and went on talking about a cowboy's life as if he had already lived it and had come back to tell the tale.

Wednesday, Billy showed up in a new pair of Tony Lama's with sixteen-inch tops stitched in four colors.

A hundred and thirty dollars, Billy said proudly, admiring the burnished orange of the calf leather in the sun.

What will Linda say? Jim asked, trying to smile as if he were kidding.

She don't know, Billy said flatly. He studied the toe, then pushed his Levi's down over the tops. Listen, Billy said, Come over on Friday this week, not Saturday, if you don't have any plans, that is.

Friday's fine, Jim answered, though he was not at all convinced. He wanted the extra day for his hands to heal further, and it made him instantly nervous to think he would have to endure the tension all day Friday, a day ahead of what he was accustomed to.

Thursday night, Billy and Linda went again to the drive-in. *Comes a Horseman* was playing. For Linda the evening was long and tedious, because Billy Jr. never went to sleep in the back seat, while for Billy the film was more than he had ever hoped for—full of long landscape shots and what were the most real-looking cowboys the movies had ever given him. Their clothes were faded and thin, lived in, and their hats were beaten into odd and responsive shapes that only long, hard use could devise. Billy was happy beyond expectation, and he tried to make passionate love to Linda after they were home in bed. She never awoke, and he spent the remainder of the night sitting at the white formica table in the kitchen smoking cigarettes and watching the dark sky through the open window.

Jim went to his least favorite bar and came back to his apartment with one of those lonely women who show up every now and again, whose life, as she told it, reminded him of the songs on the jukebox. By the time they rolled onto the bed, he was not sure if she had told him the truth or merely had taken the rhyme and the music out of a song, leaving the words to describe an unhappy life and a worse marriage hanging cold and stark in the air above them. It was so predictable that he plunged into a deep depression about how and why she was there and about how he would turn out. Both of them, he thought, were like the songs: sad and bitter at the same time.

When Jim came to work Friday, Billy was already there, hard at work beneath the hood of a '49 Cadillac coupe. Jim had not seen the car before. The windshield was cracked—spider-webbed around three bullet holes. The body was in pretty good shape, he saw, with the faded black paint showing areas of deep purple in the light.

When did that one come in? Jim asked.

It's mine, Billy said, not even looking up from beneath the hood. The engine's been rebuilt, but whoever did it messed up the carburetor. I've been putting a new one on.

As Jim walked into the garage, he heard Billy slide in behind him, then he heard only the noise of the compressor.

The truth is . . . , Billy began after lunch, but he never finished the sentence. He looked across the cars lined oddly around the concrete lot. What was the truth? He wanted to know. He walked silently among the cars. When he got to the '49 Cadillac, he leaned against the door. The truth is, he said again, that these boots sure broke in quick.

Cheap boots are the ones that take a long time to break in, Jim said quickly. He had followed Billy around the lot, listening to his footsteps in the traffic's lull. He didn't want to go back to work. His hands were not too badly banged up yet, and the morning had gone so fast that he hardly realized it was Friday. His eyes were red and dry, and the sun increased the pains behind them, but his hands were not really that banged up.

They both looked across the cars, empty, shimmering in the heat, waiting for minor repairs: a tune-up here, a speedometer cable there, a valve job.

They looked in different directions. Billy Simpson, still leaning against his car, looked west toward Route 66; Jim Byers stared toward the northeast.

Between here and Lake Tenkiller, Jim knew, was Linda, and then he saw her sitting at the kitchen table, her arms tanned and thin against the white top. He began walking back to the garage alongside the pumps, hoseless and empty and useless. Inside the garage it was dark, and he stood there, shoulders slumped, eyes red and dry, knots in his stomach.

Billy smashed the broken glass in the windshield. When he finished, only the chrome rim framed the open space.

Jim arrived at Billy and Linda's at seven after drinking three beers at his apartment while doctoring his hands. Linda met him at the door, hugged him welcome. With her arms around him for that quick moment, he closed his eyes, letting them be transported arm in arm to the wooden porch of the small frame house in the remote northeast corner of the state.

Come on back, Linda said, taking his hand, Billy is in the kitchen. He has a head start on you.

Maybe, Jim said. I've had a couple myself. He couldn't stand it, so he took his hand from hers, put both his hands in his pockets, and followed her into the kitchen.

Billy sat there leaning back in his chair behind the table. With his boots hooked to the chair legs and the chair leaned back, he looked relaxed. He wore an old flannel shirt with pearl snaps, the sleeves rolled up. He was hot and wet with sweat.

There's the icebox, Billy said. It was what he always said.

Jim moved automatically to it, grabbing a beer for Billy and one for himself. Linda, do you need one? he asked. Please, she answered.

The first long pull off the beer tasted as good as it always did, but after that, Jim was at a loss for what to say.

The three of them sat silently around the table, sweating in the heat, getting only intermittent relief as a blast from the fan atop the icebox made half-circles around the room.

The three of them made a triangle, but they were not aware of it.

Jim was connected to Linda in his dreams, to Billy at work, to Billy as a friend.

Linda saw both of them as very close to her. She loved Billy, though without the passion that once had made them inseparable. They gradually had drifted apart, he from her, she from him, and she knew that neither of them was at fault. She was away from Perry, even if Oklahoma City was not much, not even very far away. She had a real fondness for Jim; he was a close friend. She had never talked to him about the things that bothered her. She never thought about loving him other than as a friend. She never thought about any of Billy's friends that way.

Billy saw no triangle at all. He was a point. The thin line that once had connected him to Linda was no longer there. Jim was a good friend. There could have been secrets shared between them; but there were none. Billy believed Jim when he said he didn't want much.

The fan swished by Jim again. He edged his way around Linda, heading for the icebox for another beer.

Let's put the burgers on, Billy said.

He and Jim walked through the door into the backyard heat. He wanted to talk to Jim, to say things about his life with Linda, about his son, about Jim, too, but the words were not there. Listen, Billy began. He stared directly west, shielding his eyes from the setting sun. I'm glad you could make it tonight. Linda has plans for tomorrow night. And then he was silent.

None of this was true. Billy couldn't bring himself to say the things that mattered. They didn't have to be said, but he would have liked to say them anyway. What counted, what really counted, he thought, was never within earshot. Listen, Billy said finally, Don't burn those goddamn hamburgers any longer than you have to.

Billy stared a few seconds longer at Jim, looked quickly through the screened door, then walked around the house to the driveway. He peeked in the living room window to see Billy Jr. pretending the ragged green couch arm was a horse that he was riding hard and fast through some imaginary country, spurring the cushions and lashing at the back with a piece of thick rawhide.

Jim heard the Cadillac's starter, heard the deep-throated engine kick in, listened as the engine noise faded into the noise of the neighborhood. He watched the grease from the meat begin to hiss on the coals.

Linda watched Jim come through the back door carrying the plate. He walked through the kitchen toward her in slow, easy strides, his shoulders slumped, one hand stuck inside his jeans pocket. The tops of both pockets were peppered with dots of merthiolate. She watched as he set the plate carefully down. She always noticed his thick hands covered with scrapes and cuts, always painted with merthiolate. She noticed his sad eyes and his smile that creased his face in wrinkles.

Billy went for more beer, Jim said, as he walked to the icebox for another one. Looks like we had enough to make it through dinner.

He won't be long. I'll get Billy Jr. ready.

Jim watched her leave, heard her, even in the other room above the noise of the fan, readying her son. He wished Billy would return.

Halfway between Elk City, the last town of any size on the Oklahoma side of the Texas border, and Amarillo, Billy stomped on the accelerator. The Cadillac shot up to ninety miles per hour. Through the empty space of the windshield the air rushed in around his face, blowing against the wide brim of the straw Resistol that he had forced down across his forehead. The night was clear ahead of him, though to the northwest, faraway streaks of lightning bounced around an indistinct horizon. He had no clothes other than those he wore. His boots were broken in. The cool air blasting through the empty windshield cooled him, dried his shirt.

Billy had never felt better in his life. He opened a fresh beer and leaned back to enjoy driving into the West Texas night. Without a doubt, he knew that he had never felt better in his life.

Jim and Linda waited two hours for Billy. Linda fed Billy Jr., then put him to bed.

Jim drank the remaining beers in the icebox, and he and Linda sat waiting at the table for Billy to return. The grease congealed white on the plate around the hamburgers. They sat silently, staring now and again at each other, listening to the fan.

After an hour, Jim Byers and Linda Simpson lost their nervousness, but they did not eat.

Later in the evening, Jim asked Linda what her plans were for Saturday night.

Linda sat thinking about this for some time before she began to answer.

Credits